staging whiteness

staging whiteness

Mary F. Brewer

Wesleyan University Press

Middletown, Connecticut

Published by Wesleyan University Press, Middletown, CT 06459

www.wesleyan.edu/wespress

© 2005 by Mary Brewer

Printed in the United States of America

5 4 3 2 1

Library of Congress Cataloging-in-Publication Data

Brewer, Mary F.
Staging whiteness / Mary F. Brewer
    p.   cm.
Includes bibliographical references and index.
ISBN 0–8195–6769–8 (cloth : alk. paper) — ISBN 0–8195–6770–1
1. American drama—20th century—History and criticism. 2. Whites in literature.
3. English drama—20th century—History and criticism. 4. Human skin color in
literature. 5. Ethnicity in literature. 6. Race in literature. I. Title.
PS338.W45 B74 2005
812′.5093552—dc22   2005002775

To my mother, Elizabeth Rhodes, and
for Carl Muckley and Jenny Kowalski

contents

Acknowledgments ix

Introduction xi

Chapter 1: "That's White of You . . .": Civilizing Whiteness 1
Militant Whiteness: G. B. Shaw's *Captain Brassbound's Conversion* / 6
The Heart of Whiteness: W. Somerset Maugham's *The Explorer* / 11
Waving the White Flag: W. H. Auden and Christopher Isherwood's
The Ascent of F6 / 14

Chapter 2: The Borders of Whiteness in the New World 18
Emasculating Whiteness: Eugene O'Neill's *The Hairy Ape* / 27
Violating the Color Line: Langston Hughes's *Mulatto* / 30
The Grammar of Whiteness: Thornton Wilder's *Our Town* / 32
White Reconstruction: Lillian Hellman's *The Little Foxes* / 37

Chapter 3: Whiteness in Post-Imperial Britain 42
Whiteness at War: Bridget Boland's *The Cockpit* / 46
Whiteness and Polite Society: T. S. Eliot's *The Cocktail Party* / 50
Angry White Men: John Osborne's *The Entertainer* / 53

Chapter 4: Locating Race in Postwar U.S. Culture 61
Life, Liberty, and the Pursuit of Whiteness: Eugene O'Neill's *The
Iceman Cometh* / 66
Primitive Whiteness: Tennessee Williams's *A Streetcar Named Desire* / 71
Queering Whiteness: Arthur Miller's *A View from the Bridge* / 77

Chapter 5: Countercultures of Whiteness 83
White Absurdities: Edward Albee's *The American Dream* / 90
Castrating Whiteness: Amiri Baraka's *Dutchman* / 95

Whiteness as a Simulacrum of Death: David Rabe's *Sticks and Bones* / 100
The U.S. Women's Movement and Black Feminist Subculture / 104
White Talking Black: Adrienne Kennedy's *A Movie Star Has to
Star in Black and White* / 106

Chapter 6: Undigestible Difference: Powellism and New
    White Racism   111
Whiteness Made Flesh: Edward Bond's *Early Morning* / 117
Legends of White Britannia: John Arden and Margaretta D'Arcy's
The Island of the Mighty / 125
Feminism in Britain: Black versus White Responses to Women's
Subordination / 134
Colonial Metaphors of Blackness and the Reality of White
Racial Oppression: Caryl Churchill's *Cloud Nine* / 136

Chapter 7: The White Backlash: A Second U.S. Revolution   143
Postfeminism and White Womanhood: Wendy Wasserstein's *The
Heidi Chronicles* / 151
White Identity Politics: Tony Kushner's *Angels in America* / 156
(E)Racing American History: Suzan-Lori Parks's *The America Play* / 164

Chapter 8: "Swamped by People with a Different Culture": Race,
    Sexuality, and the Active British Citizen   170
White/Black Paradigms and British Gay Subculture: Philip Osment's
This Island's Mine / 176
Being Black, Seeing White: Michael Ellis's *Chameleon* / 183
The State of Whiteness: David Hare's *The Absence of War* / 188

Notes   197
Works Cited   209
Index   229

acknowledgments

This project could not have been completed without the support of numerous colleagues and friends. Many people have contributed in different ways. Thanks to Derek Paget, who, as Head of Research during my time at University College Worcester, encouraged the project, and to Baz Kershaw, who read the initial proposal. Michael Mangan talked with me about staging masculinities and provided insightful comments on Bond and Churchill. Thanks also to Mark Batty, Ross Forman, Janet Harrison, Fran Leighton, Anne Luyat, Ruth Mcelroy, and Peter Smith for dispensing advice on numerous topics, for many productive conversations, and for supplying detailed critical commentary on early drafts. Thanks again to Fran Leighton, and to Janet Harrison, this time for their practical help in looking after The Baby Genghis, which freed me up for research trips and conferences.

A huge thanks to Laura Salisbury for her advice on absolutely everything, but particularly theory, and for reading so much of the work even though she was busy finishing her Ph.D. Clive Barker commented helpfully on the whole draft and lent his support to the project from its earliest stages to completion. Ronnie Kowalski gave comments on various parts of the manuscript and passed along materials that helped me to do theater and history better. I appreciate the time Matthew Frye Jacobson took to correspond with me about his work on Whiteness.

As ever, I am grateful to Alan Sinfield. I could not have envisioned this book without the stimulating years I spent under his tutelage at Sussex University. I appreciate the rigorous way that he engaged with this work, especially his remarks on Williams and Kushner. Roy Pierce-Jones' encyclopedic knowledge and experience of British political theater helped me a great deal in conceptualizing my argument. Kate Davy's and Lynette Goddard's comments on the final draft improved the book immeasurably. I'm indebted to David Roediger for making the time to read the work and for intellectual guidance from afar. His pioneering work in the field of critical Whiteness studies inspired me intellectually, and like Alan Sinfield he has provided an inspiring example of how socially engaged criticism can be a valuable form of activism. Finally, a posthumous thank you to Jenny Kowalski and Carl Muckley, who are sorely missed. Jenny lent me time to talk through Bond's work. Carl's intellectual insights and careful editorial skills have improved the final product.

Some of this work appeared in earlier versions. Thanks in particular to Michael Worton and Nana Wilson-Tagoe, who invited me to speak on Churchill at the AHRB Gender and Representation workshop, and for the generous feedback from its participants, particularly Andrea Nouryeh. Thanks as well for productive feedback received on *Our Town* from participants at Bogaziçi University's Race, Ethnicity, and Gender conference in 2003.

I was able to write this book in large part thanks to a grant from the British Arts and Humanities Research Board, which provided me with a semester's leave. I am indebted to Judy Simons for her very useful comments on my application. The Faculty of Humanities at De Montfort University provided additional assistance in the form of a semester-long sabbatical. I'm indebted also to the librarians at De Montfort University and the British Library for their assistance throughout. Finally, I greatly appreciate the sound advice, understanding, and support of my editor at Wesleyan, Suzanna Tamminen. Thanks also to Leslie Starr at Wesleyan for her help with the cover art.

Any errors are, of course, my own.

introduction

I.

When I think about the times that I have felt myself to be White, they are usually moments when my words or actions have brought my membership in this social group into question. One such occasion in the mid-1980s involved dining out with a Black man—still an unusual sight in some parts of the deep South. The stares of the other patrons and the obvious uneasiness and disapproval of the staff made me acutely aware of my White identity, and, at the same time, my White femininity. Intuitively, I understood that we were the objects of people's attention because we were transgressing against the rules that still governed southern race-gender politics. Hence, while I felt my Whiteness manifest itself, it did so only negatively, for despite my physical appearance as a White woman, I had, for that evening, at least in the view of many present, excluded myself from this category by making a race-gendered spectacle of myself.

The genesis of this book lies partly in the moment I've just described and others like it. I am also indebted to the material produced within the growing field of critical Whiteness studies by historians, sociologists, cultural anthropologists, literary theorists, and theater scholars. This body of work has given me the tools, theoretical and methodological, to contextualize my own experience and hopefully to provide a new framework within which to analyze social and dramatic representations of race.

As Richard Dyer says in *White:* "We may be on our way to genuine hybridity, multiplicity without (white) hegemony . . . but we aren't there yet, and we won't get there until we see whiteness, see its power, its particularity and limitedness, put it in its place and end its rule. This is why studying whiteness matters" (4). Theater, I contend, enables us to see Whiteness in this critical fashion, and therefore it can contribute to a progressive racial politics.

Staging Whiteness attempts to map the complex political technology through which the category of Whiteness has been produced and endowed with cultural authority, in this case within the specific context of the twentieth-century British and U.S. theater estates. It explores the concept of Whiteness in its aesthetic and theoretical constructions and its social and political formations, illustrating where and how they intersect. My concern with representations of Whiteness is to determine the extent to which theater practices have contributed to the formation of the idea of a White "race" on a social and subjective level. What has been theater's role in reinforcing the cultural capital accruing to Whiteness in British and U.S. society by reproducing White hegemony? When and how has it worked against it? In other words, theater is examined as a site of ideological struggle over the meanings attached to race.

The book takes the position that at the levels of the social as well as the subjective British and U.S. theater practices have formed part of the discourse that precedes and enables the White subject, as well as this subject's cultural privileges. Images produced in theater function as part of the system of *langue*—the abstract totality of language—that in part forms us, and that informs our perspectives on ourselves and our society. Many people who would identify as White in Britain and the United States understand race as something that impacts only on "other" people's lives, not recognizing, as Ruth Frankenberg documents, how the system of racial differentiation constructs the identities of those upon whom it bestows privileges as much as those it subordinates (*Social Construction of Whiteness* 1). Consequently, to isolate the particular cultural location of Whiteness along a spectrum of racialized identities is to make it, and the material effects of its privileged status in society, more visible. In addition, this isolation of Whiteness demonstrates how the symbolic meanings of Whiteness shape relations of power.

Hence, one aim here is to make links between race and racism as a cultural phenomenon, something embedded in the technologies of social and political institutions, and race and racism at the micro-level of individual practices and events, in order to demonstrate how Whiteness operates. The idea behind a focus on the White subject, in addition to avoiding the treatment of Blackness as always an issue of otherness, is that examining how race and racism structure White social practices and psychology may better enable the actual mechanisms that perpetuate racism to be revealed. However, while I focus on representations of Whiteness, theorists and theater-makers have often attempted to make sense of race in a comparative context; therefore, I address also the Black/White dualism of race relations in Britain and the United States.

Because Whiteness gets staged not only in theater spaces but also on a day-to-day basis, both theater and the White "race" are addressed in their histories, with changes in the way Whiteness is represented in the theater interacting with shifts in the ideologies of racialized identities. By bringing together theater analysis and social history, I endeavor to show how the plays examined work within and sometimes against the historical limits of representation in their cultural contexts. While some of the plays demonstrate how performance texts may help replicate the status quo of White power, offering constructions of Whiteness that conform to a set of political criteria designed to preserve the social positions and privileges of selected members of society, others illustrate how theater has provided *critical* representations of Whiteness; these latter images have marked Whiteness in new ways for the spectator, opening up opportunities to resist dominant cultural processes via certain versions of Whiteness partly created through the resistance of those it denominates as its racial "others."

Concomitantly, I explore how theater has provided one of the cultural frameworks within which the spectator may recognize his/her location and level of complicity in the social conventions sustaining White power. Dominant racial discourse makes a claim for White identity as a unitary, fixed entity. To the contrary, what twentieth-century theater practice shows is that there are multiple lived experiences of Whiteness at any period in time. Indeed, the power of Whiteness is allied to what Troy Duster labels its "morphing properties": its very historic malleability (45). By demonstrating how Whiteness is a product of various power networks such as art, as well as science, medicine, religion, the media, and education, I endeavor to denaturalize the idea of the White "race." I also call into question the notion of Whiteness as a pure racial identity, pointing out its status as a constructed and hybrid entity.

Even though one can identify multiple historical inventions of Whiteness in British and U.S. culture, the fiction of a stable White identity remains a potent construction throughout the twentieth century. Race carries a real social force, because its controlling images result from certain social groups' consolidation over time of economic resources and political power, and, though Britain and the United States have very different histories, there are also some striking similarities in the way that Whiteness functions as a location of structural advantage. In each culture, Whiteness is the historical product of economic and social competition between different groups, and, as we shall see in the following chapters, Whiteness similarly connects certain institutions and social practices in both cultures.

II

This book is divided into eight chapters, each of which offers a reading of the social history and cultural developments surrounding the meaning of race alongside theater analysis. The social histories from which the plays emerge are not intended as mere backdrop; rather, they represent the condition of these plays' capacity to carry meaning.

Nearly all of the plays addressed form part of the U.S. and British twentieth-century metropolitan theater traditions, although, where necessary, some reference is made to earlier representations of race. Most of them have been staged both in New York and London. Individual plays have been chosen mainly because they point up key issues surrounding the concept of Whiteness in a particular historical period and/or theater setting. Also, I have endeavored to select plays that will be easily accessible in print and/or performance to theater students and practitioners.

Some of the works have received little, if any, recent critical treatment, while others are part of the Anglo-American canon and have a long critical and performance history. The focus of discussion is on how they reflect or call into question the prevailing myths surrounding the White "race" and how such constructions have changed over time as a result, for instance, of historical shifts such as the dissolution of the British Empire and the U.S. civil rights movement. Another key theme addresses the relation between theatricality or performance and constructions of race. The controlling images that regulate White identity, and those identities racialized as "other" within the terms of White discourse, emerge from within historical representational structures that include theatrical modes embracing elements of fantasy and projection. Thus, raced identities have a performative nature, and one can say that there is something inherently theatrical about Whiteness.

Substantively, each chapter retains its basis in a detailed criticism of the plays and period examined therein. However, in order to understand how the construction of Whiteness is embedded in twentieth-century theater practices, it is necessary to trace its historicity. I do not propose a grand theory of Whiteness; rather, I endeavor to show how the concept of the White "race" evolved over time in British and U.S. culture, and the resemblances and differences between their respective social and theatrical forms of

Whiteness. Taken together, the chapters provide a discursive history of White representations from the turn of the twentieth century through the 1990s, charting how theater-makers not only responded to changes in the social meaning of race but also offered representations of Whiteness and Blackness that figured in those changes.

The aim of chapter 1 is to chart the evolution of the dominant representation of Whiteness in British colonial discourse and the way in which theatrical representations from the turn of the century through the 1930s either challenged or reflected sociopolitical and pseudoscientific constructions of race. Chapter 2, organized within the same time frame, explores the historical development and links between Whiteness, citizenship, and expansionist ideology in the United States and their interconnections with theatrical representations of race.

Chapters 3 and 4 consider how the institutionalized myths surrounding White identity begin to be tested with greater force in the 1940s and '50s as World War II generated radical social transformations in Britain and the United States, producing a state of racial angst in both societies. In chapter 3 I examine the effect of the gradual dissolution of Britain's imperial status and Commonwealth immigration on the nation's racial and dramatic discourse, and in chapter 4 I evaluate changes in the meaning and representation of Whiteness in relation to the civil rights movement and the cold war in the United States.

In chapters 5 and 6 I address some of the conceptual changes in definitions of Whiteness produced by the social upheavals of the 1960s and '70s. I look at the way in which counterculture movements represented a potent threat to White hegemony, sometimes by those who carried the signs of its racial privilege, and how the dominant social groups in Britain and the United States responded to this threat. The emerging cultural paradigms of Black and feminist social movements and theaters are also central to these chapters. I explore how effectively subcultural movements/discourses deconstructed dominant ideological codes and posited oppositional representations of race-gendered identities.

I explore racial formations in the context of neoconservative politics in the 1980s and the new liberalism of the 1990s in chapters 7 and 8. My focus in chapter 7 is the rise of the new right in the United States, in both its secular and its religious forms, and how this movement's racial significations and preferred social structures combined to form a revised discourse of White rights. I explore subcultural responses to this new racial formation among feminist, Black, and queer playwrights. Chapter 8 concerns the development of a new White racism in British politics, and particularly how

Thatcherism advocated a certain racial narrative that excluded non-White people from the definition of Britishness. I examine the way in which this new narrative was confronted in the context of political theater, including Black and gay theaters.

The plays addressed are not intended to represent the periods under discussion in any statistical sense but to illuminate basic tensions and underlying themes that are at the center of White representations. My method of periodization is not meant to suggest that forms of Whiteness necessarily develop in a linear fashion. To the contrary, this book demonstrates how Whiteness as a category is subject to breaks, discontinuities, and revisions. At the same time, the chapter divisions do reflect certain unities within specific periods of time as events, values, and social practices share common features. The way I separate the material, therefore, is intended to make the unities as well as the dissimilarities in British and U.S. social and theatrical constructions of Whiteness more clearly visible, and to render a complex history of Whiteness and representation more easily graspable.

Staging Whiteness

chapter 1

"That's White of You . . . ": Civilizing Whiteness

The popular early-twentieth-century refrain "that's white of you" signifies a person's wish to express approval for another's admirable behavior. "Harry is a white man through and through," says a character in W. Somerset Maugham's *East of Suez* (1922), meaning that he possesses characteristics such as honesty, bravery, modesty, tolerance, loyalty, altruism, industriousness, and intelligence (209). In other words, to be White is to be culturally denominated as possessing and instantiating a set of moral and "civilized" traits and habits. That such civilized individuals overwhelmingly tend to be English and of the middle- to upper-class, male, heterosexual variety, is taken for granted not only on the world of the stage but also in the real world of turn-of-the-century England.

The prevailing definition of what it meant to be or act White at the turn of the twentieth century, which resonated up to World War II, left those who made up the category of the non-White to signify only the negative of things.[1] Though there existed some counternarratives, mainstream depictions of Africans, Indians—all those subordinated by British imperialism—generally represented them as stupid, quarrelsome, greedy, dishonest, and cunning, though, all stereotypes being equal in contradictoriness, they were also depicted as docile, irresponsibly childlike, and enjoying a doglike devotion to their masters. And always, on whatever side of the stereotypical divide they were placed, indigenous peoples were seen as governed by strong natural impulses, particularly sexual desires, that required an imposed restraint by "civilized" men, whose actions were governed by enlightened reason. Out of these paradoxical representations emerged an image of the colonized "other" that, far from static, was extremely dynamic and therefore ideologically robust, so that for any brutal act the colonizers wished to perpetrate, some combination of negative traits could be "discovered" that would excuse both the means and the ends.

However, it must be understood that English racial discourse and the concepts that cluster around the idea of racial difference have varied according to historical conditions. Winthrop D. Jordan asserts that a different symbolic register for White and Black existed in the English language before the English had in fact made contact with people who were dark-skinned. Writing about the concept of Whiteness in Elizabethan England, he states that it was already loaded with meaning and emotional impact, and, with Blackness, it conveyed some of the most ingrained values, signifying, for instance, the ideals of human beauty versus ugliness and moral purity versus evil (7–9). This, in turn, must be balanced against evidence suggesting that, although a differential set of values for Whiteness and Blackness was in place in English thought as early as the fifteenth century, these values were not yet completely consolidated in the minds of the populace. That room for alternative views existed within the symbolic register attaching to Whiteness, Blackness, and incipient notions of race is illustrated by the relatively benevolent attitudes of some sixteenth-century English colonialists toward the "Negroes" they encountered.[2]

Historical evidence suggests that early patterns of oppression based on notions of racial difference established by the English did not in the first instance solely rest on skin color. Theodore W. Allen locates the bedrock of racism in England's earliest relations with its European neighbor, Ireland, where religious difference was more important than any perceived racial difference. From as early as the thirteenth century, the ideology and practice of English racism against the Irish were based on patterns of behavior and social organization that ran counter to England's rigidly hierarchical feudal system and formal monarchy, rather than on phenotype (*The Invention of the White Race*, Vol. 1, 34).

Yet the Irish were perceived as a distinct "race," even if the concept of race was not yet fully inscribed onto the body but rather rested on perceived gradations of cultural and moral refinement. English colonialism in Ireland rested on views of the Irish as savage and uncivilized, and thus unfit for inclusion in a true Christian society. These early racial stereotypes of the Irish would come to serve as the standard of savagery that the English drew upon to justify later colonial activities among other peoples.

The idea of Whiteness as designating a natural/physical sign of racial superiority began to gain greater currency as English exploration and trading ventures in Africa, the Americas, and the Caribbean became more routine. As the trade in humans rather than in ordinary commodities became the basis of much contact with darker-skinned peoples, it became more important to English economic interests that "civilized" White traits, as opposed to Black's "anti-social" characteristics, be naturalized and, therefore, rendered unalterable. Steven Fenton locates the occasion of a systematized racism in the accelerated seventeenth-century development of world capitalism. It was the drive for profit that led English merchants to exploit existing patterns of slavery within African societies and traffic in human beings. Hence, the theory of race came after the practice of White racism (71).

As the slave trade increased and the colonial project expanded, the discrepancy between professed English Christian and democratic principles and the barbarous character of chattel slavery required stronger ideological justification. Socio-racial difference, while still resting on the nonfigurative category of the primitive, increasingly came to be registered visibly as a physical demarcator: mental and moral differences became linked to physical differences in an updated, color-coded version of the Great Chain of Being, which located White Englishmen just below the angels and Black people closer to animals.[3]

The discontinuities in English racial thought gave rise fundamentally over the course of the seventeenth and eighteenth centuries to two competing ideologies of race. The first presumed that the ascendant position of Whites and the debased condition of Blacks were naturally ordained; the second offered the possibility that Black people could be improved through contact with "civilized" Western cultures. Christianity in particular (after the Reformation, read Protestantism) was envisioned as a potential civilizing agent, one that could raise black-skinned people out of their religious and social primitivism. Whether one backed the nature or the nurture side of the argument, what was firmly established by the eighteenth century in dominant racial thought were the connections between White Englishness and socio-racial superiority, and Blackness and inferiority.

The nature versus culture debate would continue unresolved through the Victorian era. In fact, most people believed a combination of the two views, paradoxical as it was. Therefore, both notions of racial difference fed into the common understanding of the racialized subject as it came to be postulated in Victorian and Edwardian imperialist doctrines. The Victorian Empire, like the earlier slave trade, needed a rationale, one that could also sit comfortably alongside professed Christian principles. Both colonialism and Whiteness attempted to find a refuge in these principles, more specifically in the Christianity of the state. The belief that it was the White man's peculiar burden to bring the true faith to the "dark" continents eventually led to the inseparable fusion of the terms British with Christian and White in Victorian racialized discourse.[4]

At the same time, with the emergence of scientific rationalism such beliefs about racial difference as had circulated since the sixteenth century were re-inscribed by the prolific breed of ethnologists in terms influenced by the science of Darwinism.[5] Darwinism was used to stratify more precisely perceived racial differences between the White British and the diverse ethnic groups they ruled in Africa, India, and Australia. Although Indians, for example, might have been ranked higher than Aboriginal peoples in terms of their perceived racial worthiness, nevertheless the groups' culturally recognized differences were not allowed to override their containment within the inferior category of the White/Black divide. All non-White ethnic groups continued to be held in common as being beneath their White rulers. Consequently, by the time British imperialism reached its zenith in the mid-nineteenth century, Science could be added to the trio of Nation, Religion, and Whiteness as a conceptual framework for a system of colonialism buttressed by the theory of racial difference.

This gave rise to an ideological faultline in British racialized discourse, for the dominant syntactic unit pertaining to racial difference had now acquired a strong and conflicting trace of racial identity as naturally determined, subject to "scientific" validation not only on the basis of skin color but also on a growing host of measurable physical differences between White and "other" bodies and minds. Yet the residual symbolic conflation of race, religion, and nation paradoxically inferred the possibility for a person who carried natural and scientifically provable signs of inferiority on some level to successfully approximate Whiteness,[6] that is, the colonized could mimic the colonizers' cultural practices, related to religion or style of dress, for instance. This contradiction is illustrated in a statement by the founder of the Anthropological Society of London, Dr. James Hunt. He argues that the "Negro becomes more *humanized* when in his *natural* subordination to the European" (Banton 52, italics mine), thereby accepting, theoretically, at least, the idea that Blacks, though naturally inferior, could become more akin to Whites.

Although in Hunt's view Blacks would clearly remain below Whites in the social hierarchy, the notion, however tenuously expressed, that Blacks could come to resemble White Europeans brought the categories of White and "other" too close for comfort in the Victorian racial schema. Any suggestion of Whiteness as a concept with porous borders threatened the British position at the top of the colonial social order in Africa, India, and elsewhere, for their hold on power was underpinned by the presumed logical impossibility of the colonized effectively emulating the colonizers' naturally superior moral, social, and political practices. Moreover, it fed into Victorian fears that some White British subjects might "go native" and sink to the level of their colonial charges.[7]

Kenan Malik attributes the precarious and often impossible balance that the British were obliged to strike between religious, economic, political, and scientific ideologies to the relationship between race discourse, nineteenth-century capitalist relations, and enlightenment thought. A crucial part of the colonizer's mission in the age of empire was to transmit the virtues of British economic and political institutions, as well as religious ones, to the colonies. Malik argues that it was the disparity between capitalism, with its specific class and gender systems, and Enlightenment democratic ideals, combined with a dose of Victorian morality and religious ideology, that fueled a heterogeneous and contradictory mythology surrounding racialized identities (225). The inherent contradictions in British racial discourse meant that neither religion nor science could ever offer more than a partial sense of security for the White colonizers or for the discursive category of Whiteness itself, as the representation of colonialism as a civilizing mission inferred, and indeed mandated, a permeable Whiteness.

Consequently, competing versions of Whiteness and "otherness" came to circulate in later Victorian thought. The existence of these different, contradictory versions demonstrates that the meaning attached to phenotype and the meanings invested in the concept of Whiteness have always been susceptible to transvaluation according to the economic interests and sociopsychological needs of the dominant racial group. In British society race, like gender and class, has functioned as a cultural construct used to interpret social relations that feed the aims and objectives of the ruling White group. The predominant imperial construction of racial identity in the Victorian and Edwardian periods gestured toward Whiteness as a social fiction in so far as the imperial project required that White cultural practices be cast as a benign, potentially civilizing influence. Furthermore, in a neat twist, imperialism operated to further civilize Whiteness, with the British able to portray themselves as inherently enlightened given their altruistic nurturance of "other," culturally deprived races.

This conception of Whiteness coexisted with an understanding of racial difference that was never dissociated from the body in nineteenth-century discourse. Phillip Darby argues that White superiority was given a "powerful impetus . . . as a result of the spread of Social Darwinism, with its emphasis upon racial struggle and the survival of the fittest" (35). This too was vital to the cause of imperialism, as it allowed British colonialists to fall back on the argument that Black people were by nature incapable of governing their own societies. Thus we can see how, to borrow a phrase from Barthes, race functioned in British imperial discourse as "a metaphor without brakes."

Militant Whiteness: G. B. Shaw's *Captain Brassbound's Conversion*

The common understanding of the racialized subject at the turn of the twentieth century and related rationales for the subjugation of racial "others" were influenced as much by theatrical and literary ideas of race as by discussions in popular scientific magazines, newspapers, political speeches, and public lectures. Early-twentieth-century British theater enacted cultural dialogues about race by interacting with historical and contemporaneous representations from a variety of sources. Many debates about the meaning of race and ethical concerns over colonial practices that were present in late-nineteenth-century racial discourse remained unresolved in early-twentieth-century thought. From 1900 well into the 1930s, theatrical productions and their meanings continued to be critically affected by the terms of these historical debates, and, in turn, theatrical representations participated in creating and communicating a shared vision of what it meant to be a White British national.

George Bernard Shaw's *Captain Brassbound's Conversion* (1900) has as its main thrust the interrogation of the cultural myths behind colonial endeavors and the exploration of alternatives to the dominant social order. It offers a politically sophisticated and progressive scrutiny of conventional views of imperialist motives; however, the way in which it foregrounds the intersection of race, class, and gender in the construction of White imperial power produces some ideologically muddled results.

Shaw begins by putting forward the popular view of empire and the native "other" using the voice of Felix Drinkwater, a rather contrived representative of the inner-city London inhabitant. Patricia Pugh reads Drinkwater as the "average newspaper ridden Englishman" whose views on the "scramble for Africa," on "Britain's natural right" to trade "wherever it pleased," as well as the nation's "civilizing" mission (110) mirror those of the conservative press. Drinkwater perceives an unbridgeable divide between Whites and Blacks, except where he transparently projects the negative behaviors underpinning British colonial endeavors onto the Moors. Where manipulativeness and greed are concerned, he is happy to support the idea of universal kinship: "Hooman nitre is the sime everywheres. Them eathens is jast lawk you an' me, gavner" (Shaw, *CBC* 330).

However, despite Shaw's use of comedy to disarm the colonial viewpoint in the first act, the play ends up endorsing the dominant view of White supremacy by virtue of embodying the idea of British moral superiority in the play's most powerful figure, Lady Cicely Waynflete. Cicely uses her power to resolve the central dramatic problem: the kidnap of her brother-in-law, Sir Howard Hallam, by Captain Brassbound, also known as Black Paquito. Critical opinion is divided regarding Cicely's character. Shaw wrote the part as a showcase for Ellen Terry, claiming that this was the only play in which he had not "prostituted the actress" by adding a sexual interest to the character.

He based Cicely on the nineteenth-century African explorer Mary Kingsley, who was said to display a masculine "authority and knowledge of the imperial power" (MacDonald 39), and Cicely does alternate between occupying the place of White womanhood and that of Imperial Man. Sally Peters reads her as part of the Shavian tradition, offering an interpretation that celebrates female independence; she argues that Cicely's refusal to marry the captain at the end of the play signifies "a glorious escape from the marriage fate" (157–58).

By contrast, Tracy C. Davis proposes that Shaw attempts to ironize colonial relations, juggling the traditional elements of gender between Cicely and Brassbound, but that this attempt fails. A White woman, daughter of a peer, will not rule over a miscegenated, non-English, colonial pirate captain. By maintaining the one hierarchy of man over woman, the hierarchies of empires, nations, and peoples remain intact. Justice, government, and biological sex roles are all depicted as unstable, but ultimately the forces of history and incident do not succeed in changing anything ("Shaw's Interstices of Empire" 229).

I would suggest that, pace Davis, the play does subvert the primacy of the male/female hierarchy, Cicely's masculine attributes enabling her to evade the traditional strictures of her gender. Besides living independently of men, we must consider that she proves able to control all the male characters in the play and to direct major events. Nevertheless, the play's disruption of gendered hierarchies is complicated and not entirely a progressive move.

My concern is with how Cicely's position in an upside-down sex-gender system has an effect on her place in the colonial equation. How does a seemingly radical move in terms of gender representation impact the meaning and operation of Whiteness in the play? A clue may be found in a letter that Shaw wrote to Terry, which describes where he intended to locate his character in the colonial framework:

I . . . give you a play in which you stand in the very place where Imperialism is most believed to be necessary, on the border line where the European meets the fanatical African, with judge on the one hand, and indomitable adventurer-filibuster on the other, said ind-adv-fil pushing forward "civilization" in the shape of rifles and pistols in the hands of Hooligans, aristocratic mauvais sujets and stupid drifters . . . . I try to shew you fearing nobody and managing them all . . . not by cunning . . . but by simple moral superiority. Here is a part which dominates a play because the character it represents dominates the world. (T. C. Davis, *George Bernard Shaw and the Socialist Theatre*, 115–16)

Shaw's understanding of Cicely endows her with an ambiguous sex-gender status located on the borderline where masculine meets feminine. Though he claims to have rendered the character in asexual terms, nevertheless, if only because she is the sole female character, Cicely stands for the category of the feminine, and in this guise she performs the role of "other" to imperial man. Her relation to the category of "woman" is further complicated by her association with the "life-force."[8] Again, despite Shaw's insistence that the character possesses no sexual allure, the male response to Cicely consistently refutes this reading. She fits securely in the tradition of Shavian heroines whose embodiment of the "life-force" implies a potent female sexual attractiveness.

Her undeniable allure for men plays a crucial part in her ability to control them and, through them, political events, and this works to locate her more firmly in the sphere of "woman" by virtue also of aligning her with the category of the female exotic—the imponderable feminine. At the same time, however, because the hierarchy of man/woman is reversed through Cicely's controlling persona, she never fully stands in the role of exotic "other"; as stated above, she sometimes moves between masculine and feminine orders and sometimes awkwardly signifies elements of both.

Signaled in Shaw's letter to Terry is the way that her highly unstable hybridized gender status enables Cicely to occupy the borderline between (White) colonizer and colonized "other."[9] Her location at the interstices of gender, and, through gender, race, reinforces the primacy of White over Black in the racial binary, the system of color difference that maintains the borderline between colonialist and colonial, for I would suggest that her rejection of Brassbound's marriage proposal primarily reflects the need for her White racial purity to remain unsullied by cross-racial contact.

Susan Meyer points out that in Victorian racial thought what happened in the home was seen as both parallel to and necessary for the construction of empire. White women occupied an ambiguous position on the racial scales of nineteenth-century science, with their racial superiority expressed through the body as opposed to the mind (7, 19). Therefore, by maintaining Cicely's sexual exclusivity, Shaw asserts British racial superiority via the preservation of the White female body from the Black Paquito.

Ania Loomba contends that colonial ideologies of racial superiority translated easily into class terms, with the superiority of the White English implying that certain sections of people became racially identified as the "natural working-classes" (126). When Cicely adopts the position of masculine authority, her actions also work to maintain the authority of both Whiteness and dominant class positions. Her "habit of walking into people's houses and behaving as if they were her own," acquired in Africa, we are told, and her insistence that she can go anywhere safely because the people have "such nice faces" can be read in two ways. Either they signify a disregard for conventional attitudes toward class and racial difference, her avowed stance, or they provide evidence of her status as a militant female subject, who, according to Spivak, achieves her identity at the expense of the native, not-quite-human other. The play provides more convincing support for the latter interpretation.

Cicely is further linked to White colonial discourse by virtue of writing a diary of her travels for *The Daily Mail*—the same vehicle that informs Drinkwater's opinions of empire. Moreover, Cicely would have a sanitized Africa. She orders water to be brought so that Brassbound's castle may be cleaned. She would have a more hygienic working class too: she has Drinkwater forcibly bathed, in case he spreads disease. Most importantly, she completely enfeebles Brassbound. She makes something of a pet of him, refashioning him in the Anglicized wardrobe she has brought over for her brother.

Whereas Cicely symbolizes a hybridized gender construction, Brassbound represents a hybrid figure, born of a West Indian mother and a White British father—the deceased brother of Hallam. Brassbound's abduction and imprisonment of his uncle stems from a desire for revenge on several counts. However, as much as it reflects a family feud, it also speaks of his frustration at the impediment his racial difference places in the way of his enjoying full masculine privileges—the kind of power that is accorded to men such as Hallam and to a lesser degree even Drinkwater, both White and, thus, British.

Interpretations of Brassbound's racial status are a contentious matter in the play. Drinkwater describes him as a "Hinglish genlmn. Hinglish speakin; Hinglish fawther," whose "hexcursions" in Africa on behalf of the British help spread civilization (Shaw, *CBC* 328–29). The missionary Rankin, in contrast, views him as nothing better than a smuggler, one who is ill-equipped to spread civilization, neither he nor his men owning any gentle characteristics themselves. Cicely places him on the borderline between White and Black, English and Indian: she compares his behavior to Hallam's but notes that he has his "mother's complexion." Therefore, like Cicely,

Brassbound also can be said to occupy the ambiguous space between colonialist and colonized.

However, unlike her, he is not allowed to remain there. In the end, he is firmly re-placed in a subordinate role. Actually, he is blackmailed and thereby forcibly assimilated into his designated place in the Western order. The conversion undergone by Brassbound refers to his being converted from his passion for vengeance to a passion for Cicely, which climaxes in his proposal of marriage. However, while he is personally drawn to Cicely, he also needs her to censor her testimony concerning his treatment of Hallam if he is to avoid prison, and the price for this expurgation is his acquiescence in her make-over of him.

The new Western garb she provides paradoxically works to emphasize his status as racial "other," evidenced in the exchange of looks that takes place between them in the last scene. The struggle over who will be subordinator and who will be subordinated should be read as a duel between two systems of thought as much as a battle between two individual wills. The contest is not merely between "Man" and "Woman," but more importantly between a woman race-gendered as White and a man race-gendered as Black "other."

One way this is made apparent is via the heightened emphasis accorded to Brassbound's racial difference compared to earlier scenes. For most of the play, he is referred to as Brassbound or the Captain, but, in the last scene, both he and Cicely use his moniker Black Paquito. Also, the application of military language to their proposed union places their relation within the context of the actual threat of martial struggle between the White colonizers and the Moors that serves as background to acts 2 and 3.

When Brassbound proposes, for instance, he claims that he is not looking for a wife but a commander: "Don't undervalue me: I am a good man when I have a good leader" (Shaw, *CBC* 415). His view of Cicely as *naturally* suited to command over him reflects his internalization of the idea that there were people who were of superior quality by dint of blood as well as property. Fenton describes how such class-formed views paralleled racialized views in seeing a people as naturally subordinate and inherently of less quality because they were not White (83).

The final encounter between Cicely and Paquito makes it appear natural for a person racialized as "other" to serve a White person, and this logic renders the idea of a White/Black sexual pairing unnatural: "I'm afraid you don't quite know how odd a match it would be for me according to the ideas of English society," Cicely tells Paquito (Shaw, *CBC* 415–16). She reacts to his suggestion that she dismiss these conventions with a startling reversal of character, displaying her first and only show of fear. Shaw's stage directions state that she learns "for the first time in her life what terror is, as she finds that he is unconsciously mesmerizing her" (Shaw, *CBC* 416). Her unease may spring from the temptation to acquiesce or from an awareness that even she, the epitome of the unconventional Edwardian woman, is powerless to defy her society's racial conventions without suffering severe consequences.

Her mesmeric trance is momentary, however, broken by the sound of gunfire from the *Thanksgiving*—the U.S. warship—which acts to secure the dominant socio-racial order, literally and metaphorically, firstly by freeing Hallam and preventing armed resistance by the Moors, and then by bringing Cicely to her senses and preserving the sanctity of the White "race." Paquito's response to the guns, "It is farewell. Rescue for you— safety, freedom! You were made to be something better that the wife of Black Paquito," reaffirms his internalization of White racial views (Shaw, *CBC* 417). Consequently, his assertion that his power and purpose as a man have been restored proves unconvincing in the context of an encounter ultimately privileging a White cultural order that denies him access to the category of "Man."

This idea is echoed in the play's final words. Cicely's "How glorious! How glorious! And what an escape!" (Shaw, *CBC* 417) signifies that it is a reproductive union between the daughter of a White peer and a miscegenated man that cannot be imagined, even in Shaw's radical theater. Hence, Davis's argument that the maintenance of the hierarchy of man over woman keeps intact other imperial hierarchies needs to be amended to take account of the sex-gender system's racial exclusiveness, for, ultimately, it is Cicely's identity as pure White female that works to keep in place the hierarchies of nation, empire, and race.

The Heart of Whiteness: W. Somerset Maugham's *The Explorer*

Sean O'Connor suggests that W. Somerset Maugham inherited the mantle of Oscar Wilde in dissecting the character of the empire-builders, and of the parasites who prosper from British foreign policy (62). However, Maugham's play *The Explorer* (1912) does not provide a straightforward condemnation of the British imperial project but rather an ambivalent portrait of colonial enterprise. On the one hand, the play presents the virtues of White colonialism from the perspective of a quintessential Edwardian man; its leading character, Mackenzie, participates in the reproduction of White supremacist ideology. On the other hand, it bears similarities to Shaw's *Brassbound* in the way it speaks to the contradictions inherent in White racial mythology, revealing a subtle and potentially subversive portrait of Whiteness.

The play's hero, Mackenzie, is a wooden, almost comic-book representation of an Edwardian gentleman explorer. He has undertaken a number of expeditions against Arab slave traders in Northeast Africa, and, as the play begins, he prepares to embark on another. He is also represented as culturally refined, chivalrous toward women, scrupulously honest, and self-sacrificing.

This appears to earn him respect equally among White society and the natives of Mombassa, who recognize him as a natural leader among men. Mackenzie's African adventures are represented in noble terms too, with the White British depicted as friendly mentors to the natives. For example, while the Arabs would lead the Africans into chattel slavery, in a classic instance of divide and conquer the White British seek to improve Africans' lives by introducing them to the ways of 'civilization.'

Mackenzie's supposed moral conscience is said to extend to his private life. Unlike George Allerton, the drama's rogue figure, who "plays the fool" with native women, Mackenzie refrains from any such dissolute activity. In fact, despite the play's main focus, the love interest between Mackenzie and Allerton's sister, Lucy, his moral rectitude is such that it renders him strangely asexual in his approach to the White feminine.

He is, though, a heartier companion to men, including Africans, going so far as to share "Scotch jokes" in an African dialect with his native retainers. I do not mean to imply any overt manifestations of homosexuality on his part or among members of his expedition. To the contrary, Maugham carefully suggests that the cause of empire rests with "real" men like Mackenzie by providing him with a foil, the "weak and floppy" Sir Robert Boulger, who unsuccessfully competes for Lucy's affections.

Boulger's natural habitat is the drawing room. He enjoys a pampered existence. He appears as too handsome, and physically slight: one of his social set tells him "Alec [Mackenzie] could just crumple you up" (Maugham, *Explorer* 105).

Maugham endows Boulger with many of the stereotypical negative traits usually ascribed to women. He behaves petulantly. He is prone to jealousy, vicious if thwarted, and given to subterfuge, feigning headaches to escape unwanted social engagements. When he tells Mackenzie that he no longer wishes to know him, Mackenzie subtly calls Boulger's masculinity into question, offering to return his letters and photograph just as might be conventionally expected at the end of an affair with a woman.

Mackenzie, by contrast, is represented with "the will of iron and nerves of steel" needed to survive in the jungle, to build and hold an empire. When not battling against the Arabs, he and his company engage themselves in opening up and annexing new African territories for British control. These details, besides providing evidence of the imperial motive behind English disputes with the Arabs, also show how Mackenzie's character functions to link Whiteness, heterosexual masculinity, and imperial power.

However, this triad as the basis of colonial authority is eventually undermined. For example, heterosexual desire lies at the heart of the troubled expedition that results in George's death. George crosses recognized racial boundaries by having sexual relations with a Black woman, whom he later kills when she begins to make inconvenient demands. His actions provoke the Africans into defying British authority, and they refuse to fight with them against the Arabs.

Consequently, the White explorers are outnumbered; George is killed, and Mackenzie and his companions just barely escape. Whether the true cause that provokes George's exclusion from the British company of men is murder or miscegenation remains open to question. Either way, however, heterosexual desire is seen to generate an active threat to British colonial power.

Furthermore, although Mackenzie returns home to win the girl, as soon as he does he announces his departure on another colonial expedition to Africa. Clearly, he views conquest and imperial power, not domestic relations, as the natural, best destiny of the White British male, and this makes the act of colonization appear as the White man's highest personal and collective duty to self, nation, and history.

Mackenzie's final lengthy commentary on empire rings with an evangelical fervor that is clearly lacking in his addresses to Lucy:

You'll think me very silly, but I'm afraid I'm rather—patriotic. It's only we who live away from England who really love it. I'm so proud of my country, and I wanted so much to do something for it. Often in Africa I've thought of this dear England, and longed not to die till I had done my work. Behind all the soldiers and the statesmen whose fame is imperishable, there is a long line of men who've built up Empire piece by piece. Their names are forgotten, . . . but each of them gave a province to his country. And I, too, have my place among them. For five years I toiled night and day, and at the end of it was able to hand over to the Commissioners a broad tract of land, rich and fertile. (Maugham, *Explorer* 141)

That Mackenzie and Lucy will marry eventually demonstrates how heterosexuality resides at the center of colonial power insofar as the fertility of male-female unions produces the long line of men needed to sustain imperialism. Nevertheless, the privileged camaraderie enjoyed by Mackenzie's band of men, combined with his decision to postpone establishing a home with Lucy, suggests that heterosexual bonds are secondary to the ties among men, which lead to the actual acquisition of colonial territories, wealth, and power. Despite on the surface defending imperial relations by casting them in the most conventional quasi-religious terms, *The Explorer's* construction of imperial man ends up locating this subject's power within a homosocial context.

As theorized by Eve Kosofsky Sedgewick, the homosocial describes social bonds between men that include an erotic potential and possibly an element of homophobia. Instead of this erotic desire finding an outlet through homosexual practices, it plays itself out in social relations through the conduit of a woman. This triangular relationship suggests that the desire that bonds the men over the woman is as erotically invested for the men in relation to each other as for each of them in relation to her.

At the level of the individual, homosocial desire may play itself out unconsciously, but it materially manifests itself at the level of the social: it is the foundation on which patriarchal social practices and institutions are constituted. Therefore, homosocial desire is something of a paradox, insofar as it represents a form of eroticism created by, rather than repressed by, patriarchal relations and practices but at the same time depends, at the level of the social, on the "othering" (the disavowing) of openly homosexual relations (Sedgewick 1–3). By suggesting that the social bonds between Mackenzie and his men may include an erotic potential, the play lays open to question the presumed natural connection between Whiteness, heterosexuality, and power.

Waving the White Flag: W. H. Auden and Christopher Isherwood's *The Ascent of F6*

The plays discussed so far reveal to varying degrees how Whiteness and its self-proclaimed "others" are effects of a set of regulatory cultural practices fueled by the dynamics of White interests. Each play makes apparent, either by attempting to reinforce the category's imperial heritage or by deconstructing its status as naturally determined, how Whiteness constitutes a competing and conflicting deployment of identity. The final play addressed in this chapter, W. H. Auden's and Christopher Isherwood's dramatic critique of imperialism *The Ascent of F6* (1937), affords another productive illustration of how Whiteness maintains its cultural authority despite its inherent contradictions.

F6 designates a mountain peak that lies on the frontier between fictional British Sudoland and Ostnia, an imperial competitor nation. When British propaganda fails to quell Sudoese rebellion, the British mount a climbing expedition in an attempt to capitalize on a local folk belief that the White man "who first reaches the summit of F6 will be lord over both the Sudolands, with his descendants, for a thousand years" (Auden and Isherwood 22). However, the most important contest in the play is not the race between the British and Ostnian climbers but the competition between different versions of political reality. When a British general objects to the idea of the expedition as folly, preferring military action to reliance on a "fairy-tale," the colonial officer Ransom tells him that "a fairy-tale . . . is significant according to the number of people who believe in it" (Auden and Isherwood 22).

Auden and Isherwood highlight the collusion between the imperialists and the mythmaking press, with the colonial office using various media to set out their version of how the Sudoese are being treated in order to shore up support at home and rebut criticism from imperial competitors. In act 1 a radio announcer presents the British version of events: "You may have read recently . . . of riots in Sudoland, but from personal experiences I can tell you that these stories have been greatly exaggerated. . . . Hospitals, clinics, and schools have done much to raise the standard of personal hygiene and education among the Sudoese and the vast majority are happy and contented" (Auden and Isherwood 26).

Lady Isabel reprises the colonizer's viewpoint when she says that whenever anything generous, brave, or beautiful happens anywhere in the world, "we shall generally find that, at the bottom of it, is an Englishman" (Auden and Ishwerwood 41). The play makes clear how these traits are deemed the natural preserve of the White colonizers; after meeting the British climbers, Isabel comes away feeling proud of belonging to the same country and the same *race* as they. Auden and Isherwood take no dramatic liberties here. The idea that British imperialism was good for colonial peoples remained commonplace in British political discourse in the 1930s, and the announcer's words easily could have been written and read by a number of twentieth-century British politicians. Consider the view put forward by the colonialist Sir Alan Burns, who portrays British imperialism almost as a charitable act: "But when one considers colonial rule one has got to remember what was there before it started. Cannibalism, slavery, human sacrifice and various other abominations. . . . So I'm quite certain that colonialism was a good thing from the point of view of the African native himself" (Charles Allen 146).

The voice of the colonized themselves, supplied by the chorus, gives us an alternative story: "Let the eye of the traveler consider this country and weep," they state,

> For the Dragon has wasted the forest and set fire to the farm;
> He has mutilated our sons in his terrible rages
> And our daughters he has stolen to be victims of his dissolute orgies;
> He has cracked the skulls of our children in the crook of his arm;
> With the blast of his nostrils he scatters death through the land;
> We are babes in his hairy hand.
>
> (Auden and Ishwerwood 86–87)

The chorus, delivering its lines in darkness, alludes to the people's inability to make anyone see the true state of their nation under British occupation because they do not control the material means that endow White speech with force. In the final scene, the version of events put forward by Ransom, now costumed as the Dragon, holds center stage. Insisting that the British "civilizing mission has been subject to grave misinterpretations" (Auden and Ishwerwood 87), he delivers a classic carrot and stick ultimatum. While stating that the powers he represents stand unequivocally for peace and progress, he backs up this pledge of peaceful coexistence with the threat of force and a reminder of the natural position of the British as a superior culture and race.

As a polemical play, *Ascent* is open to the charge of a rather simplified assault on colonialism, sometimes making the answers to the problem of racial oppression appear too easy. Still, it provides a useful reminder of how earlier historical constructions of race may bear a continuing relevance for later social struggles. Most importantly, while it acknowledges that colonial power relies on force, as we saw in *Captain Brassbound's Conversion* and *The Explorer,* Auden and Isherwood's play demonstrates also how this power rests as much on the colonizer's ability to tell convincing stories, in this case, tales about race.

The Ascent of F6 shows Whiteness to be a fictional discursive category, with a cultural force relative to its ability to get its stories of what constitutes reality repeated and circulated as widely as possible. By calling attention to how the distorted representation of White identities enables the maintenance of its material force, Auden and Isherwood show that in order to combat White dominance it is necessary to highlight the fictional status of White stories of race and subjectivity, and this, in turn, requires a full engagement with the category's historical manifestations.

chapter 2

The Borders of Whiteness in the New World

George Rawick argues that "[m]odern racism came out of the process that marked the transition from feudalism to capitalism in sixteenth century England" (128–29). His explanation of how ideas about race emerged in relation to this transition is worth quoting at length:

> The Englishman met the West African as a reformed sinner meets a comrade of his [sic] previous debaucheries. The reformed sinner very often creates a pornography of his former life. He must suppress even his knowledge that he had acted that way or even that he wanted to act that way. Prompted by his uneasiness at the great act of repression, he cannot leave alone those who lived as he once did or as he still unconsciously desires to live. He must devote himself to their conversion or repression. In order to ensure that he will not slip back into the old ways or act out his half-suppressed fantasies, he must see a tremendous difference between his reformed self and those whom he formerly resembled. But because he still has fantasies which he cannot accept, he must impute these fantasies to the realities of someone else.
>
> The English compared themselves with the Africans and congratulated themselves for being different and superior. . . . The Africans behaved as they did because of a different innate moral constitution. What the English unconsciously realized about the Africans was not so much that they were different but that they were frighteningly similar. (133)

In the American colonies, the presence of Black slaves transformed these fears and unconscious realizations into a way of life.

Hence, from colonial times the White/Black binary, and its associated, frequently contradictory stereotypes, has represented a throughline in U.S. culture, resonating in all of its languages of socio-ideological life—historical, religious, economic, and political. While some ideas about race were imported to the Americas, racism and xenophobia quickly developed a distinct trajectory in the New World. In this chapter, I focus on the development of U.S. racial discourse in the early English colonies through the era of western expansionism. My aim is to make clear how constructions of Whiteness current at the beginning of the twentieth century relate to the colonial myth of Manifest Destiny and historical definitions of "U.S. Man," the figure that equates to the ideal U.S. citizen.

Matthew Frye Jacobson's compelling account of the U.S. historical vision and re-visioning of Whiteness locates a tendency to conflate political and racial identity, at least implicitly, "in the earliest documents establishing a European political order in the New World. . . ." The duties of citizenship were articulated over and against White English encounters with "savage Indians" (23). The colonial view of the Native American as barbarous rested in the first instance on differences between social practices, not physical bodies. Although their darker skin was noted, this did not bother the White settlers as much as the perceived iniquity of their lifestyles. In particular, their communal patterns of social organization, in terms of ownership of land and commodities, conflicted with White English capitalist forms, and the perceived looseness of their familial and sexual relations went against the grain of Christian morality.

The White English further differentiated themselves based on where they lived, the settlers' perspective being entwined with their views on nature: the vast uncharted wilderness regions of the Americas. They were suspicious of the Native American way of living in harmony with the land, rather than parceling it out among themselves and subduing it, as set out in Biblical doctrine. Their occupation of uncultivated land, combined with tribal spiritual practices, consolidated Native Americans with satanic forces in the minds of the mainly Puritan White settlers; the Devil, it was feared, also lurked in this untamed natural space.

While the settlers were faced with the real prospect of danger from disease, starvation, and in some cases extinction by the indigenous population, which sought to resist further settlements, they also imagined themselves as facing a threat to their souls in what they perceived to be a metaphysically threatening environment. This equation of the wilderness with evil potentialities, which were then embodied in the Indian race, comes through in William Bradford's account *Of Plymouth Plantation*. In 1620, he described the colonists' first reaction to the land: "what could they see but a hideous and desolate wilderness, full of wild beasts and wild men. . . . For the summer being done, all things stand upon them with a weatherbeaten face, and the whole country, full of woods and thickets, represented a wild and savage hue" (176). It was not long before the colonists largely abandoned their professed mission to "reclaim" the Native Americans for God (after having failed at attempts to enslave them) and began to see them rather as obstacles to their colonial designs that would have to be overcome or removed.

Colonial notions of racial and cultural difference, while formed against the character and practices, both real and imagined, of indigenous peoples, cannot be understood without reference to the presence of African slaves. In the seventeenth century England alone could not supply the labor power needed to colonize its share of the New World, and for this it relied upon slavery to supplement the population of indentured servants. Further, in the seventeenth and eighteenth centuries the colonial elite was made up of a small band of "plantocrats," men who owned large tracts of mainly agricultural land. Within this economic context, slavery favored capital accumulation among the plantocracy; consequently, in the eighteenth century the performance of agricultural and unskilled physical labor became concentrated among an ever-increasing population of enslaved Blacks.

This left a significant number of White laborers, who had earned release from their bonds, in a precarious position. Also, it made the question of how to maintain control over this class of worker an urgent one for the ruling elite. These White laborers, male and female, were too many in number to be accommodated within the class of the petty bourgeoisie. As a result, the landowning class lived with the constant threat of rebellion. Their fears were justified, given the history of resistance in the colonies, sometimes violent, by groups of poor White servants.

Theodore Allen elaborates on how the promotion of race-consciousness over class-consciousness was used to avert the possibility of White and Black laborers acting collectively. The result was a new concept of Whiteness: "nothing could have been more apparent than that the small cohort of the ruling elite must have a substantial intermediate buffer social control stratum to stand between it and possible 'rebellion' by the poor White freeman." The White "race" was invented to serve as the social control formation, and "[w]hat distinguished this system of social control, what made it the 'white race,' was the participation of the laboring classes: non-slaveholders, self-employed smallholders, tenants and laborers" (Allen, *The Invention of the White Race,* vol. 2, 240–51).[10]

As the regime of chattel slavery became entrenched, an altered concept of racial difference came into being as a response to the threat of class rebellion and the unconscious processes of identification noted by Rawick. This racial schema was less ambiguous than the discourse of savagism, for it made difference immediately detectable by inscribing it onto the skin, the hair, the lips, and so on, of people of color.[11] Within this socio-racial system, Whiteness and Blackness were founded first on a difference in physicality, whereby white skin functioned as a sign of superiority and black skin functioned as the external marker of an internal mental and moral inferiority.

In the eighteenth century colonial slaves were Black Africans, who, regardless of their knowledge of Christian practices, could never transcend this classification, and by the nineteenth century this view had hardened to such an extent that Blackness became synonymous in dominant thought with the category of the subhuman.[12] This meant that anyone located within the category Black was deemed a natural candidate for slavery, in perpetuity. Thus, in contrast to British imperialist discourse, the definition of racial difference in the colonies was becoming less entangled with residual notions of religious and cultural difference. The presence of "other" racial groups on what the colonists saw from the outset as their home territory meant that the contest over what it signified socially to be White as opposed to Black had a greater sense of immediacy and political and economic urgency than might have been felt by British colonialists occupying territories outside their homeland.

This sense of urgency was also heightened by the growing debate over slavery in the nineteenth century. In the 1840s and '50s, scientific explanations of the nature of racial difference came to play a leading role in arguments for and against emancipation, with the supposed objectivity of ethnology making it a very useful tool for both sides. [13] Monogenecists held that humans shared a common ancestry, and that racial differences were attributable to differences in social environments (for example, savagery versus civilization). Polygenecists, in contrast, believed that there existed several races that had been created separately and were in fact distinct species. Among pro-slavers, the argument for plural origins was preferred. This occluded any prospect of biological or political mobility for Blacks, and it conveniently denied the possibility that the White race might be subject to degeneration. Polygenesis offered pro-slavers a potent weapon in their argument that Whites were naturally fit to rule. Further, it allowed them free rein in how they treated Blacks.

After the Civil War, when Blacks gained equal rights, at least on paper, the polygenecist position gained more adherents, even among some who had opposed slavery. The principal cause of this shift was the challenge that Whites faced in how to integrate a free Black population within the U.S. (White) body politic. During Reconstruction the North had adopted a weak brand of paternalism toward Blacks, while the South became increasingly negrophobic, fostering a culture of extreme racism. Yet despite this difference in attitude and tone, the stakes surrounding the status of free Blacks following Black emancipation were now felt by both sides to be quite similar.

Recall that the category of Whiteness in U.S. discourse not only refers to physically measurable differences between social groups but also indicates a degree of freedom by signifying the relation of a group's members to the concept of the ideal U.S. citizen, and all of the privileges attendant on this identity. After the failure of Reconstruction the Northern victors deemed it expedient to normalize relations with the former Confederate States. The idea that Blacks were a different species from Whites made it easier for the North to placate the South by turning a blind eye to "Black Codes" and "Jim Crow" laws that were used to reinstitutionalize White supremacy. Moreover, by dividing the races into separate and unequal species, the ruling elite could better unify support for the status quo among Whites of different classes, both North and South.

If the social control stratum was to be maintained, a firm distinction needed to be drawn between what it meant to be a free White person and a free Black person.[14] While science and the physical "proofs" it was believed to offer were used theoretically to reinforce the political power of Whiteness, what distinguished the positions of Whites from Black freemen on a day-to-day basis was the kind of work each group performed. This was especially true for White immigrants.

Jacobson suggests that the republican equation of Whiteness with fitness for citizenship was generally an untroubled one until "'free white persons' of un-dreamt of diversity and number dragged ashore in the 1840s and afterward" (38). Thousands of refugees from the Napoleonic Wars and victims of the Irish famine migrated to the United States, followed by waves of immigrants from southern and eastern Europe and Asia. The latter migrants were perceived as particularly threatening by the WASP citizenry because, like the Irish, they tended to be Catholic, or worse not Christian at all, and many were dark skinned and/or did not speak English as a first language. These successive waves of immigration led to fears of cultural contamination that were most often expressed in racialized terms. It was this anxiety about preserving the essential White Anglo–orientation of U.S. culture in the face of large numbers of diverse immigrant cultures, joined with the need to sustain White power over African Americans, that would give rise in the 1860s to the notion of variegated Whiteness.

The case of Irish immigrants offers a clear example of the link between labor and race, as well as the increasing malleability of Whiteness as a discursive category. Upon first arrival in the United States, the Irish often worked with Blacks at the same jobs. In addition, they lived in close physical proximity, frequently socialized in the same places, and sometimes inter-married. For this reason (and for others embedded in Anglo-Irish historical relations), Irish immigrants were characterized commonly as "niggers turned inside out."[15]

In *How the Irish Became White,* Noel Ignatiev shows that skin color made the Irish only eligible for admission into the White "race"; it did not guarantee them a place. As with other immigrants, the Irish soon became aware of the considerable material as well as psychological advantages of regularizing their ambiguous position in the socio-racial hierarchy and earning acceptance in mainstream U.S. culture. They would earn their right to be called White by declaring their difference from and superiority to Black Americans. Mainly, this was accomplished by associating Irish workers with occupational roles that were perceived as naturally suited to White laborers. The main criterion for work to be designated White was not so much the nature of the work itself (though Whites did adamantly insist on their right to skilled occupations) but the fact that Blacks were ex-cluded from performing it.

Ignatiev argues that in every period of U.S. history the category White included only groups that did "white man's work."[16] Certainly by the nine-teenth century whether immigrants would be viewed as White was not simply a matter of their physical characteristics: rather, White marked a particular kind of class relation, a category mediated through distinctive forms of labor that could not exist without an opposite or Black "other." Immigrant groups (for example, Italians, Poles, Jews) with questionable racial credentials would follow a similar pattern to that of the Irish, access-ing Whiteness by dissociating themselves from Blacks both in the work-place and in their home environments.

However, as W. E. B. Du Bois reflects in *Black Reconstruction,* the wages of Whiteness for many of these immigrants were nearly all psychological (which is not to say imaginary) but of little consequence in economic terms. Yet despite the contradiction that could exist between a group's identification as White and its continued relative substandard of living, the policy of using race to unite Whites of different classes worked for those in power. David Roediger documents how "race and class are so imbricated in the consciousness of working-class Americans that we do not get class if we do not get race" (*Toward the Abolition of Whiteness* 9). This intimate connection helps explain how widespread support among working-class immigrant populations first for the institution of slavery and later for apartheid was generated.

The identity of "U.S. Man," that "true American" citizen who, by virtue of his race, gender, heterosexuality, and rugged individualism, possessed the capability of aiding his nation in realizing its special destiny, was inextricably tied to his willingness to oppress, violently and otherwise, people racialized as "other." While the U.S. social elite was working out new institutional mechanisms for controlling the free Black population, Whites were also engaged in "winning the West." The settlement of the western territories illustrates how White America conceives of itself as a nation via its belief in Manifest Destiny.[17]

The term "Manifest Destiny" refers to the belief that North America represents a "new Jerusalem," that Americans are God's new chosen people, and that the United States as a nation has a divine mission to spread its religious and, perhaps more importantly, economic and political principles across the North American continent and indeed the globe. From the seventeenth century onward Manifest Destiny has been the most important doctrine in the campaign to justify a host of U.S. imperialist activities, economic and otherwise. In the nineteenth century these colonial activities included the systematic displacement and genocide of Native Americans.

Whites in the United States needed an ideological justification for their activities, one that could be squared with the dominant Protestant religion. This 1873 account by William Gilpin, first governor of Colorado, exemplifies how western expansionism was rationalized:

Since 1608 we have grown from nothing to 22,000,000: from a garden-patch, to be thirty States and many territories!

This occupation of wild territory, accumulating outward like the annual rings of our forest trees, proceeds with all the solemnity of a Providential ordinance. It is at this moment sweeping onward to the Pacific with accelerated activity and force, like a deluge of men, rising unabatedly, and daily pushed onward by the hand of God. (232–33)[18]

The presence of significant numbers of Native Americans in this "wild territory" was one of the reasons why the U.S. Government was willing to grant entry to large numbers of immigrants who were not of pure Caucasian descent, which was defined as Anglo-Saxon or Teutonic ancestry. If the Indian Wars were to be won, sufficient numbers were needed to fight them. Western expansionism meant that *place* would continue to play an important role in the construction of the White "race" through the end of the nineteenth century, for "civilizing" the West by conquering Native lands offered some immigrant groups another opportunity to qualify as White.

By 1890, with the Indian Wars mainly concluded, the western frontier was announced officially to be closed. The remaining Native American population, drastically decreased in number, now endured a precarious existence, partitioned off from the White population on reservations. As Native Americans became less visible in White society, the figure of the "Red Indian" came to occupy a less prominent role in U.S. racial discourse.

As the century drew to a close, the dominant representation of the "Negro" would come more and more to be designated as the primary racial "other" against which White America defined itself. The stereotype of Blacks that predominated at the turn of the century crystallized during the period of racial hysteria that swept the South in the wake of the Civil War. Southern ideology endowed Blacks with a dual identity: docile and amiable when enslaved or kept in proper subordination but likely to turn ferocious and murderous when free or allowed to get above their natural station.

Blacks' presumed guilelessness was especially feared for the danger it posed to democracy, because it would make them easy prey for manipulation by demagogues. Black people were also viewed as having a propensity to violence and generally lacking self-control, being gluttonous and licentious—Black men prone to sexual violence and Black women unchaste. They were portrayed as disliking work, whereas Whites had initiative and enterprise, and while Whites were honest and open-hearted, Blacks were ruthless and cunning.

The idea that Blacks were a degenerate race—"degenerate" signifying immorality as well as an active state of psycho-physical deterioration—was central to late-nineteenth-century racial ideology. This concept, which rested in part on a crude reading of Darwinism, suggested that, once free, Blacks would revert to a savage state, prove unable to sustain themselves, and ultimately become extinct. Some Whites, North and South, welcomed economic competition from free Blacks. It was assumed that their degeneracy (especially sexual degeneracy, which led to disease) would render them incapable of winning such a competition, and in this way the problem of what to do about them would solve itself.

To an extent, this proved a self-fulfilling prophecy, because White representations of Blackness served to excuse the government from supporting programs that might enable Black people to escape poverty. If Blacks were by nature doomed to die out, then, rather than assist them in becoming full members of society, the task of Whites would be to prevent their own society from becoming contaminated through contact. This line of reasoning provided a convenient rationale for new and overtly oppressive state policies, and it rationalized the continuing exclusion of Blacks from the political sphere, thereby preserving the U.S. body politic as a White racialized entity.

Compared to both "Indian" and "Negro" identities, constructions of Whiteness in the nineteenth century proved conveniently flexible, prone in their historical terms to rapid fluctuations in signification, due to the necessity of assimilating a host of immigrant communities that were deemed racially/culturally different. As a result, for most of the period and continuing into the twentieth century there existed a ladder of Whiteness in U.S. racial discourse. That White Anglo-Saxon Protestants should occupy the top rung passed for the cultural common sense.

This did not mean that a particular immigrant group's place on the ladder was solely determined by their resemblance to the dominant cultural group. As important, if not more so, was the degree to which the immigrant group could show itself as different from African Americans, and, too, the group's relative fitness for U.S. citizenship compared to other racialized immigrant communities. For example, whether the Polish qualified as U.S. citizens was in part decided by the degree to which they could distinguish themselves from Blacks, and by comparing the relative unsuitability of other immigrants, such as the Italians. The number of rungs on the ladder of Whiteness was virtually unlimited. Therefore, when one group of immigrants joined it or moved up, it did not necessitate removing another group, but it did mean that for a time one might be positioned further from the ideal of Whiteness and its relative privileges.

Paradoxically, by 1900 the theory of an unadulterated Whiteness also held a firm place in U.S. racial discourse. The division between the categories of White and Black would be sharpened through the 1930s, even though immigrant groups who arrived with the status of quasi-white would continue to be gradually assimilated into the superior category of Whiteness. In other words, while the category of Whiteness could be infiltrated by "intermediate whites," in relation to Blackness its boundaries, both psychological and material, would be represented as impregnable. Andrew Hacker documents the way in which all "intermediate" White racial groups have been allowed to put a visible distance between themselves and Blacks, with none of the presumptions of inferiority being permanently imposed on other ethnicities the way that they have been enforced on Black Americans (18–19). Only the figure of the African American "other" would remain positioned at the bottom of the U.S. socio-racial hierarchy in both the nineteenth and twentieth centuries.

Emasculating Whiteness: Eugene O'Neill's *The Hairy Ape*

Turning now to the production of Whiteness in U.S. theater, I address firstly Eugene O'Neill's *The Hairy Ape* (1922). My reading considers how O'Neill gives us in Yank, the play's main character, a figure whose experience plainly displays the gaps between White identity's available positions within U.S. society in the early decades of the twentieth century. Combining expressionist and realist features, O'Neill counters any tendency in the spectator to sympathize with Yank, leading one instead to evaluate critically the systemic conditions that produce his individual circumstances. Yank functions as a sign, and exactly *of what* has occupied critics' attention since the play's first production.

Margaret Loftus Ranald sums him up as representative of the "unthinking, voiceless working-class" (62). Keat Murray reads Yank as an animated version of Rodin's *Thinker*, a person searching for order in the "seeming formlessness of life" who seeks to "create a new self-conception in a new reality" (108). Whether viewed as a modern-day working-class hero calling for revolution or new-world Neanderthal illustrating the futility of violent resistance, Yank has attracted only scant critical attention to his racialized identity. Race has rarely been deemed central to the play's meaning, yet the way in which Yank's Whiteness punctuates his position in the class system proves critical in determining his experience.

The economic and cultural conditions that form the backdrop to O'Neill's play are those of the industrial era: the period between Reconstruction and the Great Depression was characterized by White efforts to solidify economic and racial domination through various forms of juridical, political, and social discrimination (Wilson 4). These sociopolitical circumstances are reflected in the mise en scéne of the play's opening. Here O'Neill pays careful attention to race, describing the men in the forecastle as belonging to the "civilized white races." His reference proves ironic, as this episode elaborates a catalog of ethnic groups that historically have struggled to attain White status. Accordingly, as the men register among themselves their different ethnicities, they are concerned also to establish their difference from the "nigger" (O'Neill, *THA* 137).

The perceptions of Yank and his men are those of people reared in the knowledge that to be a *normal* U.S. citizen is to be masculine *and* middle class *and* financially successful *and* independent—all of which come together to spell White, that is, Whiteness of a particular variety. I posit Yank as representative of variegated Whiteness, whereas Mildred's anemic persona represents a purer White identity, with these distinct instances of Whiteness tied to the characters' different class and gender identities. In contrast to Roediger, who views the exchange of looks that pass between Yank and Mildred in the stokehole (scene 3) as marking the moment when Yank is rendered non-White after previously having personified "All-American manhood" ("White Looks" 37), I suggest that his encounter with Mildred reveals the contradiction that exists between being White and working class in U.S. culture. O'Neill never provides Yank with a firm foothold in the category of U.S. Man but only a slippery position on the ladder of Whiteness. Mildred serves as the vector through which he becomes aware of his *relative* White status and the reason why he cannot garner recognition of his full humanity.

O'Neill interpolates Yank as a variegated White figure through the savage guise of the "primitive."[19] Yank's brutish disposition shows itself most clearly in scene 3, during which he becomes aware of Mildred through the eyes of his men. He turns to see what stands behind him "defensively, with a snarling, murderous growl, crouching to spring, his lips drawn back over his teeth, his small eyes gleaming ferociously." O'Neill's stage directions state that Yank perceives her "like a white apparition," and beneath her gaze he is "turned to stone." Also temporarily paralyzed, she is crushed by the impact of this "unknown, abysmal brutality, naked and shameless" (O'Neill, *THA* 157).

Yank's bestial pose stamps his exchange of looks with Mildred, as well as his subsequent obsession with her, with sexual connotations, and it aligns him with the recognizable stereotype of the Black male rapist, a figure prevalent in the political discourse and literature of the day. Consider also that throughout the play he appears literally blackened: he is the only crewmember who does not wash, and hence the coal dust seeping into his skin gives Yank the appearance of a "piebald nigger."

Paradoxically, as Yank grows to be more simian he becomes less rather than more powerful, supported by the fact that meeting Mildred signals his emasculation. In dominant terms, were he a White man in the fullest sense, Mildred would stand as his "other" and he would have free access to White femininity. By contrast, what so disturbs Yank is how Mildred's gaze "others" *him.* For this reason, his attempts to create a secure self-identity depend as much on his ability to reverse the relations between himself and Mildred-as-woman as they do on his capacity to topple the owners of Fifth Avenue. However, as a not-quite-White working-class male Yank occupies an inferior position in the sex-gender as well as the class systems; therefore, his power to approach legitimately the pedestal of White womanhood is just as limited as if he were a caged animal.

The play demonstrates that while class is a question of owning capital and controlling repressive state apparatuses (consider Yank's treatment by the police), it also involves owning the knowledge that enables one to participate in a range of dominant cultural practices. Yank is excluded from the cultural landscape housing the White well-to-do. Scene 2, for instance, shows him lacking the competence to participate in the display of etiquette between Mildred and her aunt. His exclusion both in economic and in culturally material terms is what renders him politically impotent. In the end, his resistance amounts to nothing more than a childlike rant that aims to tear down what actually he desires but knows that he can never possess; thus, he attempts to degrade Mildred by branding her a "white-faced slut," by reducing her to nothing more than a "skoit."

The play reveals how U.S. political discourse correlates class to race in order to obscure both White privilege and the operation of class in society, and Mildred's relation to Yank illustrates how the feminine may serve this ideology. *The Hairy Ape*'s subversive force lies in its making visible the unity among the links of race, class, and gender in the chain that signifies the White "race" in U.S. discourse. O'Neill dispels the smokescreen of White mythology by turning the race-gender system upside-down: it is Yank who signifies "lack," who does not have the ingredients necessary to competently perform White masculinity.

O'Neill also draws out the way that the dominant social group obscures how economic inequalities generate social differences by fostering the belief system that anyone can make good—if they try—and those who fail to thrive in the great U.S. meritocracy are personally inadequate. Yank's experience undermines this doctrine, revealing how social reality for the working class or the poor cannot match the dream, for without the difference they represent U.S. Man could not recognize himself.

The play challenges the myth of the American Dream by demonstrating that not even all White people share equally in its promised rewards, but White power maintains itself because a majority of people, of all classes and colors, buy into the myth. To aim for inclusion in the category of White masculinity would necessitate Yank accepting a value system that allows those in power to dupe him in return for a very limited set of rewards. However, he can neither alter nor accept the conditions that degrade and distort his humanity, and it is his inability to either transform or come to terms with his relative White status that leads to his annihilation.

Violating the Color Line: Langston Hughes's *Mulatto*

U.S. society expresses acute anxieties surrounding cross-racial sexual relations. The instabilities in White identity that the figure of the racial hybrid brings to light are made manifest in Langston Hughes's *Mulatto* (1935).[20] The play charts the story of Robert Lewis, the mixed-race son of a White plantation owner, Colonel Robert Norwood, and his black female servant and mistress, Cora Lewis. It demonstrates the way in which people of mixed race (who, by virtue of the one-drop theory, are deemed Black) threaten the White social order by carrying on the body visual signs of the illusory boundaries of raced categories.[21] In other words, the category Mulatto by its very existence operates to disable the binary construction of race.

As Richard K. Barksdale notes, the play focuses on the sociological impact of mixed-race identity from a Black cultural viewpoint, unusually, rather than a White perspective (196). *Mulatto* addresses Robert's attempts to cope psychologically and practically with his White father's refusal to recognize him. Robert rejects Black identity, obsessively scrutinizing himself for signs of Whiteness. He mimics White speech and behavior, hoping to fix himself as a White man in the eyes of society. His pursuit of Norwood's public approval, which, he believes, would validate his possession of an authentic White masculinity, signals a quest for the social privileges attached to the ruling race. Ignoring the dangers of violating the color line, Robert repeatedly tries to cross the boundary separating "light mulatto" from full-blooded White male.

His first transgression takes place at age seven, when he refers to Norwood as "papa" in the presence of White company, earning a beating for his audacity. As an adult, Robert shows himself to be even more determined to press his White pedigree. He greets his father by sticking "out his hand fo' to shake hands with him!" (Hughes 34). To avoid further conflict, Robert is sent away to school, but when he returns relations between him and Norwood quickly degenerate, as Robert becomes bolder in asserting what he believes to be his rights as the colonel's only male heir. When he enters the colonel's house by the front door, nearly colliding with him, a showdown takes place. Robert directly asserts a claim to Whiteness by pointing out his physical resemblance to Norwood. The security of his race-gendered status at risk, Norwood struggles to reestablish White authority by compelling Robert to accept his status as absolute Black "other."[22]

Norwood points out the signs of his racial difference, symbolized by his "yellow skin" and "rusty elbows." Also, in terms of White culture's operational principles, if Robert truly embodied the signs of Whiteness then certain material benefits would logically pertain. To the contrary, Norwood reminds Robert that those social privileges he enjoys, such as his education, have come out of Norwood's indulgence rather than any system of entitlement. He challenges Robert's ability to see himself clearly by citing his White neighbor's response to Robert's actions: "How come they threw you out of the post office for talking to a white woman?" (Hughes 47).

Although it privileges the Black experience, *Mulatto* does not ignore how the material boundaries maintained between Whiteness and Blackness function to shore up White psychic identity. Hughes suggests a continuity between Robert as an individual African American and the Black community. In the same way, Norwood instantiates one link within a conceptual chain designating White as a particular class of being. The harder Robert tries to force Norwood to recognize the visual evidence of his paternity, the more the White man must defend the unbridgeable distance between the races.

When discursive strategies for supporting the color line fail, violence erupts. Robert's continued refusal to back down to his assigned place in the racial hierarchy, and the intense need for each man to be seen as White by the other, raises tensions to such a pitch that Norwood threatens to shoot his son. Enraged, Robert attacks him and chokes Norwood to death. Rather than fall into the hands of a White mob, Robert uses Norwood's gun to kill himself at the play's end.

Robert's refusal to "see" Norwood's representation of himself may be viewed both positively and negatively. His desire to resist the stereotyped portrait of the "black buck" is laudable, but his selective vision of himself is also prompted by a deeply internalized racism. "Look at me," he tells his mother. "See these grey eyes. I got the right to everything everybody else has" (Hughes 38). In reality, seeing the world through "grey eyes" for Robert means participating in the representation of his Blackness as nonbeing; for in so doing he tacitly accepts the White vision of Blackness reflected back to him by Norwood.

Because White eyes will only ever see him as a swaggering figure of mockery or as a sexual embarrassment and a threat to White social order, Robert's best chance of surviving as a mixed-race figure in a White-dominated world is to align himself more closely with Blackness. Repairing his ties to the Black community could offer him a space to revalue Blackness and thereby resist the most damaging psychological effects of racism. Instead, he tries to function, in a colloquial sense, as a racially schizophrenic figure, which only leads to his demise.

What is more interesting, however, is the way in which Hughes casts

Norwood as equally divided in himself. While sexual relations between White men and women of other races met with a surface disapproval, double standards came into play to give a measure of protection to the White man's status. Nevertheless, Norwood, by the indulgence he shows to his black children, places himself in an unusually close relation to Blackness, something that disturbs his White peers. Norwood's friend Higgins warns him that with "Nothing but blacks in the house—a man gets soft like niggers inside. And living with a coloured woman! . . . for a man's own house you need a wife, not a black woman" (Hughes 31). Sometimes Norwood's Whiteness appears tainted, like his son's. Hence, the war of Black against White takes place within as well as between the two characters, with their heated final exchange demonstrating how it is essential for the maintenance of White security, psychic and otherwise, that race be absolutely, not relatively, defined.

Moreover, it is essential that definitions of White and Black are set by the White patriarchy, given that the dividing line between them has always been a convenient conceptual and linguistic division that has no basis in nature. The play draws a connection between Robert's and Norwood's personal narratives and U.S. socio-racial history: as their individual stories are disclosed on stage, likewise a narrative of U.S. Whiteness unfolds, one in which it becomes clear how, ultimately, Norwood's White identity depends on Robert's status as Black "other." That is, the play posits Whiteness as devoid of any intrinsic identity, which accounts for the tenacity with which Norwood and his compatriots defend the dividing line between White and Black.

The climax of *Mulatto* posits an interconnection between the representation of race as an organic creation and its social construction, as well as its relation to other forms of identity, such as class, gender, and nation. Further, it foregrounds the frequently contradictory White discursive strategies for masking how one construction engenders another. Black and White are presented as written on the body, and while Norwood never denies race as a natural fact, at the same time he insists that the truth of identity manifests itself largely through social confirmation. Thus, *Mulatto* shows that while race is tied to skin color, it is also more than skin color in U.S. society: Blackness and Whiteness are ways of thinking and acting, and of perceiving and being perceived.

The Grammar of Whiteness: Thornton Wilder's *Our Town*

Mulatto presents a case where Whiteness uses the presence of Blackness to determine itself. In contrast, Thornton Wilder's *Our Town* (1938) provides an example of how Whiteness may be actively constituted on stage in the absence of the racialized "other." As Richard Londraville points out, in terms of the dramatic canon *Our Town* is considered to be "quintessentially the American play" (365). However, in his preface Wilder asserts that the play offers a picture of *humanity*, a generic account of people's failure to perceive the true value of life, and not a snapshot of small-town American society (12). Despite his insistence that the play explores universal human experience (itself a contentious category), spectators and critics have tended to read the production as an exercise in nostalgia, a soothing treatment of an idyllic small-town "American way of life." Indeed, given the custom among members of the dominant U.S. culture to conflate their experience with the universal, Wilder's claim may even encourage conservative readings.

Nancy Bunge provides a useful survey of critical responses to the text, demonstrating two strands of interpretation that are similar in content but ideologically opposed. On the one hand, critics have applauded the text's power to reawaken American's common cultural memories, its celebration of a golden age of social and economic stability, and the hope it raises that "traditional" values may yet enjoy a renaissance. On the other hand, unsympathetic analyses criticize it for its lack of social awareness, its narrow focus on two self-sufficient, middle-class WASP families, its endorsement of bourgeois domesticity, and its support for outdated mores based on an agrarian lifestyle (Bunge 349–64).

Some recent criticism finds in *Our Town* a more radical thrust. Addressing the play as social critique, Lanford Wilson describes it as a "deadly cynical and acidly accurate play." What most interpret as a "golden community in fact consists of people terrified of change who not only stifle themselves, but give no signs of confidence or hope in others" (Bunge 358, 360). Wilson's summary invests the play with a grimly tragic note. He renders the inhabitants of Grover's Corners as literary descendants of Rawick's sixteenth-century exemplars of repressed desire, whose constricted vision makes them willing to accept what they would like to believe represents a comfortable position in a benevolent capitalist order, but what in fact signifies suffocating routine and a forfeit of freedom and pleasure.

The way in which *Our Town* is taken to be a reflection of American society, whether one considers it as representative of the "American-way-of-life," or a radical critique of this dreamscape, depends in part on the spectator's particular relation to the dominant culture. To what degree does s/he resemble the idealized portrait of the U.S. citizen? What is his/her relative degree of access to the American Dream?

The role played by political geography in the play's construction of identity, which replicates the function of place in marking racialized identity, also significantly contributes to the shaping of the spectator's response, for marginality in the play proves to be relational.[23] Consider the Stage Manager's introduction to Grover's Corners:

Up here—is Main Street. Way back there is the railway station; tracks go that way. Polish Town's across the tracks, and some Canuck families.
Over there is the Congregational Church; across the street's the Presbyterian. Methodist and Unitarian are over there.
Baptist is down in the holla' by the river.
Catholic Church is over beyond the tracks.

(Wilder, OT 21–22)

This mapping of Grover's Corners represents a construction of cultural otherness, in which one's difference is indicated by one's distance from the center—Main Street. The railroad tracks mark an ideological as well as a physical divide between the town's "normal" citizens and its social misfits: the poor, non-Protestants, non-Whites, or intermediately White. Even before the main action begins, we discover Wilder's *universal-particular* modern society to be rigidly and hierarchically divided according to class, ethnic, and racial identity. *Our Town* presents a model of the American homeland that is permeated with "otherness." Whereas the town's WASP citizenry will be individuated, the Poles, Catholics, and Native Americans remain reduced to collective nouns in this restrictive nation space. However, the character of the town and its inhabitants is defined by these communal figures of exile, whose displacement from Main Street renders the center of Grover's Corners a White, Protestant, middle-class, and, as we shall see, masculine space.

The Stage Manager's discourse, then, signifies a territorial act, an aggressive colonization of the concept of home as both foundation and property. It claims on behalf of U.S. Man the right to name difference, to support or undermine another group's sense of social belonging as well as to shape "others'" life experiences, and, as such, it represents a moment of symbolic violence in the play.

Further, *Our Town's* spatial model of identity asserts that difference is recognizable and solid, and therefore mappable. "In our town [it is possible] to know the facts about everybody" (Wilder, *OT* 24), and Professor Willard duly registers the inhabitants in terms of a set of anthropological data. The registration of their gender, class, ethnicity, political affiliation, and so on enables the isolation of those labeled "different"; in turn, setting apart the "other" lends form to White identity and allows the town's true citizens—the White middle class—to maintain power.

Our Town reveals White power as an organized hierarchical cluster of relations that goes unrecognized because of its representation as ordinary, everyday life. This is emphasized by Mr. Webb, patriarch of one of the town's two principal families, who assumes that he does not reveal so much as remind the spectator of something s/he already knows about how society operates when he describes the town as being run by a board of *Selectmen*. He begins his description by saying "I don't have to tell you . . ." This appeal to an audience's common sense represents an attempt to involve the audience in the further entrenchment of Whiteness by drawing it into a relation of intimacy.

However, the status of women in Grover's Corners lays open to question the logic of White establishment tradition. The play's construction of femininity, while reinforcing the idea of the town's racial, class, and sexual exclusivity, also gives material form to Whiteness, and thus it threatens the presumed invulnerability of White authority, which rests on its invisibility.

In *Our Town* feminine and masculine identities are performed within an unquestioned framework of concretized gender distinctions. In act 2, the Stage Manager instructs the audience about the married woman's social duties: cooking three meals a day, bringing up children, washing, and cleaning the house—"with no summer vacation" (Wilder, *OT* 50). Women, like the racialized "other," are excluded from the public sphere; all men vote at age twenty-one, while women vote "indirect," presumably by means of any influence they carry with their husbands (Wilder, *OT* 34).

The power of masculinity and heterosexuality, like that of Whiteness, is ubiquitous in Grover's Corners, as emphasized by the Stage Manager's introduction of the main female characters. Like Webb, he appeals to common sense: "I don't have to point out to the women in my audience that those ladies they see before them . . . " (Wilder, *OT* 50), and what goes without saying is that the women spend their lives serving the physical and emotional needs of men. It also implies a sameness of identity for women that resembles the collective identity attributed to the racialized "other": women, like Native Americans and Catholics, can all be contained in neat categories.

While on the surface *Our Town* appears to naturalize dominant race-gender constructs, heterosexuality, and bourgeois social tradition, the play also shows such arrangements to be products of coercive social structures. The Stage Manager informs us that "Almost everybody in the world gets married—you know what I mean?" and he continues, "In our town there aren't hardly any exceptions" (Wilder, *OT* 50). The organization of society into heterosexual pairs and their offspring is put down to nature, which, we are told, pushes and contrives things so that young people fall in love and get married.

In fact, Emily, the "brightest girl in school," whose ambition is to "make public speeches," gets pushed into marriage by her father despite her reluctance and fear of it.[24] Her intended husband greets their union with the same lack of enthusiasm. Mrs. Gibbs makes the point that marriage stifles women, regretting that she will never venture beyond Grover's Corners because her husband fears that travel, especially "traipsin' round Europe," will only lead to discontent at home.

Women's multiple experience of place in the White social order, as linchpins of the WASP nuclear family unit, yet, like the racialized "other," relegated to the borders of the body politic, renders identity per se subject to a shifting set of contexts in the play, and each of these frames of reference involves a host of others. The meaning of White identity, at least White female identity, depends on a set of elements including the family, economic structures, educational and religious institutions, and political ideologies. The way in which the play engages in the (re)production of White femininity signals the complex and often contradictory relation of the play to White mythology.

Our Town aids the naturalization of Whiteness by its appeal to the category of the universal, which is marked as White, heterosexual, and masculine. At the same time, it challenges the hegemony of White masculinity by positing the concept of White feminine identity as contingent and historical, for the security of the former depends on the fixity of the latter. The play's involvement in the political meaning of Whiteness and the "American-way-of-life" is also ambiguous.

In an essay called "Toward an American Language" Wilder writes that "It is difficult to be American because there is as yet no code, grammar, decalogue by which to locate oneself" (12). In another essay, he writes that story is essential to the invention of identity. For Wilder,

we seek our place in myths. Myths are the dreaming soul of the race, telling its story. Now the dreaming soul of the race has told its story for centuries . . . and there have been billions of stories. But the myths are the survival of the fittest of the billions of stories, most of which have been forgotten. No chance survival there. The retelling of them on every hand occurs because they whisper a validation—they isolate and confer a significance. ("Joyce and the Modern Novel" 176–77)

Wilder's reading of myth implies a connection between nation, culture, race, and literature. His use of quasi-Darwinian terms to discuss the role of myth in the construction of U.S. identity suggests a code of national community in which theater would form part of the project of securing hier-archically organized racial, class, gender, and sexual differences among people. The grammar of American identity employed in *Our Town* follows a similar code. The spatial model of identity narrated by the Stage Man-ager clearly affords no room on Main Street for the location of the "other." Accordingly, Wilder's retelling of U.S. identity validates it as a signifier of universal Whiteness, and *Our Town* as theater functions as a means by which one comes to experience oneself as a member of the White "race."

Still, the different "truth" of White feminine experience expressed in the play complicates this fantasy of U.S. Man. White motherhood, his literal author, ends up positioned alongside Native Americans and the Polish on the borders of White discourse. In this way, the representation of femi-ninity reveals how White womanhood functions as an ideology of White supremacy. Further, by demonstrating the integral connection between sex-gender subordination, racial oppression, and class domination in U.S. society, Wilder's play challenges the ideality of the White code where it lays claim to a utopian White democratic order held together by a coherent and whole White self.

White Reconstruction: Lillian Hellman's *The Little Foxes*

In *The Great Family of Man* Roland Barthes asserts that the myth of the human condition rests on a very old mystification, "which always consists in placing Nature at the bottom of History" (108). The idea that the White social order, while patriarchal, may be nevertheless wholesomely egalitar-ian—not in the sense of democratically equal but through the stratifi-cation of society in such a way that each member fulfills his or her natural role—rests on this myth. In U.S. discourse, the myth is frankly exploited in White Southern ideology. Paul M. Gaston writes that the South has fos-tered two images of itself. One myth features a romantic account of the Confederacy as a "Lost Cause." This casts the *ancien regime* as a beneficent plantation tradition, sustained by a code of honor in which chivalric White gentlemen protected innocent White womanhood and ruled over a class of contented slaves. The alternative vision, while taking pride in the sedate grandeur of the Old South, promotes the idea of a dynamic New South, committed to social and economic progress, commercially inclined, and socially united (Gaston 6–7).

On the surface, Lillian Hellman's *The Little Foxes* (1939) is not a play concerned with race relations, but it clearly taps into both mythic representations of Southern Whiteness. Many critics and spectators have variously interpreted the play as being about besieged agrarianism and thus sustaining the dominant antebellum viewpoint. Others read it as a critique of the region, presenting it as exemplary of social backwardness—in other words, an argument for social reformation. Hellman, however, claimed that the play's setting was "purely incidental," useful because it lent credence to a "certain naïve and innocent quality" she wished to impart to some of her characters.[25] Whatever the reason for her choice, it cannot be denied that White Southern mythology provides the context for making sense of experience in the play, both in terms of how characters view themselves and each other and how audiences have viewed them.

Set in 1900, the play addresses the interaction between an impoverished Southern aristocracy and a rising commercial class, represented in microscopic form by the marriage of Birdie, who descends from the "highest-tone" plantation owners, and Oscar Hubbard, whose wealth comes from trade. Birdie's family could not keep their plantation going after the war, and the Hubbards now own Lionnet. The reasons behind the character's personal and familial difficulties (for example, the lust for power and greed) have been discussed at length.[26] The focus of my analysis will be on how the play reflects the context of White racialized discourse, sometimes replicating it ideologically, sometimes negating it.

While dramatic events arise out of familial enmity, interpersonal rivalries play themselves out within the terms of opposition between distinct socio-racial orders—Old versus New South and a hybridized South versus mainstream U.S. society. Birdie represents the determination of the Old South to preserve its traditional ways, a system of values that apparently clashes with the Hubbards' belief in unchecked free enterprise. She expresses a constant longing for the past, describing Lionnet before the war in Edenic terms and begging Oscar to restore it. Naïve, certainly, but far from blameless, she also fosters a legend of Southern innocence, maintaining that slavery was a better state for Blacks than emancipation: "We were good to our people. Everybody knew that" (Hellman, *TLF* 13).

Though he despises his wife, Oscar needs her, or rather he requires possession of the cultural capital that comes with her class position and the concomitant brand of Whiteness that she represents. Whiteness is mobilized in the play through the exchange of women that results in Birdie's marriage to Oscar, which takes place at the intersection of class as well as race-gender difference. Without his connection to Birdie, Oscar would be viewed as no better than a carpet-bagger, who were often termed "White niggers," feeding off the corpse of the Old South. Birdie's racialized class privilege, however, conjoined with his wealth, bestows the full privilege of White masculinity on Oscar.

While in one sense Birdie's position enables her husband's rise in New Southern society, her embodiment of Old Southern mores acts also as a potential threat to his financial empire. Marshall, the Northern industrialist whose financial backing Oscar needs, views Southerners as addicted to leisure pursuits, unable or uninterested in finding time to do business (Hellman, *TLF* 8). Accordingly, Oscar and his brother must negotiate between the needs to be viewed as both like and unlike Birdie's social group. They mimic the social forms and activities associated with the Southern aristocracy while at the same time emphasizing their commercial pedigree: the fact that the family wealth derives from their father and grandfather, who worked in trade.

The floating nature of Oscar's race-gendered status illustrates the ideological elasticity of White identity, a malleability that proves to be a double-edged sword: while it may help sustain White power, if this malleability becomes too transparent it threatens the stability of White identity by pointing to its provisionality. Its contingent nature is further amplified when one considers that even though the Hubbards may access the full privileges of Whiteness within the context of New Southern society despite their allegiance to the ideal of U.S. abundance, they reside on the edge of American national identity. Hellman's characters are displaced within the larger U.S. social and political order, occupying a discursive space ancillary to the category of U.S. Whiteness, with their ambivalent relation to Whiteness based not on ethnic difference but on regional identity.

In the post-reconstruction period Southerners served as one of the "others" against which American-ness was secured. Whether according to the terms of Southern identity posited in Confederate or in New South mythology, the security of the Southerners' White racialized position was vulnerable. White U.S. identity entails industry, responsibility, and fiscal prudence, with the racialized "other" serving as the archetype of idleness, improvidence, and irresponsibility (much of which can be said about some of the Hubbards). The slow and easy pace of antebellum life, founded on the forced labor of Blacks, was far removed from the Protestant work ethic promoted by dominant U.S. discourse. Southerners were seen to have further erred by wasting their prewar abundance of wealth cultivating an overly opulent lifestyle.

Many in the New South no longer fit the criteria for automatic and full inclusion in the category of Whiteness: "you Southerners occupy a unique position in America," Marshall tells the Hubbards (Hellman, *TLF* 8).

Recall that to be White in the nineteenth century meant to be a member of the advanced race, someone at the top of the social order, an author of civilization through the acquisition of territory and/or the advancement of science and industry, and, in this way, a creator of wealth. Southerners, in contrast, were a conquered people whose land had been occupied. Most of the planter class was bankrupt, and many middle-class Whites were reduced to working in jobs considered beneath their socio-racial station. Southern culture could boast of few contributions to industrial development.

Within the context of wider U.S. culture, Southerners were perceived as socially, technologically, and economically backward. The North held them guilty of threatening the security of the Union, not to mention of the sin of slavery. Thus their way of life was considered not only anachronistic but also un-American, with the fitness of White Southerners for U.S. citizenship—that which they had themselves so recently rejected—being questioned. All of these factors placed Southern Whites in a peculiar relationship to the category of Whiteness itself and to the larger myths of U.S. Man and Manifest Destiny.

Hellman's play reveals how some Whites could live within the United States in terms of its geographical borders and the boundaries of control of its political institutions while nevertheless maintaining a disjointed relation to U.S. citizenship. American nationalism imagines a community of people with shared interests as well as a common culture, and although the Hubbards might wish to claim a common future with U.S. Man, they shared with him neither a common past nor a collection of social symbols and customs. Southern ethnonationalism rendered Whiteness in the South a different mode of ethnicity, one distinguished from U.S. Man by its historical context and its distinct economic and social structures. Consequently, one aim of New Southern mythology was to reconstitute Southerners as desirable citizens by reinventing the idea of White national unity and entitlement, thereby establishing new cultural as well as economic ties to the North. The Hubbards try to reconcile Whiteness and Southern identity by redefining progressive symbols and themes in ethnonationalist terms, as in, for example, their aim to make Southern cotton mills the "Rembrandts of investment."

The taint of not-quite-White that attached to Southern identity after the Civil War would eventually dissipate because White power depended as much on categorical as on other forms of domination. If significant numbers of Whites in the South could not be firmly categorized as such, the entire system of social classification could be undermined. The campaign to prove White Southern suitability for citizenship succeeded because the unification of the White experience was in the interests of the dominant culture as a whole. The myth of the New South would eventually help bind together Whites of different classes, including former slaveholders in the South and non-slaveholders in the North and South, while bringing a majority of the White Southerners back into the family of Whiteness.

Like *Our Town,* Hellman's play provides an example of how myth may serve as a device for papering over the ambivalences and complexities of social relations. To say that White Southern mythology forms the intellectual and moral foundation of *The Little Foxes* does not necessarily mean that it ultimately endorses this version of reality. To the contrary, the drama proves interesting for the way it demonstrates, especially through the use of irony, the tensions between the mythic view and the social reality, and for the way it highlights the process by which White discourse is able to sustain the viability of its mythology despite some rather obvious disparities.

chapter 3

Whiteness in Post-Imperial Britain

World War II provided the primary experience molding the shape of modern Britain. On a positive note, the postwar social consensus that produced the welfare state inaugurated new economic practices and institutions that benefited particularly the working class and the poor. However, victory would bring about a number of destabilizing changes as well; the aftereffects of war heralded the beginning of the end of Britain's role as an international power of the first order.

Kenneth O. Morgan suggests that the war's ambivalent legacy contained elements of social unity and division, but, he argues, "it was the symbols of national unity and consensus which gained most attention" (11). The war effort in Britain required the temporary papering over of social divisions. E. Ellis Cashmore concludes that this led to a strengthening of faith in existing institutional arrangements: "There was little room for self-criticism; Britain was still in many people's eyes a 'world power' (14).

As I made clear in chapter 1, one of the most potent unifying symbols in British society historically has been its empire. In addition to providing Britain with a host of material benefits (for example, protected access to a colony's natural resources, guaranteed trade links, and soldiers), for several generations of all classes the empire gave meaning to White British identity.

Although they may have felt subordinate at home, the working class could claim, to borrow a phrase from U.S. historian Du Bois, a "psychological wage" accruing from the subjection of a host of colonial societies. Accordingly, British wartime politics were profoundly motivated by its leaders' imperial vision.[27] This conception of national identity entailed three distinct but related notions of empire: the empire of prestige that determined Britain's image of itself as a world power; the empire of "kith and kin," consisting of the White dominions and the European settlements in east and central Africa; and the economic empire of tariffs barriers and the sterling area (Philip Murphy 28).

Beginning in 1946, when Jordan gained its independence, this vision would be repeatedly challenged. Nationalist movements began to exert enormous pressure on Britain to relinquish power. In 1947 India gained autonomy, followed by Sri Lanka and Burma (1948), Israel (1949), Sudan (1956), and Ghana and Malaya (1957). From then on the empire would steadily shrink, and with it so too would British prestige.

The reasons for the decline of empire are contested. Some historians argue that domestic politics were opposed to its continuation because it was perceived as a financial drain and a political distraction from domestic social reform. However, Stephen Howe argues that the overwhelming characteristic of public perceptions of colonial issues after the war was sheer ignorance (20). John Darwin concurs, finding little evidence of any clearcut public opposition to empire. Yet he maintains that political leaders of the postwar era firmly believed that the public was far from indifferent to the loss of empire, and so they went to great lengths to avoid or conceal any open reverse of British world power (*Britain and Decolonisation* 168).

Another argument is that there was a new postwar liberalism opposed to the means of sustaining colonial power as well as its underlying assumptions about colonial peoples. While Nazi atrocities had eroded the acceptability of the most blatant racist justifications for empire, they had by no means completely eliminated popular imperial sentiment. Darwin writes: "There was an old and powerful public doctrine of trusteeship, stretching back to Edmund Burke and the eighteenth century, which had provided one of the most satisfying justifications for British rule; this was the idea that the Empire 'brought peace and humanitarian reform to communities battered by war, slavery, or barbaric social practices'" (*End of the British Empire* 19).

Whether one accepts the resistance of colonial subjects, the need to focus on rebuilding British communities, or a shift in attitude toward colonial peoples as the primary factor facilitating the passage of empire, one must also take into account that the country's postwar economy simply could no longer afford to maintain direct control of the colonies. Middle-class Britain was beginning to enjoy access to new leisure industries and labor-saving consumer goods after the war, but to a much lesser extent than its wartime ally the United States, and there was widespread rationing in Britain well into the 1950s.

Unlike the unfettered economic boom enjoyed by the United States, Britain would face a number of economic crises in the late 1940s and '50s that would further test its hold on its empire.[28] The colonies had always required a strong military presence. Given the demands of cold war politics in the 1940s and '50s, and, more to the point, the demands of successive U.S. administrations, Britain was now forced to devote massive resources to the defense of Western Europe against the perceived threat of Soviet expansion.

In the 1950s this diminution of power came to be felt at home: a sense of British vulnerability developed as weaknesses in the domestic infrastructure became more evident. Nevertheless, there was reluctance on the part of politicians and many ordinary British citizens to recognize the nation's diminished international role, even in the face of continuing colonial losses. David Sanders notes that Britain had not suffered the same sort of external trauma, defeat in war, as other former European powers, and thus people were not forced to undergo the same fundamental role reappraisal (72).

There was, though, recognition of the need to reposition the nation on the international stage. After 1945, political practitioners attempted to sustain a strong voice by aligning Britain's interests with those of U.S. foreign policy. This unequal trans-Atlantic partnership, the so-called "special relationship" with the United States, offered a poor substitute for the realities of imperial power, and it never contributed as much to how people experienced their British identity as the empire had.

After the war, the role of race in determining modern British identity becomes amplified. The most important factor influencing the way in which Whiteness would increasingly function as the replacement unifying symbol for large segments of British society was the arrival of Black immigrants from former colonies.[29] The war left Britain with a severe labor shortage that emigrants from the newly emerging commonwealth were deemed appropriate to fill. The arrival of the ship *Empire Windrush* in 1948 generally marks the inception of the postwar migration of colonial subjects. It also marks the beginnings of significant levels of racial antagonism and conflict in modern British society.

During the war, the colonies offered vital support to the British cause, providing supplies and labor power. As Britain's need for active war personnel became more urgent, Black men and women were accepted as full participants in the war effort. While few would deny that racism existed in the military, Black soldiers and nurses reported being treated largely with respect by both military personnel and the civilian population. This situation altered dramatically after the war. As Caribbean officer Dudley Thompson remembers, "when we first came over here, we were more or less welcomed because we were in the uniform of the King. But when the war . . .

ended . . . some of the other people tend to say to themselves, well, you come over here to help us to win a war, now the war is over, isn't it about time you go back?" (Phillips and Phillips 51).

While jobs were plentiful after the war, housing was scarce, and from the outset the new arrivals were resented as competitors for this and other social services; when the economy declined, migrants also began to be viewed as rivals for jobs to which White British were rightfully entitled. As the number of Black immigrants increased in the 1950s, so too did public anxiety and hostility.

Over the course of the decade, the racist discourse that had once been used to justify imperial conquests gained new currency. This was true of both popular and official language. In 1950, for example, government minister Hugh Dalton described the colonies as "pullulating poverty stricken, diseased nigger communities" (Phillips and Phillips 75).

As it became clear that Black immigrants did not intend to return to their countries of origin, British society began to mirror U.S. racist practices. Whites often refused to rent or lease to Blacks. Signs and adverts stating "No Niggers" or "Whites Only" became commonplace. Banks often refused to grant Blacks mortgages. There were few pubs, Anglican churches, or other public leisure facilities where Blacks were welcome. Their skin color made the immigrants easy targets for street racism, and they were routinely subject to verbal harassment and the threat of physical violence.

Black migrants were generally trapped in the least desired, unskilled, manual positions, or they were the first to be made redundant. There was commercial segregation also, with Black-owned businesses located primarily in residential areas with high migrant numbers. Therefore, although in principal Blacks enjoyed the same legal rights and protections as Whites, Britain in the 1940s and '50s was a de facto segregated society.

This is not to say that Whiteness maintained its position at the epicenter of the nation's social and political life unchallenged in this period. For some White British, mainly the working class and the poor, living and working alongside the new immigrants meant that they could not reproduce the larger pattern of racial separation that governed White middle-class life. This created new and ongoing conflicts for these segments of White society, the people who had once relied upon the Whitening practices of imperialism to perpetuate their position in the racial hierarchy. With the loss of empire, however, some Whites would struggle more than others to maintain their difference from Blackness and to negotiate a firm and clear relation to postwar British national identity.

Whiteness at War: Bridget Boland's *The Cockpit*

The developing color bar in British society in the 1940s and '50s was reflected also in the arts. Playwrights were at the forefront of exploring the feelings of White Britain toward the social changes provoked by the war. Some contributed toward the effort to recover or rehabilitate the White imperial self; others sought to unravel how the image of Black immigrants functioned in the subjective and social construction of modern White British identity.

Bridget Boland demonstrates an awareness of writing at a critical moment in British history as the imperial era was giving way to another, more uncertain one. Her 1948 play, *The Cockpit,* explores the crisis conditions in which Europeans, including the British, would need to forge a postwar identity. The play is set in May 1945, in a provincial German town under British military control. The action centers on a group of nationally and ethnically diverse displaced persons who are being temporarily accommodated in a theater building.

The Cockpit was first published in a collected volume titled *Plays of the Year: 1948–49,* and the editor's introduction by J. C. Trewin gives important clues as to how the play might have been received by contemporary spectators. Its initial London run was not successful, perhaps because, as Trewin contends, there was "No lounge-hall, French-window stuff here." However, when it toured the regions, playing to working-class audiences in halls throughout Wales and the Northeast, it "held every audience" (Trewin 9). Trewin alerts us to the way that contemporary audiences could interpret the play as a historical document, a political critique of life in postwar Europe and Britain's role therein. Although metropolitan audiences may have been put off by Boland's social realism, other segments of British society whose social location did not afford as many opportunities to cushion themselves from the consequences of war were more open to engaging with her disturbing images of a chaotic and crumbling world order.

Trewin's commentary also affords insight into the way in which the play intervenes in the postwar production of racial codes. This is how he describes the plot: "Here, in this document-drama, are members of the warring races (and the warring sub-divisions of those races). . . . Whatever the British officer and his sergeant—working, earnestly, by rule-of-thumb—can do, racial angers and jealousies will mount in a frantic hubbub" (8). His analysis assumes that the play presents the audience with a number of racial types and that people's actions are motivated by characteristics derived from specific racialized identities, a largely redundant notion of racial difference in 1948.

Still, the play makes clear that the source of discord among the displaced is racial or ethnic difference, aggravated by cultural and ideological disagreements. On close reading, however, there is no evidence to suggest that the play conspires in the reproduction of regressive codes of race. If *The Cockpit* contains a political message, it is certainly a liberal one; it tries to work against reductive racialist interpretations, making a plea at least for racial tolerance.

Even while providing a relatively balanced and unbiased portrait of the different ethnic groups it represents, though, the play centers racial ambiguities on the presentation of its British characters. On the surface, the play enables a comforting view of the White British subject as the last bastion of strength in a fractured world order, who once again is destined to look after other, inferior social groups. Alternatively, it also affords an oppositional reading, one that undermines cultural notions of White British superiority and dominance.

First, I will explore how Boland's attempt to make sense of Britain's place in the postwar world feeds into a conservative frame of reference. Of all the different groups represented—the "whole of Europe under one roof"—only the British escape definition as a racial or ethnic type. Just as they are raceless, the British characters are also the only nationality not weighted down with political or ideological baggage. To the contrary, the behavior of Captain Ridley, officer-in-charge, Sergeant Barnes, and Saunders is said to be governed by the spirit of reason and a natural feeling for democracy and justice, supported by a level-headed pragmatism. Throughout the fighting in the theater, they remain calmly above the fray, apparently shocked and dismayed at the friction within the community of displaced persons; hence Ridley's wondering comment, "Do you suppose we should fight like this at home?" (Boland 62).

When the group bickers over food provisions, Ridley lectures them: "It doesn't matter a hoot in hell what your politics are, or your profession, your religions. . . . Democracy is what you've been fighting for, and Democracy is what you're going to get—and that includes food for people who don't agree with you" (Boland 63). Only the British are shown to be free of such foolish political prejudices and capable of the moral objectivity needed to establish social harmony.

Even though British identity is not explicitly designated as a racialized or even an ethnic position, if we examine the attitudes attached to this particular social group in the play then it becomes obvious how the characters are marked as White; that is, they appear White in so far as Whiteness is applied as a metaphor for morality. White imperial discourse shapes their standard of morality, and it is this metadiscourse that provides the common frame of reference to which Ridley refers when he speaks about the extraordinarily peaceable nature of British society.

This bias is recognized by the displaced. They see the British claim to a privileged rationality, to a monopoly on the "truth" of the postwar situation—indeed, most of what Ridley tells them—as stemming from ethnocentric and upper-class arrogance. They are able to point to the cultural insularity and elitist political ideology at the heart of the British position (which is really an *English* position). The Frenchwoman, Marie, surprises Ridley when she tells him: "It's you who cause all the trouble, with your amateur theories, trying to reorganize Europe according to the British Public School Code" (64–5), and later, "You English have spent hundreds of years playing Empire Builders all over the world. What do you know about us at home in Europe?" (Boland 65).

When they become the objects of attention, the British drop their polite, earnest working style. Surprised and angered by her words, Barnes retorts: "That's enough lip! Infernal nerve!" She refuses to back down, prompting Ridley's patronizing response: "My dear girl, no one is sorrier than we are, but we really can't leave Europe to be sorted out by the French. Why, since 1940, you've hardly been a first-class power" (Boland 65). Besides denying the change in their position in the world order, Ridley's comments foreground the reality of British chauvinism.

Michel Foucault proposes that power is tolerable only on condition that it masks a substantial part of itself; its success is proportional to its ability to hide its own mechanisms (*History of Sexuality* 86). After the British and their socio-racial mechanisms are exposed, they struggle to maintain their tenuous grip on things. In act 2, Ridley and Marie engage in another in-depth political argument. Their exchange follows her accusation that Ridley automatically considers the belief systems of the various displaced persons to be "all wrong." He responds:

I believe I think that belief itself is wrong. . . . But theories are harmless, a theory is a thing you can hold lightly, you can balance it, hold it up to the light and look at it, compare it with your neighbour's. Belief is dangerous, it is the arm flung out in salute, the clenched fist you use to knock your neighbour down if he doesn't believe the same. (Boland 89)

This speech reveals the language games that the British enact with the displaced and, indeed, themselves. It also highlights the way in which the explanatory power of White British discourse to make sense of and order the material world is a game of semantics. Despite dismissing the concept, Ridley subscribes to a *belief* in an external absolute standard of reality that supports the British theory of democracy and moral right.

He invests the British approach to "the thankless task of reorganising" European lives with a transcendent truth, a status beyond the immediate sphere. Theory is a more acceptable label than belief because it sanctions the British claim to act based on principle, that is, logically, rather than based on irrational desire. In this way, the play foregrounds how White British rules of behavior are largely self-validating. Further, White British identity, secured through the practice of these internalized conventions, is shown to be based on the unverifiable belief in natural British superiority over a "squalling pack" of "sulky brutes"—Ridley's opinion of the "common people of all the back streets from Marseilles to Harbin" (Boland 34).

The dominant definition of White British identity is further called into question by the play's final event. The British are engaged in transporting the displaced when a dispute arises between two groups: a group of Westerners are rushing some eastbound trucks. Ridley refuses to quiet the situation by allowing the displaced to assist in organizing the transports. Throughout, he has demonstrated a blindness to cultural differences among them and has refused to admit that their recent wartime experiences render his superficial doctrine of "common humanity" difficult to accept. Rather, he is intent on pressuring them into adopting the proverbial British "stiff upper lip" and just getting on with things. Thus he compels people to work together in what for many of them represent fearful combinations. He is so convinced of the rightness of his theories that he relies on the ostensible force of British moral authority rather than the use of arms to quell the uprising, confidently stating that "There'll be no shooting" (Boland 177). The "prolonged burst of firing" that follows shatters the validity of his grand narrative.

Dan Rebellato points out that Boland's play foreshadows what happens once the claim to truth is lost (135). When the language games in which the British engage fail to make an effective claim to veracity, the counter-narratives of the displaced invalidate the tenets of White British discourse as universal or ahistorical. They overtly cast doubt on the power of the White British example to shape the postwar world. In *The Cockpit* we see clearly that the "truth" of White British identity is produced through language, through the will to know and thus control the "other" by constructing a particular view of reality that works to the White subject's advantage.

Whiteness and Polite Society: T. S. Eliot's *The Cocktail Party*

Wartime conditions had a negative impact on culture industries in the United Kingdom. Bombing raids had caused the closure or destruction of many theaters in London (as well as across the regions), which seriously curtailed theater practices throughout the country. The disruption of metropolitan theater effected the regions because, before the war, most regional theaters staged plays in the run-up to or following a West End production. Despite the postwar establishment of the Arts Council of Great Britain in 1946, Arthur Marwick records that there was on the whole a reversion to the conditions of productions of the 1930s. Many of the same playwrights predominated, the only new alternative being "verse drama" (*Culture in Britain since 1945,* 25).

Verse drama had actually been established in the 1930s, T. S. Eliot's *Murder in the Cathedral* being the leading example, but it did enjoy a revival in the 1940s and '50s. In 1949, Eliot's poetic drama *The Cocktail Party* was produced at the Edinburgh Festival. It opened in London, and then opened on Broadway in March 1950, where it enjoyed considerable financial and critical success.

Arnold P. Hinchliffe attributes the popularity of verse drama to a postwar desire for "colour, fancy and escape" (33). Rather than seeing verse drama as a form of escapist fare, John Elsom describes most of it as having a social aim, often a pious, moralizing one, that is forwarded through a set of derivative literary values and conservative social ones (64). Both definitions suit *The Cocktail Party* and its reception by contemporary audiences. Set in London, the play focuses on the marital relationship of Edward and Lavinia Chamberlayne, a barrister and his society wife. Hence, it is essentially a comfortably recognizable drawing-room piece; its subtext, however, adopts a high serious tone to explore the divide between postwar secular and traditional spiritual values.

In *The Idea of a Christian Society* (1939) Eliot writes that "we have today a culture which is mainly negative, but which, so far as it is positive, is still Christian" (13). Behind both the negative world symbolized by the Chamberlaynes and their social set and the larger, more obscure Christian British society lies imperial Britain and its attendant values. In a contemporary review William Arrowsmith observed that "A necessary part of the description of a Christian society is its relation, not only to the secular states with which it is involved, but to other and non-Christian societies" (391).[30] The role of the "other" in *The Cocktail Party* is filled by the indigenous population of

Kinkanja, an island whose inhabitants have been split by British colonization into those who remain faithful to their indigenous beliefs and those
who have been more successfully "colonized," that is, Christianized.

At yet another cocktail party hosted by the Chamberlaynes, Alex, a colonial inspector, returns from a tour of the colony. He characterizes Kinkanja as
a strange, frightening, and sinful place. Conversation revolves around the
usual insulting stereotypes about "the natives," who are described as heathens
of limited intelligence, as is evidenced by their veneration of monkeys; among
the barbaric practices ascribed to them are torture, murder, and cannibalism.
Kenneth Asher interprets their characterization in terms of a "mid-nineteenth
century churchman's notion of Darwinism" (114). That such views continue
to form a residual part of the postwar popular imaginary is borne out by
contemporary reviews of Eliot's play, which either accept uncritically his notion of the savage "other" or treat the natives as inconsequential figures.[31]

The play's most dramatic event occurs offstage. Alex announces that
Celia, Edward's former mistress, is dead, a victim of the Kinkanjans (following the end of their affair, Celia adopted the vocation of a missionary
nurse). In reality Celia is a victim of the British divide and conquer policy,
for she gets caught up in the conflict between those who have succumbed
to British rule for profit and those who continue to resist. The Christianized colonists have taken on British economic as well as religious values,
and in order to protect their crops they have begun to kill and eat the traditionally sacred saffron monkeys.

This provokes the "heathen" element into a revolt, during which Celia
and two other missionary women are taken captive. One dies in the jungle,
another is rendered unfit "for normal life again," and Celia suffers a more
ironic fate: crucifixion. Alternately described as her "duty" and a way to
work out her own salvation, what Celia perceives to be her spiritual destiny
in Kinkanja is tantamount to taking up the burden of Whiteness. Presumably she sacrifices herself for the benefit of those not fortunate enough to
have been born White British.

The values endorsed in the play demonstrate that the basic premises of
the British belief in racial superiority survived the war. The natives of
Kinkanja are the objects upon which Celia can validate her White subjectivity. Her destiny is equivalent to that of the nineteenth-century White
British subject who, recall, embodied muscular Christianity and, in the
case of the female subject, was fated to care for lesser peoples.

Arrowsmith recognizes that *The Cocktail Party* puts forward a test case
both "for the colonial administration and for Eliot's Christian society." The
problems the missionaries encounter on the island, he argues, are "insoluble

by ordinary political methods" because they are religious in origin. For this reason, when Alex, described as "the agent of a neutral and benevolent government," employs the laudable methods of the British Council, the only result is delay and an "interim report." In contrast, Celia's martyrdom, Arrowsmith concludes, evokes acceptance by the natives and heals the social divisions wrought by the British presence (391–92). However, there is no evidence in the text to support his reading that after her death Celia is "accepted by the natives and harmonized with their cult of the taboo saffron monkey."

To the contrary, by the manner of her death Eliot stages a return to moral darkness that reinforces the validity of the imperial doctrine of trusteeship: for a "handful of plague-stricken natives/who would have died anyway" (Eliot, *TCP* 169), Celia, White Lady Bountiful, is crucified on an ant hill. Just as humanitarian aims were put forward as excuses for imperial expansion at the height of empire, British imperialists after the war masked their opposition to the transfer of colonial power by portraying British rule as a necessary, albeit unappreciated, system of benevolent caretaking. Opponents to nationalist movements warned that, bereft of British protection, the colonies would descend into chaos and return to the kind of "darkness and death" that Eliot ascribes to the non-Christian people of Kinkanja (Darwin, *End of the British Empire* 20).

Arrowsmith's interpretation suggests that in the future, having mystically assimilated Celia, the people of Kinkanja will accord their British rulers the same veneration as the traditional saffron monkey enjoys. This reading, which splits the religious and the political impulses, means that Eliot's Christian society emerges as the winner of the contest between secular and spiritual values. Yet the two are inextricably linked in imperial discourse, with Christianity functioning as the interior colonial mechanism, balanced in turn by the exterior economic and political forms of subjection brought to bear on colonial peoples.

In *The Cocktail Party* Eliot, the quintessential Anglo-Saxon subject, produces a cultural text that attempts to validate the experiences and feelings of prewar imperial Britain. The play reconstructs the values informing the White imperial subject in a comforting manner, leaving the belief in the divine right of the British to racial ascendancy unchallenged. In Eliot's conception the postwar White British subject would remain defined by a stable body of systematic ideas with a clear historical trajectory.

Given the historical conditions of its production, what is remarkable about this play—what reveals it as a volley on the battleground for competing ideologies of racial identity in the postwar era—is what remains unstated about the changes in the structure of British society and the altered place of the British in the postwar world relative to its colonial societies. As Raymond Williams detects, the play is concerned more with the salvation of a particular social group than with any one individual (263). When conflict breaks out between the local people and the White imperialists, the distinction between private and public self breaks down. What happens to Celia is personal, but its context is a structural system within which White middle-class British subjects construct their collective racialized identity.

Celia does not so much choose her vocation as she is directed to it by Reilly, one of Eliot's social guardians (in the tradition of Plato's philosopher-kings) whose role is to overlook and organize the lives of the characters. He deputizes Celia as a representative of her class and race, willingly offering her up as a White sacrifice so that her presence in Kinkanja may aid the reinforcement of British colonial power as well as reproduce the axioms of White racial difference that underpin the system. However, classic colonial tensions remain unresolved at the end of the play. Neither the religious nor the secular institutions of British imperialism prevail, rendering *The Cocktail Party* ineffective as a palliative for those seeking to reestablish the security of a fixed White imperial identity.

Angry White Men: John Osborne's *The Entertainer*

In the 1950s it became more common for playwrights to examine how changes in the relations of power brought about by the war had irrevocably altered the position of the White British subject in the order of things. Alongside the classbound conservatism of the West End, an oppositional theater movement was gaining momentum. The year 1956, which saw the production of John Osborne's *Look Back in Anger,* is generally taken as a watershed for alternative British theater. New radical writers were overtly questioning the paradigms, racial and otherwise, that had been at the heart of British imperialism.

One of the centers of alternative theater was London's Royal Court. Unlike West End theaters, it did not stage plays based on their commercial potential. Work was sought that spoke frankly to the problems of the day and that appealed to younger audiences who might find mainstream theater redundant. Osborne featured as a key writer at the Royal Court, where his play *The Entertainer* opened in 1957.

Premiering one year after the Suez Crisis, it ranks as one of the decade's most politically provocative dramas. In July 1956, in response to the Egyptian government's legitimate nationalizing of the Suez Canal, Britain and France sent troops into the region. Opposed to the invasion, the United States worked behind the scenes to create a run on sterling, assuming that economic instability might force the British to retreat. Britain was also denounced overwhelmingly by the United Nations as an aggressor. These pressures combined to force the British into withdrawing from Egyptian territory.

Kenneth O. Morgan describes the Suez military venture as among the most humiliating in British history; in addition to damaging relations with the United States and the United Nations, it brought British economic stability into grave question (154). The Suez debacle also deepened anxieties surrounding British national identity, concerns that are echoed in *The Entertainer.* The relevant question here concerns how the cultural shift toward a post-imperial society is shown to impact on the symbolic acts through which the White British subject orders his or her experience.

Sander Gilman contends that people construct an acceptable order for their experiences through the use of a symbolic language taken from the society in which they live: "The roots of this symbolization are in the need for order, its form is the essential symbolic language of any given world view." This ordering, which is retrospective, uses symbols, with all their public meanings, to provide a context for establishing a unified sense of self. The language applied is found within the tradition of the representation of reality, which includes literature, art, science, and religion (*Inscribing the Other* 3). *The Entertainer* demonstrates how the symbolism of racial fictions operates to constitute modern White British identity.

The play centers on the life and art of Archie Rice, an aging music hall entertainer. Penny Summerfield cites the nineteenth-century music hall as a "fount of patriotism." She notes a common observation among contemporary social commentators that the music hall functioned to manipulate working-class opinion, particularly in favor of exploitative imperialist policy (17). Therefore, Osborne's note to the play—"The music hall is dying, and, with it, a significant part of England'—refers to the loss of empire and to the associated loss of a measure of identity for the British White working class.

Michael Anderson considers that the play equates popular entertainment with the state of the nation's soul (38), which makes Archie a microfigure of the nation-state. Interspersed with scenes of his solo performances are naturalistic scenes featuring him in a domestic setting. Because the whole Rice family figures as a microversion of British society, their domestic exchanges, like Archie's performances, also comment explicitly on the nation's state of affairs, and judging from the condition of Archie's career and family, Britain appears in severe decline.

No longer the main attraction, he has been reduced to serving as filler between acts that spectators have really paid to see—scantily clad female dancers who present their disreputable show before half-empty, disintegrating houses. By juxtaposing Archie's brand of titillating consumerism with the career of his father, Billy Osborne further emphasizes Britain's deterioration. As a product of the Edwardian era, Billy represents a sentimentalized narrative of past national glories, artistic and otherwise. He reminisces about the days when he ruled the boards like Britannia ruled the waves.

John Russell Brown reads the character Britannia as representing "god and country" in the play; she is the "final appeal" of many of Archie's songs and Billy's memories and the "living equivalent of the Union Jack that drapes Billy's coffin" (142). Archie's show, however, features a nude Britannia, stripped of all majesty. Rebellato sketches the connection between her despoiled state and the loss of empire: "Prestige is all that Britain has left, but when even that evaporates, as it did during Suez, we are revealed naked underneath the tattered finery" (139–40).

The figure of Britannia serves to illustrate how Archie and Billy's psychology has been shaped by different social representations of White Britishness. Their self-images and ways of relating to others are rooted in these interiorized representations. Billy's persona is constructed within the mythic language of imperial power. Osborne describes Billy's speech as "not an accent of class but of period," referring once again to the accessibility of imperial discourse as a mode of validating one's White Britishness regardless of class background.

Billy's discourse refers both to his particular use of language and to the philosophical presuppositions that attend it. His first speech is a rant against the threat of socio-racial difference: "Bloody Poles and Irish! I hate the bastards. Dirty, filthy lot. I'll bet they left the front door open. Born in fields, they are. . . . Animals. Like animals" (Osborne 13–14). He continues his rant to his granddaughter Jean: "Bloody farm-yard. They want locking up. And you know what now, don't you? You know who she's got upstairs, in Mick's old room, don't you? Some black fellow. It's true. I tell you, you've come to a mad-house this time" (Osborne 15). While the creation of stereotypes mirrors a process that all people undergo in becoming individuals, Billy's crude representation of Blacks, Poles, and Irish is pathological. His process of othering is a desperate attempt to place a buffer between his desired image of himself and the realities of his position in post-imperial

Britain. This is necessary because White discourse no longer carries the same cultural authority it did in the Edwardian era.

Luc Gilleman identifies the significance of Billy's lament for the demise of the music hall, for the "shared laughter at predictable moments and targets" generated by this social text (text in its widest sense) created a "comforting impression of cultural unity" (75). At the height of his fame, Billy enjoyed a certainty of identity: "We all had our own style, our own songs, and we were all English. What's more we spoke English. . . . We all knew what the rules were" (Osborne 81).

Billy's sense of loss is always measured against this mythic time of fullness, when there was a perceived universality or at least commonality to White British experience and when the British occupied a position from which they were able to do what they liked on the world stage, just as Billy could sing his own songs in his own style. Britannia's place on this stage having altered, Billy is unable to negotiate the realities of life in modern Britain. He strives to make sense of it all, without success: "What d'you make about all this business out in the Middle East? People seem to be able to do what they like to us. Just what they like. I don't understand it. I really don't" (Osborne 17). Consequently, in order to replicate the vanished unity and force of White Britishness Billy needs to perpetuate a sense of difference between himself and the racial "other," but the play makes clear that his practice of stereotyping offers a very slippery kind of psychic security.

Archie too embodies the fragility of White identity in postwar Britain. "Don't clap too hard,—it's a very old building" (Osborne 59), he warns his audience, invoking once again the analogy between the decaying music hall and the nation-state. While Archie represents a debauched figure who is in violation of many of the traditional values his father celebrates, he too professes a sentimental longing for past certainties. He alternates between a resigned acceptance of his personal and cultural defeat and a schmaltzy, only half-cynical appeal to jingoistic "truths": "For I'm sure you'll agree,/ That a fellow like me,/Is the salt of our dear country" (Osborne 60). Through his performances, he tries to reinvoke the commonality of White British experience enjoyed in his father's day, positioning himself in terms of the average White British man: "Now I'm just an ordinary bloke/The same as you out there" (Obsorne 60). However, his efforts evoke no hearty applause.

Archie's supposed ordinariness is constructed against a backdrop of the racialized "other." Though with more subtlety than Billy, he still vocalizes the racist tendency to collectivize ethnic "others," such as the "wogs." He attempts to bind himself further to Whiteness via his appeals to the category of the normal: "Thank God we're normal, normal, normal/Thank God we're normal" (Osborne 61). That he appeals in vain is made abundantly clear by the fact that he delivers this in front of an image of a nude-woman in Britannia's helmet, holding a bulldog and trident.

The play's Brechtian episodes encourage the audience to share in the process of self-conception that is integral to Archie's experience. Katherine J. Worth proposes that Osborne

> gets his audience into the same position as the actors: We are Archie's audience now, reacting with him to . . . the nude Britannia with the bulldog and trident. We can choose to laugh or not to laugh at her and at Archie's jokes . . . . But either way our response is prepared for and taken into the play. The feeling of being *really* in it together is uncomfortably communicated. (76)

The postwar condition shared by actor and spectator (symbolized by the nude Britannia) is characterized by an inability to recreate the sense of psychic plenitude that accompanied Britain's imperial status. A principle factor working against Archie and Billy feeling at ease in postwar Britain is the literal presence of the "other" within their homespace; that is, Blackness occupies an unacceptable degree of proximity to this symbolic White British family.

The family was the focus of social reconstruction in the postwar era, and the recoverability of British greatness was believed to reside in its success. Gilleman, considering the reduced circumstances of the Rice family, notes how their position in the new social geography is expressed in terms of lack. Their house, described as a monument to the past, is situated in a coastal resort, but in a "place where tourists never venture. Its neighbourhood can only be defined in terms of . . . what it is not, no longer or just barely" (66). And what it is no longer is purely White.

As immigrants in the 1940s and '50s have attested, Whites were highly reluctant to rent rooms to Blacks or other social groups Whites judged to be inferior. The Rices, however, cannot afford this illusion of an absolute dividing line between White self and "other." To violate the set boundaries of racial categories by taking in the wrong type of lodgers amounts to more than just placing oneself on the lower end of the social scale; it means also casting doubt on the resurrection of White British dominance. By allowing the incursion of the "other" into previously White-only space, the Rices refute the fiction of White British integrity as well as solidarity.

Metaphorically sleeping with the "other" negates the mythic idea of White British brotherhood, the belief that Whites in Britain were more

united in race than divided by class or other forms of difference, for it is
the Rice's poverty that dictates their mode of living. Compared to Billy,
Archie and his children are dissociated from the privileges of Whiteness:
their position in relation to Whiteness makes clear a major postwar shift in
the construction of British identity, namely that Whiteness as the glue
binding together various class factions within British society is losing some
of its adhesiveness.

This raises questions about the nature of the play's message, especially
in regard to its patriotism. John Russell Taylor provides a balanced summary of the play's political stance, pointing out that in *The Entertainer* Osborne writes

of something, like the Edwardian splendors of India, which he cannot possibly remember himself and which becomes therefore, for him, a romantic legend to be
longed for as an alternative to the indecisions and false values of modern life. The
intelligent man of left-wing sympathies in Osborne tells him—and us—that it
was the faults in this ante-diluvian world which brought our world into existence,
but the incorrigible romantic looks back admiringly. (50)

Taylor describes the play in terms of a battleground on which these *two* Os-
bornes fight it out. While *The Entertainer* clearly mourns some of the
changes in postwar British society, neither Osborne the sentimentalist nor
Osborne the radical prevails, thereby delivering no definitive endorsement
of either traditional or modern values.

He does not give us a partisan account of what precipitated the flood.
Instead, what the play makes clear are the consequences to individual subjects of the underlying ruptures in the White social structure that result
from the loss of empire, and the concomitant invalidation of its core racial
identity, which was both producer and product of imperial discourse. It is
through the younger generation of the Rice family—Jean, Mick, and
Frank—that Osborne show us the complexity of the identity strategies
needed to negotiate a modern White British position, as each struggles in
a different way to survive intact in their postdiluvian world.

Osborne condenses and displaces onto the younger Rice generation a
whole range of anxieties about White British identity that were prevalent
in the 1950s. The well-trodden path of service to "God and country" in
which Mick evinces faith is challenged for the family and the spectator
when, having answered the call for military service, Mick is captured and
killed by "bloody wogs." His death is portrayed by his sister not as a heroic
sacrifice but as a pointless waste of life: "Why do people like us sit here,

and just lap it all up, why do boys die . . . is it really just for the sake of a gloved hand waving at you from a golden coach?" (Osborne 78).

In contrast to his brother, Frank sees no future for himself or anyone of his generation in Britain: "Look around you. Can you think of any good reason for staying in this cosy corner of Europe? Don't kid yourself anyone's going to let you do anything, or try anything here, Jeannie" (Osborne 67). This bleak view of his position in his home country makes him unwilling to fight, preferring a prison sentence to serving Britain.

Eventually his pessimism, worsened by the deaths of his brother and grandfather, spurs him to emigrate. When Frank gives up on his country, he appears to endorse the view that responsibility for Britain's tired state can be blamed as much on internal as external factors. This position was adopted by subscribers to the British right in the 1950s, who argued that young Britain was more unwilling than unable to fulfill an imperial destiny because it lacked the moral fiber and self-discipline of previous generations.[32]

Jean presents the most interesting psychological response to the postwar circumstances. Neither pure traditionalist nor pure modernist, her ambivalent location bordering old and new Britain, the right and left, throws into relief the conflict between the established symbolic order and the desire to reform that order that marked the 1950s in Britain. On the one hand, she subscribes to a liberal set of ideas. She foregoes marriage to the socially ambitious Graham, objecting to his unequal view of women. She opts to work at a low-paying but socially useful job teaching art to underprivileged children at a youth club, and she pins some hopes on the efficacy of political action to bring about positive social change, attending a rally in Trafalgar Square.

At the same time, she clings to the redundant sentimental narrative of Britishness espoused by Billy and Archie. She has imbibed also the older generation's reactionary bigotry, saying of Frank that "He'd have been better off, in the Army—sticking a bayonet into some wog" (Osborne 31). Notwithstanding her bitterness, only she seems to hold out any promise for the future of Britain, as is evidenced by her decision to stay at home and look after Phoebe while Archie serves his prison term for failure to pay income tax.

Whether Jean will be able to "make a go of it," despite the empress no longer having any clothes, Osborne leaves open to doubt. The failure of the younger Rices to establish successful lives clearly belies the notion, unquestioned by Billy's generation, that there are superior qualities natural to

White Britishness. Further, the play suggests that the White British project to redeem its future by reinscribing the values of its imperial past through a process of stereotyping and scapegoating the racialized "other" is both deluded and futile.

When Phoebe complains about having to consort with "down and outs," she foregrounds the contradiction that would become more glaringly apparent in the 1960s between White British endeavors to define racial difference and their increasing inability to exercise the power needed to legislate the material boundaries of that difference. This helps place Jean's final thought in an appropriate sociohistorical context: "Here we are, we're alone in the universe, there's no God. . . . We've only got ourselves. Somehow, we've just got to make a go of it. *We've only got ourselves*" (Osborne 85).

Critics have sometimes read Jean's words as optimistic, but it is more likely that they suggest a resigned acceptance on her part. The feeling of extreme isolation she expresses relates to what has been lost since Billy's generation—namely, Britain's imperial referents. Colonialism, with God at its apex and human colonial subjects at its base, contributed toward a feeling of security and psychological wholeness for many White Britons. After empire, however, Jean suggests that what White Britishness means is nothing more than what one can make of it in the face of very unfavorable external conditions that are largely outside of one's control.

chapter 4

Locating Race in Postwar U.S. Culture

he social context of race was altered in the United States during
World War II as a result of the interaction between military and national policies, which resulted in changes in both.[33] This war marked
the first time in history that the willing participation of Blacks was vital to
the U.S. success story. Their labor was needed at home as well as in the
armed forces, and the war effort required of everyone a heightened sense
of national unity. World War II offered Black Americans the greatest possibility for social gains since reconstruction—a second opportunity to access the category of U.S. citizenship. Accordingly, military service was an
integral part of the campaign for civil rights, in the opinion of many Black
leaders.

At the start of the war, the military establishment accepted the general
cultural criteria that dictated that Whites were innately superior to Blacks,
and it set its policies accordingly. The roles assigned to Blacks matched the
traditional racial division of labor that historically functioned to police
the boundaries of Whiteness and Blackness in the larger society. Relegated
mainly to segregated noncombat units and denied leadership positions,
Blacks were seen fit to provide primarily manual labor: digging latrines,
collecting trash, or working as cooks.[34]

Nevertheless, the war created a political climate in which Black Americans could more effectively resist discrimination, and the 1940s saw an increase in Black lobbying groups and a new militancy in the Black press and
trade unions. Over the course of the war, the nation's need for its Black citizens grew; coupled with an intensified level of political activism, this produced a series of qualitative and quantitative gains in race relations.[35] In
the short term, the wartime economy provided new job opportunities and
more financial security for Black Americans, while their large-scale migration to the North offered new educational chances as well. These gains
translated into a new level of self-sufficiency and a more positive commu-

nity identity among the Black populace. Among some segments of White society, too, the Black community's contribution to the war effort gained them added respect.

Still, in the long term wartime experiences did not effect a recognition of Blacks as first-class citizens. Indeed, throughout the war there was substantial resistance among Whites to Black participation, either through military service or civilian activities. Despite a shortage of labor at home, White workers and unions fought changes to the racialized division of labor in industries, fearing the threat such changes posed to working-class White identity. Also, there was fierce competition for housing, health, and leisure facilities across the Northern states where Black migrants settled.[36]

In some cases, White communities violently defended these geo-racial turfs. White antagonism to Blacks' advancement, Neil Wynn records, led to 242 racial battles across forty-seven cities in 1942–43 (67–73). Manning Marable recalls another series of "hate strikes" in 1943 and '44 against the integration and/or upgrading of Black workers in industry (14).

As the 1940s progressed, so too did the intensity of struggle over the meaning of race. Once White society registered the threat posed to the system of race and class relations that had been in place since the turn of the century, an intensified campaign ensued to contain or roll back the gains Blacks had achieved during the war years. White America acted by reinforcing the impermeability of the color line, principally through accelerating the process of segregation.

At the turn of the century, it was not uncommon for Whites of all classes and Blacks to live in close proximity to each other. Working-class people in northern cities might live side by side; Black sharecroppers and servants in the South often lived on their employer's estates or near the homes they served. As Black social migration increased in the 1920s and '30s, so too did their physical isolation from the rest of U.S. society. Douglas Massey and Nancy Denton observe that the "outlines and form of the modern black ghetto were in place in most northern cities by the outbreak of World War II." Similarly, in many southern areas laws existed mandating the separation of cities into White and Black districts. The process of ghetto formation in the 1940s would increase the White/Black divide to new extremes. By the end of the war, racial segregation was a permanent structural feature of the spatial organization of the United States (Massey and Denton 43).

Despite the containment of the Black populace by physically sectioning it off from White society, the United States became a culture increasingly ridden with race-related anxiety. Added to racial pressures at home were threats from abroad. The postwar years witnessed the beginnings of the cold war and the nuclear threat it contained, a much harder challenge than race for those in power. In one sense, Blacks had been easy to suppress historically because the color divide rendered them so conspicuous as the "other." More alarming to the dominant culture were those enemies of the "American-way-of-life" who could not be so readily identified because their skin color belied their ethnicity, placing them on the periphery of the White/"other" divide.

The war in Europe had produced tens of thousands of refugees. Large numbers of people migrating to the United States now came from Eastern European countries. As always, there was opposition to the new immigrants. In this case, the basis for resistance was named the threat of communism.

In a 1946 speech that clearly anticipates the full-scale paranoia that would erupt in the 1950s, Captain Eddie Rickenbacker characterizes the new immigrants as a kind of viral presence in the U.S. body politic. These "sinister agents of the refugee army" represent a horde of alien bodies intent on destroying the "American-way-of-life" from within. He contrasts the refugees to previous economic migrant groups. The latter had come to help build the United States, and when the (now assimilated as White) Irish and Germans had said "gimme," it meant "give me work . . . opportunity . . . a chance." For war refugees, in contrast, it was taken to mean "gimme what you got or else." "It is time to stop the breach. It is time to plug the leak," Rickenbacker states, and, blind to the paradoxes of his own position, he concludes by arguing: "It is time to take steps against undeserving aliens . . . hostile aliens who are now in this country, aliens who are horsemen of the modern Apocalypse of intolerance, division, hate, suspicion, and strife" (554).

This speech illustrates how after World War II the Eastern Bloc countries become the dark and menacing child of Europe in the popular imagination. Also, it sheds light on the underside of the U.S. mindset in the late 1940s. Despite enjoying an economic boom and having attained superpower status, the United States was still capable of envisioning itself as a ship in peril, one that might be sunk if it took on board the wrong social elements.

The changes in U.S. society activated by the war provoked anxiety among the majority White populace because they suggested a possible future in which Whiteness would no longer correspond to an unalterable dominance. These anxieties would be exacerbated further in the 1950s. There existed side by side in the 1950s two world views that in many ways were at odds with each other—the United States was a vulnerable political entity *and* it was the world's most successful nation.

Some feared a third world war, possibly nuclear, that would be fought against the world's other superpower, the Soviet Union. Added to the dangers perceived to lie outside its borders, the United States felt vulnerable to attack from subversive agents within. There was concern about a possible covert "Red" invasion, that is, a Soviet infiltration into U.S. life in ways other than military. This gave rise to the infamies of the McCarthy era, during which the House Un-American Activities Committee (HUAC) interrogated U.S. citizens about their possible links to communist organizations. The communist "witch hunts" focused intensely on figures from the arts, with film, music, and theater viewed as likely sources of communist propaganda because they could easily "disguise, deodorize, and attractively package Moscow's revolutionary products" (O'Neil 110).

Anticommunist dogma frequently merged with racial politics in the 1950s. This decade signaled the growing importance of Black civil rights to the U.S. political process. Black resistance began to organize under the banner of the civil rights movement, and minority voices were poised for the first time to become a powerful social force for change. While liberal Whites would play an important role in the success of the movement, among the majority of Whites the Black demands for social justice sparked a backlash against the ideals and policies of the New Deal era and precipitated the growth of right-wing conservatism in the 1950s and beyond.[37] Hence, by the 1950s the dominant White culture could no longer ignore the problems created by the rigid White/Black social divide.

Since the 1930s the communists have been recognized by many working-class Blacks as allies in the fight against racial prejudice and segregation.[38] During the cold war, the unequal treatment of Blacks provided the Soviets with a potent weapon with which to embarrass the United States on the world stage. Also, while denying it publicly, the head of the FBI, J. Edgar Hoover, was convinced that communist agitators had infiltrated civil rights groups, even conservatives ones.

Even though a number of prominent individual Black leaders and numerous middle-class groups actively participated in anticommunist activities, this counted little in their favor. In some ways, middle-class Blacks played into the hands of the racist establishment, because anticommunist rhetoric proved a useful tool for impeding advances in race relations. It allowed those in power to collectively label anyone seeking to reform the U.S. system as subversive, in effect, un-American. Irrespective of class, then, Blacks could be viewed as a threat to the "American-way-of-life."

Another factor contributing to the feeling that Whiteness was under siege was the encroachment of Black culture into White lifestyles and especially youth culture. The middle class particularly feared that an exposure to Black cultural practices, such as music, would "mongrelize" and thus destroy the Anglo-Saxon race. Elvis was touted as the clearest example of the "debasing effects on a good, god-fearing mother-loving country boy of over-exposure to black culture" (Ward 202).

Wini Breines documents how rock and roll was central to the White teen experience in the 1950s, regardless of class. She characterizes the story of rock and roll as the badge of postwar White teenage culture, and as a racial tale: "another version of whiteness constructed against blackness, of a Herculean effort to contain, transform, even erase, black culture from white life" (151). Some Whites attempted to combat Black influence by suggesting that the popularity of its art forms with White audiences could only be accounted for by a communist conspiracy.

Tom Engelhardt elaborates on the way in which the element of disorder and sexuality historically associated with Blackness and now personified by the racially ambiguous figure of Elvis mingled with fears about a communist menace. The racial border crossings possible within the arena of popular culture were analogous to crossing the line of political probity. Just as communists were traitors to the "American-way-of-life," so too were the Whites who consumed Black culture, thereby destabilizing, even eroding, the racial boundaries supporting White supremacy. Thus while the processes of segregation were working to secure the color line, there were other covert elements present in 1950s society that the dominant order feared might lead to its breakdown.

Despite economic optimism in the United States, immigration remained a source of apprehension as well. The Maoist revolution led to an influx of Chinese immigrants, and Hungarian refugees started to arrive after the 1956 rebellion (Olson 232). Once again, it was felt that this foreign presence was a threat to dominant U.S. cultural values—in other words, the White hegemony.

Paradoxically, Americans like to remember the 1950s with fond nostalgia as a golden time of economic prosperity, youthful innocence, and social cohesion, encapsulated, for example, in the long-running TV sitcom *Happy Days*. Indeed, many in the United States did enjoy an unprecedented period of materialism and optimism. The United States had become the world's richest nation. It ostentatiously made up for wartime privations, at least for its White inhabitants; despite having only 6 percent of the world's population, it used half of the world's production of energy.

Consumer spending was at an all-time high. The United States produced half and consumed much more than half of the world's manufactured products.[39]

However, the phenomena of "conspicuous consumption" wrought a host of detrimental social effects. Within dominant discourse, the new level of prosperity was offered as a proof against socialism. A notion of the "people's capitalism" developed, a system that was supposedly erasing class divisions by making everyone middle class. In reality, as Ronald Oakley makes clear, the United States suffered from a severe case of economic myopia (203).

Although the number of people falling into the economic range marking the middle class increased, huge inequalities in wealth remained. The poor were still present in large numbers.[40] While their plight was largely ignored, the increased visibility of Black culture and the new waves of Eastern European immigration could not be. Combined with generalized fears about communism and Soviet aggression, these changes generated widespread anguish and paranoia, and they contributed to a highly pressurized atmosphere among Whites to conform to the dominant notion of "Americanism."

Life, Liberty, and the Pursuit of Whiteness: Eugene O'Neill's *The Iceman Cometh*

Developments in staged representations of Whiteness played a part in the racial contests of the 1940s and '50s in the United States, participating in the redefinition of what it meant to be part of White America at this time. Some dramatic representations from the period exhibit a strong continuity with images that predominated at the turn of the century and that functioned to endorse the system within which Whiteness carries the highest social value. Others, consciously or not, contributed toward a moderated version of Whiteness by making visible the paradoxes within White ideology and destabilizing the illusion of the White subject's integrity.

Eugene O'Neill's *The Iceman Cometh* marks a shift in imaginative encounters with White identity. O'Neill began drafting the play at the end of 1939, as war broke out in Europe.[41] Travis Bogard records that it was withheld from production during the war because, as O'Neill explained, the "pity and tragedy of defensive pipe dreams would be deemed downright unpatriotic. . . . But after the war is over . . . American audiences will understand a lot of *The Iceman Cometh* only too well" (418).

The play marked O'Neill's return to the Broadway stage after a twelve-year absence. Despite his much-anticipated homecoming, the play's reception was lukewarm, and it closed after only 146 productions (Berlin 85). To understand this disappointing commercial and ambivalent critical reception, one must bear in mind the social conditions surrounding its appearance.[42]

When it premiered in 1946, the nation as a whole was in the midst of celebrating the Allied victory, which had ensured the preservation of the "American-way-of-life." In addition, the United States had assumed a new position of supremacy among Western nations, and its mission to export its philosophy of life was accelerating. Against this social backdrop, *Iceman's* themes—the illusory nature of truth, the impossibility of redemption, and the futility of individual action—were simply unpalatable to a postwar audience.

Moreover, if, as I will argue, being American in the play equates to being White subject in *Iceman,* O'Neill stages a very unsettling representation of Whiteness, one that would have been seen as alarming given the active threat to White identity and privilege during the war years.[43] Consequently, O'Neill's realist-symbolist construction of Whiteness, which works against the essentializing dynamic in White discourse,[44] as by connecting Whiteness with self-delusion, dependence, dissipation, and death would have been read as highly troubling.

However, as my reading will demonstrate, the play's representation of Whiteness is sometimes at odds with itself. In some instances Whiteness is coded through a set of normative assumptions; at other times it is depicted in terms that provide a form of critical opposition to this dominant formula. Yet the overall effect of this contradiction is to point up the relationship between the fictive and the real in dominant understandings of White U.S. identity.

Most criticism of the play addresses the experiences of the three central figures: Hickey, Larry, and Parritt. My reading focuses on the character types with whom O'Neill peoples Hope's Saloon. Implicitly, the American Dream is the umbrella fiction for all of the character's individual pipe dreams. However, the dreams of the choral figures illustrate most clearly how they relate to the construction of race in U.S. society and to each character's relative place on the ladder of Whiteness.

The choral figures offer the spectator an economy of identification. O'Neill's strategic use of stereotype differs according to the character's race and follows the Nature/culture, civilized/primitive binary intrinsic to White discourse. White characters are drawn through the allocation of cultural attributes. Cecil, for O'Neill, is as obviously English as "Yorkshire pudding." Piet is a Dutch "farmer type." In contrast, Blacks and variegated Whites are physicalized. Rocky, a Neapolitan, is identified by his "flat swarthy face and beady eyes," while Joe represents the "mildly negroid in type."

The action of the play lies in the characters' repetition of tales. Most of the stories relate how *tomorrow* the person will be able to tap the psychological and physical capacity needed to reestablish their place in society. *Iceman* dramatizes Stuart Hall's observation that "identity is always constructed through memory, fantasy, narrative and myth" ("Cultural Identity and Diaspora" 226), for it is through relating their fictionalized personal narratives that each character can create a self-image that, with enough drink, makes their lives just bearable.

The reiteration of their pipe dreams represents a kind of gaming among the characters—a competition for ascendancy within the community of Hope's Saloon. "It's a great game, the pursuit of happiness," Larry says, echoing and mocking Jefferson's words in the Declaration of Independence (O'Neill, *TIC* 14). Until the arrival of Hickey, the unspoken rule for residency at Hope's is that each patron, by supporting the others' illusions, enables them all to retain a façade of respectability.

However, once Hickey's evangelical crusade to debunk their dreams gets under way, the social psychology of the group alters significantly. The primary way of boosting one's self-esteem shifts from colluding in everyone else's fantastic accounts to degrading each person, verbalizing how someone else is less equipped than oneself to make good in the world outside. As the group dynamic deteriorates and the characters lose faith in their dreams, conflicts erupt, due to the differences of race, as well as gender and class, that have always simmered beneath the surface.

As one pipe dream after another gets shattered, what becomes degraded as much as the individual characters is the dominant idea of Whiteness. This occurs in two ways. Most of the minor character's dreams are highly individualized in their aims. For instance, McGloin wants to win back his old position on the force. Willie, a failed lawyer, wants a job in the district attorney's office. These are concrete proposals that, given the right combination of personal attributes, represent achievable aims. Yet all of these characters fail to attain what is clearly attainable for White subjects within the mythology of the American Dream.

Their failure refutes the reality of U.S. Man by challenging the idea that there is something innate to American character that makes anything doable. When unmasked to themselves by Hickey, the White characters choose to pursue happiness in the form of the ideal, self-sufficient masculinity that U.S. sociopolitical discourse presents as a White birthright, only to realize that Hickey's naked "truth" about their capacities is just as deluded. In this way the play foregrounds the internal contradictions of Whiteness.

White masculine identity promises much but delivers very little for the characters. Once Hickey departs, the characters, unable to break their self-destructive cycle, return quickly to a state of consoling ignorance and drunkenness. Their capitulation to a failed destiny makes the play's imaginative encounter with Whiteness an unattractive and threatening one, especially in an immediate postwar context, for again it denies the "truth" of the American Dream, the very ideal for which people believed they had fought.

The second way in which *Iceman* stages a reconfigured White subject is by endowing the White characters with a self-consciousness based on self-loathing, as well as a crippling sense of guilt and fear. As they sober up, these feelings translate into increasing conflict within the group. The atmosphere becomes poisoned with bickering, threats, and actual violence. Hatred for the other ultimately turns in on itself, and personalities start to disintegrate, with character's swinging between vengeful posturing, hysterical fear, maudlin ramblings, and incoherent bouts of laughter. By demeaning the characters in this way, O'Neill also racializes them; because these types, meant to represent a cross-section of White U.S. society, now fall into the civilized/primitive binary as primitives.

O'Neill rewrites the racialization process that makes White dominance possible, firstly by making Whiteness visible onstage, and secondly by lending it a corrupted appearance. The instability of Whiteness as guarantor for the "American-way-of-life" is emphasized further by the way in which Rocky and Joe are positioned in relation to the great American *pipe* Dream. Their aspirations stand out as distinct from the White figures', for neither man would be capable of realizing his dream regardless of personal improvement.

At no time in the play do the choral figures occupy an equal place in the "Tomorrow Movement" (the men's ironic title, meant to express their affinity), and the differences among them translate into a racialized pecking order that mirrors the wider society. Rocky, as a Neapolitan and therefore a variegated White, is positioned on the margins, which reflects his tenuous place on the ladder of Whiteness. Despite his individual shortcomings, Rocky's presence at Hope's may be attributed as much to institutional factors as to personal characteristics. His inability to realize the American Dream has deeper structural roots than that of the other characters, and it needs to be seen in relation to the way in which he is fixed within the historical terms of White racial discourse.

Rocky embodies the paradoxical notion that one may be white and yet racially distinct from the category of Whiteness. In keeping with U.S. racial history, his proximity to Whiteness is determined partly by Joe's distance from it as a Black male, but Rocky is endowed also with traits that correlate to Whiteness in dominant thought.[45] Rocky's dream relates to improving and stabilizing his place in the socio-racial hierarchy, which, as I demonstrated in chapter 2, would not have been an impossible object for Italian immigrants in the 1940s. Following the tradition of such immigrant groups, he tries to raise his status by basing his identity on a legitimate form of labor—bartender-cum-bouncer. Therefore, it makes some sense for Rocky to be at Hope's, because it provides a possible avenue to a more privileged social identity, as well as bed, board, and access to steady cash.

However, within the majority White "Tomorrow Movement," Rocky's ethnic difference continues to register above all else. For example, he is prejudged to be an ineffectual figure by Hope, who believes his Neapolitan ethnicity precludes him from adequately carrying out his role as minder, with "Dago . . . order" characterized as "like bedlam in a cathouse." Even his closest allies Chuck, Pearl, and Margie, themselves racial outsiders, render him as a sign of socio-racial illegitimacy—a "dirty little Ginny" pimp.

One must also take into account O'Neill's description of Rocky as a "Wop" (without papers). This may be intended as just another example of an ethnic slur, or it could mean that he is an illegal immigrant. In the latter case, his opportunities to Whiten himself through work would be more limited, and this may account both for his occupancy at Hope's as well as his role of pimp to Pearl and Margie, from whom he derives the bulk of his income. That he relies on the women's labor to support himself further problematizes his relation to Whiteness. It mars his potential to resemble U.S. Man, for the ideal form of White subjectivity he seeks to inhabit correlates to a White masculinity that depends on the ability to pull oneself up the economic ladder through one's own efforts and to carry, rather than be carried by, a woman.

Even more than Rocky's, Joe's experience offers a counterpoint to the national White imaginary. Because Joe dreams of equality with White men, he metaphorically dons white face in the play. In the past, his identification with Whiteness has brought him some social rewards. For instance, he was the "only coloured man dey allows in de white gambling houses" (O'Neill, *TIC* 45). Ultimately, though, the cost of impersonating Whiteness outweighs the gains for Joe.

Because his mask of Whiteness is always poised to slip, he exists in a state of psychological disaffection. The danger that he may catch sight of his Blackness in the eyes of others is everpresent, as is illustrated when

Lewis, awakening from a drunken stupor, voices his shock at seeing himself seated next to a "Kaffir." After Hickey transforms the characters' relations, Joe can no longer hide from his Black identity because there is a particularly vicious turn to the way he is treated. Chuck threatens to "moider de nigger!" Margie objects to his "noive": "Just because we act nice to him, he gets a swelled nut! If dat ain't a coon all over" (O'Neill, *TIC* 47). When he tries to intervene in a quarrel between Chuck and Rocky, they turn on him "*as if their own quarrel was forgotten and they became natural allies against an alien*" (O'Neill, *TIC* 145).

Joe's White mask fools no one but himself and only serves White interests by making him easier to exploit. Whites perceive him as a *good* Black because his desire for the privileges of Whiteness makes him useful in controlling other Blacks. Even so, by making Joe appear to undergo White experience, O'Neill makes the character an effective agent for challenging racial difference as it is fixed within White discourse.

By playing Whiteness, Joe opens the category to a wider range of meanings. Most significantly, his identification with Whiteness reveals White identity to be something provisional, something that may be performed rather than a natural and static subjectivity. Rather than enhancing the White characters' qualities—the usual role of Black characters in literature of this period—Joe's impersonation of Whiteness affords a gap in how it is ordinarily perceived. For instance, when the Big Chief, the local reigning mobster, allows him to run his own gambling joint, Joe proves his Whiteness, as vouched for by Harry Hope, by paying his "sugar on de dot" (O'Neill, *TIC* 46).

On a surface level, Joe's desire for Whiteness may seem to reinforce the dominant idealized view of White identity, yet in fact it makes Whiteness proximate to dissolution. By licensing a Black man to perform Whiteness in this way, *The Iceman Cometh* dislodges the White subject from the center of moral discourse. This is a deeply subversive move, because U.S. social and political discourse posits a higher morality as the source of White power at home, and increasingly after the war the special virtues of the "American-way-of-life" become the justification for U.S. imperialism abroad.

Primitive Whiteness: Tennessee Williams's *A Streetcar Named Desire*

Felicia Hardison Londré describes Tennessee Williams's *A Streetcar Named Desire* (1946) as a "play about people trying to build lives for themselves in the changing postwar world" (48). The play explores the construction of postwar U.S. identity from a number of perspectives. It offers a multilayered portrait of race that illuminates how it intersects with gender, class, sexuality, and sociopolitical space. It makes White ethnicity noticeable by displaying its hybrid status, shedding light on the way in which White identities were being reconfigured as the result of historically specific shifts in postwar society.

Streetcar may be described as a text of sameness and otherness. Thematically, the structure rests on a number of binary oppositions: White/Black, masculine/feminine, hetero/homosexual, culture/nature, civilized/primitive, Old/New South. These categories, and their social causes and effects, are primarily refracted through character. As the play opens, we are plunged immediately into a racialized *mise en scène*. The first characters we see are Eunice, a White woman, and her "colored" neighbor, who are "taking the air on the steps." (Williams 11). Such physical proximity of White to Black would alert the contemporary spectator that the characters reside in an(other) space compared to normative U.S. society.

Eunice's proximity to Blackness places a question mark after her White identity, for a *nice* middle-class White woman, particularly a Southern one, would not be found in this situation. The scene locates Eunice within the category of "white trash." Matt Wray and Annalee Newitz describe this category as more than just a racist slur; it is also a racial epithet that marks certain people quasi-white, that is, a breed apart from Whites (1).

In addition to character, the binaries structuring the play's narrative are refracted through physical space. Writing about the gaze in Williams, John Timpane describes how it encompasses place as a construction of identity. It is "a metaphor for the chaotic determination of identity," with Southernness acting as a metaphor for a kind of conflicted identity (751–52). The different values of the sociopolitical spaces coded as New versus Old South provide a framework within which the play's principal antagonists, Stanley Kowalski and Blanche Du Bois, enact their contest for personal and political supremacy.

A progeny of Belle Reve (beautiful dream), Blanche stands as a repository of White genteel culture.[46] She clings to a way of life whereby one's character is judged by one's birth (read race) and allegiance to prescribed high cultural practices and attainments (a certain set of racialized class values). Her association with the plantocracy and the civilized arts of poetry and music, and her addiction to what Williams terms "magic," lend her an ethereal and ephemeral air. These things mark her difference from Stanley, who incarnates the thrusting and coarser spirit of the urban postwar South.

Blanche embodies the paradoxes of southern belle femininity. On the one hand, Williams endows her with a stereotypical emotional dependence on "the kindness of strangers." This is most clearly illustrated in the final scene, where Blanche runs from the nurse but accepts the attentions of the male physician, or in other words the Old South system of patriarchy. On the other hand, despite the airs, graces, and material accoutrements of femininity that Blanche displays, she plainly veers far from the ideal of White womanhood in her sexual rapaciousness.

To violate the limits of conventional female sexuality as prescribed within patriarchal terms, however, does not entirely alienate Blanche from the category of White womanhood. David Savran argues that the phallus and all that it symbolizes belongs to Stanley (122).[47] He notes that the phallic male in Williams differs in terms of social class, ethnicity, and temperament from the White protestant bourgeois paradigm so feverishly promoted in popular culture during the postwar domestic revival (*Communists, Cowboys and Queers* 122–23). I would argue that Blanche provides a model of White femininity that differs from the bourgeois paradigm as much as Stanley's brand of masculinity. What makes Blanche different from her sister, for instance, is the way that she is partly invested with the power of the phallic function usually reserved for the White male.

Certainly Williams writes Stanley as a character whose being is largely determined by his sexual potency: "Since earliest childhood the centre of his life has been pleasure with women. . . . He sizes women up at a glance, with sexual classifications, crude images flashing into his mind and determining the way he smiles at them" (24). Nevertheless, to wield with force the most privileged conventional model of the phallus (that is, its function as a womanizer par excellence) is not the same thing as having full access to its symbolic values, the material privileges that attend to full White masculine subjectivity.

In Split Britches's collaboration with Bloolips on a queer reinscription of *Streetcar* entitled *Belle Reprieve,* Blanche is played by a gay man; this aptly demonstrates that part of what Williams asks us to consider in relation to Stanley and Blanche is *who is* as opposed to *who has* the phallus.[48] Jacqueline Rose discusses how Lacan posits phallicism to be an "unconcious phemonemon" that has nothing any more natural about it for a boy than for a girl. Because men and women are socially constructed through language, Lacanian thought allows phallic sexuality to either gender (Mitchell and Rose 135).[49] Therefore, one's place in the masculine/feminine binary, within which the subject has the phallus and the "other" is defined as being it, is to a degree fluid.

Until the rape scene, Stanley's position in relation to the phallus is tenuous. One thing that he seeks in his battles with Blanche is proof that he possesses what he suspects s/he may have. His distaste for her is provoked in part by his fear of feminine difference, as well as a class antagonism. Stanley dreads being emasculated, even infantilized, by Blanche, particularly through her attempts to remodel his behavior and appearance. In addition, he fears her power to take Stella away from him, to separate them as surely as any male rival might. Hence, when Stella begins mimicking Blanche's superior attitude by pointing out that he eats like a pig, ordering him to "go and wash up and then help me clear the table" as if he were a wayward child or a servant, Stanley reacts violently in an effort to reestablish the masculine/feminine hierarchy within his household (Williams 90).

Moreover, Stanley realizes Blanche's power to make him appear to be something less than fully White—which is, in effect, true. His determination to be rid of her hardens when he overhears her attempt to drive a wedge between him and Stella by pointing up the *natural* divide separating them: "He acts like an animal, has an animal's habits. There's even something—sub-human—something not quite to the stage of humanity yet. Yes, something—ape-like about him." When Blanche implores Stella to leave her husband, to "hold as our flag" the standards of civilization, she is appealing to her race as well as her class loyalties (Williams 59–60).

Numerous critics and directors have noted the Black aesthetic permeating the play, from the "Negro" music that punctuates the heterogeneous social intercourse that is a staple of life on Elysian Fields to the shape of a character's political unconscious. Just as a White aesthetic may be said to form Blanche, critics have suggested that Stanley's character relates to notions of Blackness, and a number of productions have cast the role with a Black actor.[50] Savran identifies a tendency by Williams throughout his work to represent Black masculinity in genital terms (127). In this sense, connections between Stanley and the figure of the Black male "other" may certainly be drawn, most notably in Stanley's categorization as "the gaudy seed-bearer" (24).

Clearly, Williams means to cast Stanley in primitive terms: Blanche describes him as "Bearing the raw meat home from the kill in the jungle" (Williams 59). His mere presence invokes "inhuman jungle voices" (Williams 111). Also, both Blanche and Stella perceive him as a *species* apart from themselves. While this reference in scene 1 obviously relates to Stanley's class difference, it taps also into residual social Darwinian terminology and conceptions of the differences between Whites and "other" racial types.[51]

One must be careful, however, not to overvalue Stanley's relation to Black masculinity. It is not necessary that he be read as a cipher of Black manhood in order for him to be dangerously different from the men

Blanche and Stella went out with at Belle Reve. His Polish identity alone suffices to render him a possible destabilizing presence in genteel White society. In social terms, it is historically more appropriate and potentially dissident to interpret Stanley in terms of a variegated, alien Whiteness, for he, like Eunice, can be fitted into the category of "white trash."

Alan Sinfield argues that *Streetcar* "embodies a powerful instance of male oppression of women in heterosexual relations, and displays some of the pressures on women to collude in that" (*Out on Stage* 190). To add the element of race to his analysis opens further political dimensions to the work in terms of its construction of U.S. identity. The contest of wills between Blanche and Stanley is one of masculine versus feminine value systems, but their heterosexual gender relations are constructed relative to racialized identities. The difference between Blanche and Stanley is between that of a person racialized as White compared to someone categorized as variegated White. In the same way that social pressures exist that compel women to collude in their own gender oppression, pressures exist that encourage women and men to collude in the system of White privilege and possibly their own racial oppression.

Nineteenth-century White discourse positioned the Irish as "white niggers," and in the 1940s Eastern European immigrants occupied a similar place in U.S. society. As a "Pole," Stanley is viewed as only quasi-White, and thus quasi-American. Returning to the relation between space and identity in the play, it becomes evident why Williams locates him in the Vieux Carré: his racialized status necessitates the couple living in one of the few spaces where the "intermingling of races" (and classes) is tolerated.

Blanche's opposition to Stella's marriage and her dismay at her sister's pregnancy may be read as personal jealousy, but it may also stem from a desire to preserve an undiluted category of Whiteness and the Du Bois's position within it. When they lose Belle Reve, they lose one of the principal means of sustaining White heritage: property. Consequently, Stella's sexual relations with a "Polack" and their expected mixed-race product gravely threatens the sisters' racial status, and, indeed, within dominant U.S. racial discourse such unions threaten the future of the White race. That Stanley poses a threat to the purity of White identity comes out clearly when, following sexual intercourse, Stella's eyes and lips are described as having "that almost narcotized tranquility that is in the face of Eastern idols" (Williams 52). Consequently, Blanche's opinion of Stanley and her response to him, often read purely in terms of her mental instabilities as well as through a masculine/feminine divide, appears as simply the dominant White stance when considered in the light of U.S. postwar race relations.

Without a doubt, Blanche is eaten up by her own internal demons, but this is not motivated by personal trauma alone. Her motives are the same ones driving the dominant political worldview, in which class and race hatred and a fear of difference are the norm. Elia Kazan, who directed the film version of *Streetcar,* recognized her as a "social type" (Bigsby, *A Critical Introduction* 49), one obviously representative of a dead civilization and also, I would argue, one formed by a 1940s White racial narrative that spans North and New South.

Therefore, while Blanche may appear as the symbol of non-reason in the world of the play, she represents at the same time the corrupted reason behind the racial politics of the 1940s. As C. W. E. Bigsby points out, Williams is aware of the "suffocatingly hypocritical model of the feminine role" contained within Old Southern mythology. "The woman was essentially a passive creature, alternately a chaste symbol, a social icon *who played her role in concealing a more anarchic and brutal reality*" (*A Critical Introduction* 63, italics mine). Vestiges of this brutal reality could still be glimpsed in postwar U.S. society. It gave rise, for instance, to the resurgence of the Ku Klux Klan, which menaced Catholics, Jews, and those Whites identified as race traitors, as well as Blacks, and the Klan is an enterprise in which White women played a seminal role.

Blanche's position within White discourse makes her as necessary to Stanley as she is dangerous, for his ascension to full White masculine status depends on her recognition. Stanley requires the reciprocal gaze of the White woman to cement his identification with U.S. Man, hence his persistent impassioned objections: "I am not a Polack." He defines himself as "one hundred per cent American, born and raised in the greatest country on earth and proud as hell of it" (Williams 93). In spite of this, without the validation of the White feminine "other" Stanley will remain a partial subject—or a non-subject even—like the Black male "other" onto whom is projected a rampant sexuality though he is never granted the phallus that authorizes White masculine power.

Accordingly, Stanley's possession of the privileged signifier of phallic sexuality should be seen as merely endowing him with the potential to own the phallus—that is, attain the highest form of White subjectivity. At the end of the play, this potential is finally realized through the symbolic castration of Blanche in the rape scene, the phallus and castration being counterparts like masculine and feminine. Until the moment of Blanche's physical violation, however, Stanley occupies an uneasy space between the poles of Blackness and Whiteness, masculinity and femininity.

Ruth Bleier describes how women are socialized to be "exquisitely sensitive to the social cues from those on whom they are taught to depend for love and approval; that they learn to define themselves only or primarily in relation to a multitude of others" (202). This is undoubtedly true of Blanche, and to an unusual degree it appears true of Stanley as well. *Streetcar* reverses the dualism of masculine and feminine where the "truth" of Whiteness is concerned.

Racial history is an ideology of male supremacy in the United States as much as an expression of White authority. Thus, Stanley and Blanche's opposed epistemological stances are molded by their racial *and* gender differences. Until the rape, Blanche's Whiteness allows her to enforce the male-constructed rules by which race-gendered identities are verified. Only by reversing the dualism of nature and culture, by allowing Stanley's enactment of primitive man to achieve Blanche's subordination, does the "truth" of race become contingent once again on a masculine action. It is only his psycho-physical ruin of Blanche that enables Stanley to move from being a white male to being seen as a White Man, for the act of rape provides him and the spectator with proof that he has it and she doesn't.[52]

Thus, the rape is the crucial event in the play, destabilizing the either/or of gendered and racialized identities as they are conventionally configured. It is also the device that operates to direct the spectator's gaze to a reconceptualized Whiteness. Because Blanche will be lobotomized after being raped, Whiteness now encompasses a metaphoric move via desire toward desolation and spiritual death. Also, the rape seals the equation drawn between Whiteness and the uncivilized, thereby undermining notions of White's society's superiority.

For most of the play, Blanche represents the ruthlessness of the White female subject, who accepts her role as the reproducer of White power through her sexual commerce with White men. Historically, this role is tied to the use of White womanhood as a justification for Black oppression, extending to its most barbaric forms, such as lynching. The Whiteness symbolized by Blanche then corresponds to the savagery of sexual violence enacted by Stanley. As a result, whichever way it plays out between them, the struggle between Blanche and Stanley works to reposition the White subject outside the moral center by linking at different points both the White feminine and White masculine with moral corruption and brutishness.

Queering Whiteness: Arthur Miller's *A View from the Bridge*

Surveying U.S. literary discourse, Toni Morrison argues that "images of Blackness can be evil *and* protective, rebellious *and* forgiving, fearful *and* desirable—all of the self-contradictory features of the self. Whiteness, alone, is mute, meaningless, unfathomable, pointless, frozen, veiled, curtained." (59). This statement renders both of the plays examined so far unusual in the way that they articulate Whiteness by shedding light on the ideological processes through which White power sought to solidify a battery of cultural assumptions and practices. In the 1950s theater continued to make provocative points about Whiteness, despite an increasing political conservatism.

Against the volatile social and political backdrop discussed in the first section of this chapter, the contest between 1950s U.S. Man and his "other" was played out in the literature, film, and theater of the period. In drama, what it meant to be American in the 1950s was explored most notably by Arthur Miller, who vied with Williams for the role of preeminent U.S. playwright. Bigsby describes Miller as a "playwright who has consistently sought to translate the social world into private anxieties. . . . Because he has chosen to write about a world of moral dilemmas and because he has always proved so sensitive to the pressure of history he has been seen as elevating himself to the position of social conscience" (*A Critical Introduction* 136).

His assessment is demonstrated in Miller's *A View from the Bridge*. First produced as a one-act play in New York in 1955, it was rewritten in two acts for its 1956 London premiere.[53] Critics have drawn attention to how the play's subject matter—the protagonist Eddie's betrayal of two illegal immigrants to the authorities—obliquely refers to McCarthyism. It is well known that, unlike Eddie, Miller risked his reputation and freedom rather than name names when in 1956 he was called to testify in front of HUAC.[54] However, critics are divided concerning the extent to which the play should be read as a political parable. Miller himself denies that the play is about a political informer: "The situation in the . . . play is not analogous, is not even pertinent to that kind of dilemma" (Brenda Murphy 217).

I am not concerned here to explore the play as a social text about U.S. anti-communist purges. I am interested in the view that Miller affords the spectator of the way in which the color divide operated in the 1950s, and of the different constructions of gender, particularly masculinity, that were in circulation at the time. My reading, therefore, aims to show the relations between its representations of race, gender, and sexuality, especially the connection that the play makes between Whiteness and homosexuality.

The plot hinges on the feelings of Eddie Carbone for his niece Catherine. Involved in a sexless marriage to Beatrice, he appears to harbor an unconscious sexual desire for Catherine. His feelings gradually come closer to the surface when she becomes romantically involved with Beatrice's cousin

Rodolfo. Rodolfo and his brother Marco have illegally emigrated from Sicily, and they have been given shelter in Eddie's apartment. When Catherine and Rodolfo become engaged, Eddie informs the immigration bureau of Rodolfo's whereabouts in order to prevent the marriage. Rodolfo is arrested, and Eddie's act of betrayal results in his alienation from his Italian American community and his eventual death at the hands of Marco.

Donald P. Costello reads the play in terms of a set of "circles of responsibility." He contends that the central question motivating Miller is "How can a human being work out the interconnections among the ever-widening circles of . . . self, family, society, the universe?" (444). In the course of the play, Eddie violates these circles of responsibility, and in violating self and family he necessarily violates the codes of his society. Thus, Miller gives us in Eddie a glimpse of the human struggles and forces that animate history. But whose history does Eddie represent and what social codes does he breach?

The play is set in Red Hook, a waterfront slum. The bridge of the title refers to the Brooklyn Bridge, which overlooks the waterfront and tenement buildings where the characters work and live. Metaphorically, the bridge spans two cultural divides—the Old World of Sicily, which still holds ties for many of Red Hook's inhabitants, and the New World of twentieth-century America. It represents the division between the disparate White world and that of the dark-skinned Italian "other." Albert Wertheim describes it as stretching from ethnic Brooklyn to the "cosmopolitan, urbane, Manhattan area settled by New York's original Dutch colonists," and from "a Brooklyn of social taboos, of family and clan allegiances . . . to Manhattan's City Hall and courts, to a social contract . . . regulated by codified laws and government institutions" (109).

According to Miller, it is not possible to understand Eddie apart from his relation to his "neighborhood, his fellow workers, his social situation. His self-esteem depends upon their estimate of him, and his value is created largely by his fidelity to the code of his culture" (Griffin 83). Yet it is also important to consider the way in which Eddie's family uncomfortably straddles two cultures, for they and the other recent immigrants of Red Hook reside on the borderline of U.S. identity.

Eddie demonstrates as much fealty to White Anglo-Saxon cultural codes as to Italian codes. He works to educate Catherine so that she may assimilate into mainstream U.S. society. When she suggests taking a job near the navy yard, he tells her: "I want you to be with different kind of people. . . . Maybe a lawyer's office someplace in New York in one of them nice buildings. I mean if you're gonna get outta here then get out; don't go practically in the same kind of neighborhood (Miller, *AVFTB* 19). Eddie's personal history might lie in his Sicilian roots, but his present allegiance is as much to an Americanized history and a White-defined future.

Bigsby relates that Miller composed the play at a time when he felt completely out of sync with U.S. society; he had come to believe that "he and his country were so fundamentally at odds as to have little to say to one another" (*Modern American Drama* 103). What Miller does say about 1950s Americanism is littered with inconsistencies. In particular, the figure of Catherine contains two opposing drives in relation to Eddie and Rodolfo that together contribute to the appearance of a White paradox. The play suggests that Catherine may provide an avenue to a normative U.S. identity; and, as such, she points to the multiplicity of sites of power between men and women as well as between different types of men.

Undoubtedly, Rodolfo's attraction to Catherine is motivated in part by the passport, literal and otherwise, that she offers to White American terrain. The emphasis placed upon her education, seen as having primed her to enter White society, has the effect of asserting Whiteness as a universal aspiration, thereby stabilizing the category and reifying its power. Catherine's association with White subjectivity may also account for Eddie's protectiveness toward her. His wish to prevent her from being defiled by a marriage to Rodolfo may represent a desire to assimilate by demonstrating an allegiance to the dominant ideology, the centerpoint of which was the sanctity of White womanhood. In this sense, Catherine's womanhood needs to be theorized as an instrument in the service of White control and supremacy.[55]

However, Catherine is also positioned as a passive object in relation to both Rodolfo and Eddie. She may be read as the object of Eddie's antisocial sexual desires,[56] and she is the vehicle Rodolfo hopes to use in order to gain entry into the category of U.S. Man. Her status as something to be maintained by Eddie or obtained by Rodolfo positions Whiteness in turn as something that may be accumulated, contained, and controlled. If those on its borders can assert power over it in this way, then Whiteness appears as unstable: it becomes particularized, rather than symbolizing something amorphous or universal.

Most significantly, the play succeeds in particularizing Whiteness as something potentially queer. Colorism is an important factor in Eddie's estimation of Rodolfo's sexual character. Physically, the two men are poles apart and represent strikingly different kinds of masculinity. Eddie is "forty—a husky, slightly overweight longshoreman." He is dark, with a stereotypically masculine gait, demeanor, and way of speaking. Rodolfo, in contrast, is a "blond guy. Like . . . platinum." Eddie appears obsessed with Rodolfo's color difference, but in an uncommon way, for it is not a difference marked by dark skin that concerns him; rather, it is his resemblance to Whiteness that Eddie believes makes Rodolfo look like a young "chorus girl" (Miller, *AVFTB* 35). Suspecting that his hair color is not even natural, Eddie hints that Rodolfo may be unnatural in other ways too. Unusually, then, we are presented with a character whose phenotypical Whiteness is the first sign that designates him as sexually subversive.

The men's mode of action differs as well. Eddie enacts the part of head of the household to his wife's role as supportive housewife. Rodolfo falls somewhere—and for Eddie, suspiciously so—between the masculine/feminine divide. He holds a job on the docks, but he also cooks and sews. While working alongside Eddie on the ships, Rodolfo is prone to bursting into song, which he does in a high-pitched voice. His behavior, tainted as it is with feminine overtones, makes him a figure of mockery on the piers: "Paper Doll they're callin' him, Canary," and later "Blondie now" (Miller, *AVFTB* 35, 47).[57] When Eddie tries to teach him boxing, Rodolfo shows a preference and greater flair for dancing, which leads Eddie to conclude that "he ain't right" (Miller, *AVFTB* 47)—a statement clearly meant to mark Rodolfo as queer.

Rodolfo's presumed queerness renders him a political threat. U.S. political discourse in the 1950s was deeply hetero-normative, and the threat of communism and of perverse sexuality was seen to go hand in hand. McCarthy, for instance, often used homophobic rhetoric in his denunciations of those deemed un-American: the "pitiful squealing" or "egg-sucking phoney liberals," he charged, "would hold sacrosanct those Communists and queers" who had sold China into "atheistic slavery." Promising to purge the "prancing mimics of the Moscow party line" from the state department, he railed against those who "whined," "whimpered," and "cringed" before communism (Wittner 95).

Furthermore, as an illegal immigrant Rodolfo represents the tip of the alien invasion, making him, ironically, a danger to the established White order in which he conceivably could physically pass. In this way, the play reverses the normal order of things, with the dark "other" acting as the gatekeeper of the "American-way-of-life," as Eddie does when he facilitates the job of the immigration officials. However, signs of homosexuality also attach to Eddie, which further complicates the situation.[58]

Questions about Eddie's heterosexual virility emerge early on in the play, when it becomes clear that his marriage to Beatrice is in trouble because he will not/cannot have sex with her. Thus, by the time he kisses

Rodolfo the audience has been prepared for the possibility that there is something different about Eddie's sexuality as well. The kiss has been read in two ways: either it represents Eddie's unconscious desire for Rodolfo, or Eddie intends the kiss as an insult to him, meaning in this way to brand him publicly as a homosexual (de Jongh 84).

Savran argues that Eddie's kiss reveals more about the structure of cold war masculinity than about any peculiarities of Eddie's psyche. More than any other Miller play, he suggests, *A View from the Bridge* demonstrates how the fear of effeminacy slides into homophobic panic, which, almost inevitably, slides into homosexual desire (*Communists, Cowboys and Queers* 41–42). This reading places the relation between Eddie and Rodolfo on homosocial terrain.

This *man* (Eddie)—*woman* (Catherine)—*man* (Rodolfo) triangle suggests that the desire that bonds the men over Catherine is as erotically invested for them in relation to each other as for each of them in relation to her. The homosocial potential between the men results, once again, in the queering of Whiteness. When Eddie informs on his wife's relatives, he abrogates the White voice. The fact that his motive in speaking stems from his desire to split Rodolfo and Catherine's heterosexual union renders it a sexually suspect action, and by representing a kind of racially queer voice it allows for the possible slide into homosexual desire that Savran mentions. Therefore, as often as Eddie's predicament leads him to act in a way that legitimizes the dominant White perspective, it leads him to queer White codes as well.

A View from the Bridge offers a narrative in which the tensions among its human agents, the political and social institutions within which they negotiate their relation to a normative White national identity, and a White sex-gender discourse cannot be reconciled favorably within a dominant conceptual framework. Its central conflict is not only between two men but also between two different race-gendered discourses. Thus, the play's manner of exploring sexuality and race as a cultural formation queers a host of things that supported 1950s Americanism, including the capitalist mode of production, the patriarchy, marriage, and the family.

chapter 5

Countercultures of Whiteness

T he U.S. economy continued to be extraordinarily resourceful in the 1960s. Esmond Wright's précis of conditions notes very low unemployment, business and national incomes at peak levels, increased educational opportunities, and more mechanical conveniences, cultural opportunities, and leisure time (354)—that is, of course, for White Americans. Ever-increasing numbers of Whites enjoyed access to not just the proverbial good life but the better-than-good life, and this excessive abundance led to a restructuring of the social order and a refashioning of White American character as well.

The complexion of U.S. labor was changing. Blue-collar jobs were diminishing, and white-collar occupations were rising. Even working-class people, however, could afford the material perks previously limited to the middle class: house, new car, a full range of appliances, family vacations, and so on. Changes accelerated in the residential patterns begun in the 1940s. M. J. Heale documents the suburbanization of the U.S. landscape, with suburban populations overtaking those of cities in size (31). Provided you were White and could afford it, most suburban neighborhoods were open regardless of other social differences, such as class background, occupation, or religion, and this helped spread the middle-class lifestyle.

It also meant that U.S. cities were increasingly relegated to impoverished African American and immigrant communities. Because many businesses followed the flow to the suburbs and their greatly diminished tax base, "White flight" translated into fewer urban workplaces. Even with the U.S. economy at its highest point in the mid-1960s, Blacks, whether educated or not, still found it hard to get and keep a job. This process generated a sea change in U.S. politics, too, as the center of power now focused on filling the wish lists of middle-class suburban voters. Therefore, although the changes in occupation and residential patterns were creating a U.S. society less stratified by class than it had been in previous eras, racial differences were hardening, even despite the changes brought about by the civil rights movement.

In the early 1960s, most social commentators were as silent on the topic of inequality as they had been in the prior decade. For many, faith in the American Dream was at an all-time high. Yet dissenting voices were on the increase, and what would set the 1960s apart was the degree of White dissent that would erupt toward the end of the decade.

Critics of the status quo questioned the moral worth of the new, self-expressive lifestyle then being celebrated, for the principle way in which one was encouraged to express oneself was through the acquisition of more products, a process heavily mediated by advertising. Moreover, suburbanization was contributing to the creation of a conservative national culture to be consumed by equally homogenous suburban dwellers. This lifestyle of unrestrained consumer pleasure marked a change from the styles of living associated with earlier forms of capitalism. The Protestant work ethic had privileged self-sacrifice and discipline in exchange for family and social security. Thus prosperity posed something of a conundrum for White America, one that David Farber relates to the necessity of demonstrating hedonism to be a moral, not an immoral, choice since general prosperity was based on fruitful consumption (16).

The rejection of mainstream values and institutions was also inspired by the increased activity of civil rights activists. This decade saw a considerable alteration in the tone and methods adopted to resist White supremacy. Some Black leaders continued to promote legislative changes as the best way forward, and Blacks continued to score important legal successes in the 1960s, with the 1964 Civil Rights Act and the 1965 Voting Rights Act, which effectively removed the legal basis for American apartheid. The problem was that legislative changes were often not adequately implemented, so that in practice people continued to face a significant level of discrimination. The discrepancy between the de jure and de facto statuses of Blacks was generating a broader-based social movement to combat racist practices.

A more confrontational grassroots movement, however, also emerged in the 1960s. These more radical groups eschewed the process of institutionalization favored by their predecessors. They preferred working outside the system, employed more radical acts of civil disobedience, and sometimes even operated outside the law.[59] The provocative rhetoric of leaders such as Malcolm X and Stokely Carmichael ensured a high media profile, which made them more worrying to the dominant White culture than the milder-mannered Martin Luther King Jr.

What most concerned the established White order was that many Black activists were starting to reject the policy of nonviolent resistance and the goal of assimilation. This new separatist mindset was also reflected through the changing status accorded to Whites in the movement, which differed depending on the goals of particular groups. Though liberal Whites continued to play a key role in many moderate organizations, they were frequently unwelcome in more radical groups. Malcolm X and the Nation of Islam, for example, advocated an explicitly anti-White stance. In "God's Judgement of White America" (1963), Malcolm X characterized White society as "a wicked world . . . ruled by a race of devils" (124). Elsewhere, he labeled Whites the "common enemy," "oppressor," "exploiter," and "discriminator."

In the 1960s a new philosophy of resistance known as Black power came to the fore. Stokely Carmichael and Charles V. Hamilton describe the new politics:

a call for black people in this country to unite, to recognize their heritage, to build a sense of community. It is a call for black people to begin to define their own goals . . . It is a call to reject the racist institutions and values of this society.

The concept of Black power rests on a fundamental premise: *Before a group can enter the open society, it must first close ranks.* (44)

Black power urged the rank and file of African Americans to take the fight to White society, arguing that the language of 1950s freedom struggles, such as progress, nonviolence, integration, or fear of "white backlash," was unproductive (Carmichael and Hamilton 50).[60]

Moderate leaders such as Dr. King frequently couched their demands within the terms of dominant discourse, the most famous example being his keynote address of the March on Washington in 1963. He declared his dream for a United States in which people would "not be judged by the color of their skin but by the content of their character." He acknowledged this as "deeply rooted in the American Dream" (104). In contrast, radical Black discourse urged people to emphasize how they were different and to take pride in their Blackness and the unique values of African American culture. The discourse of Black power rejected White-defined versions of Blackness as deviant, pathological, and deficient, instead defining themselves as valuable members of society—captured in the popular phrase "Black is beautiful."

It became more common for Black activists to emphasize how racist practices connected with other forms of subordination, such as class prejudice and imperialism. They openly contested the validity of the American Dream, painting it as the great "American Lie" for Blacks. It was often cited that cooption in the 1950s had produced little in the way of improvements for the vast majority of Black people, who continued to lag behind Whites across a range of socioeconomic indicators. Parallels were drawn between the position of Blacks in the United States and colonial peoples under European control, with White America accused of fostering an internal system of colonialism.[61] Echoing African nationalist sentiments, Amiri Baraka stated "It's Nation Time," portraying the Black power movement as a U.S. version of the decolonization movements that had arisen in Africa, Central America, and Southeast Asia in the 1950s.

Critical analyses of White culture have always circulated within Black communities, but their public airing, sometimes in mainstream media, signified a revolutionary moment in U.S. race relations. The impact of radical Black discourse, therefore, was by no means restricted to the Black community; it influenced mainstream thought as well, sometimes negatively, sometimes progressively.

As the Black movement was perceived to grow in militancy and influence, the White backlash feared in the 1950s did materialize. In the early 1960s, despite intensified scrutiny from Washington and the international community, there was an increase in brutal acts of oppression across southern cities by White mobs as well as the civil authorities against those who challenged Jim Crow.[62] Although violent response was less common in other parts of the country, as Carl M. Brauer makes clear, the White backlash was not confined to the south. Northern hostility to civil rights was an important factor in the electoral process in the 1960s and '70s (301–2). Also, by the mid-1960s the backlash was being fed by violent images of race riots in urban ghettos that were regularly flashed across the country's television screens, giving rise to fears of a race war.

Whereas some segments of the White populace favored counteroffensive attacks, there are clear indications that the Black movement was contributing to a reformation in White identity. A significant number of White middle-class people were being exposed to images of overt racism for the first time, either directly on southern streets or via increased televised news coverage. These images could provoke a sense of outrage and sympathy; they could also provoke embarrassment and a sense of guilt, in so far as one was forced to acknowledge a shared racial identity with the perpetrators.

Responses of White liberal guilt, though well intentioned, were not politically useful. Acknowledging the way in which one benefited from the dominant racial order was an important first step in changing the consciousness that maintained the status quo, but stopping there did little more than make some people feel better about themselves. Initially, many White activists brought a missionary attitude to their work, which stemmed from an inherent belief in the paternalism of their race. There are numerous recorded complaints from Black activists about Whites' insensitivity.[63] No doubt some left with their chauvinism little changed, but the experience of living and working alongside Black people curbed this paternalistic propensity for significant numbers of White activists, leading to radical changes in outlook.

For the first time, growing numbers of Whites began to critically consider the meaning of their own racial identity and to draw connections between their individual prejudices and institutional forms of racism, especially those people who had some contact with or interest in civil rights. Doug McAdam records that the first change in feeling for many White activists related to their views of the established order, for example, the Justice Department and the FBI, as well as their views of the Democratic Party, which liked to present itself as the party of civil rights. Further, their experiences undercut fundamental relationships to social institutions such as churches and schools, as well as their own families.

McAdam quotes Pam Parker, a young, White, upper-middle-class woman, who in 1964 expressed her newly felt alienation from mainstream society: "I feel like a marginal person. I am not happy nor comfortable in white society any longer nor am I fully comfortable in Negro society, and I know at least for myself, it has been a very lonely, isolated year because of this" (134).

She describes feeling estranged from her family, now perceiving them as part of a class that is morally culpable for a variety of social ills: "Coming out of Mississippi and into the 'civilized white' world was hard. It was like culture shock or something. Like I didn't feel like talking to anyone. I was in a kind of daze . . . I don't know quite what I am saying except that I am against much of what my family stands for" (135). Parker's reassessment of her place in the social order illustrates how White faith in the American-way-of-life was beginning to be undermined. By the end of the decade, the painful ambivalence toward her own culture that Parker expresses would be shared by increasing numbers of young Americans and would culminate in the wholesale rejection of dominant values by those who formed the 1970s counterculture movements.

While the civil rights movement influenced some to reject the mainstream, the counterculture had other origins as well, most notably resistance to the Vietnam War, which by 1966 was beginning to dominate U.S. foreign and domestic politics. U.S. involvement in Vietnam cannot be divorced from the nation's mythic perceptions of itself as an exceptional society or from its fictions about race. U.S. political discourse expressed a sacred duty to export its principles and the benefits of the American-way-of-life across the world. However, the special relationship it posited with the divine was not the only reason the United States believed it could defeat any enemy; this idea was based also in its conception of itself as a White nation: U.S. superiority was believed to reside in White racial difference.

Among the many factors behind the U.S. defeat in Vietnam, the assumption on the part of successive administrations that they understood the Vietnamese people and what was best for them is seminal. Edward Said uses the term "Orientalism" to describe such assumptions in the Western European construction of non-White, non-Western cultures (1–2). The Vietnamese people were viewed in the same way that the Black "other" was perceived. Both social groups were collectivized on the basis of their racial difference from Whites. It was assumed that as a collective mass the Vietnamese could be easily read and thus dominated. Thus, to a degree, the war was an extension of U.S. racial discursive history.

The war connects to racist practices in other, more substantive ways too. The ground campaign was fought disproportionately by Black soldiers. Whether they were draftees or recruits, Blacks were more likely to be assigned to combat units, and consequently they suffered far higher rates of injury and death. When race relations at home became more fraught, tensions in the field also increased, both between White commanders and majority Black units and Black and White GIs. As Black leaders came out in opposition to the war and the Black power anticolonialist message spread, Black soldiers began to identify with the Vietnamese as another oppressed race, seeing the White Man back home as the real enemy.

Nevertheless, the antiwar movement was a biracial one. A large proportion of activists comprised the children of Whites who had settled the suburbs in the 1950s. Now college age, they turned university campuses into centers of protest. Their resistance to the war stemmed from a belief in nonviolence that was increasingly tied to anti-imperialist and anti-capitalist politics. The activists perceived the U.S. government as complicit with corporate capitalism in the production of a death machine: imperialist wars were good for U.S. capitalism because they provided markets for munitions and other goods.

Although generational conflict raged in the late 1960s, opposition to the war was not limited to the young. By the end of the decade, no resolution to the war was in sight, and it was becoming clear that the end might not mean victory; as a result, the frustration grew to include a wide cross-section of society. By 1972, during Nixon's presidency, a majority of the United States was antiwar.

The turn in public opinion came about also as accounts of U.S. war crimes started to filter home. The My Lai village massacre in 1968, which involved the killing of hundreds of unarmed civilian Vietnamese, including elderly men, women and children, was the most outrageous atrocity. However, beatings, torture, and civilian deaths could form part of routine missions as well, not to mention the regular bombing of civilian areas and the use of chemical agents like napalm. Ronald Ridenhour, a U.S. GI who testified about My Lai, wrote: "As far as I was concerned, it was a reflection on me, on every American, on the ideals that we supposedly represent. It completely castrated the whole picture of America" (Engelhardt 218).

The nature of the warfare in which U.S. military personnel were engaged irrevocably altered the way in which White Americans were able to identify themselves. As John Morton Blum explains, once people learned of the atrocities being carried out, it was no longer possible to believe in the innocence of the American-way-of-life (245). Moreover, as the Vietnamese continued to resist and U.S. casualties mounted, Stanley Karnow argues, the U.S. sense of invincibility was eroded: the war fundamentally challenged the country's absolute confidence in its moral exclusivity and, thus, its Manifest Destiny (9).

For U.S. leaders, however, the real threat to U.S. Man and his power was not the Vietcong but a distorted form of that Man himself, who occupied the home front. Nixon viewed the antiwar activists as aiding the enemy. He appealed to "the great silent majority of my fellow Americans—I ask for your support.... North Vietnam cannot defeat ... the United States. Only Americans can do that" (Blum 355).

When the police bludgeoned activists senseless at the Democratic Party Convention in Chicago in 1968 and National Guardsmen shot student protestors at Kent State University in 1970, the morality of state authority was wrecked. Nixon himself would make a startling contribution to the general erosion of faith when his involvement in the Watergate scandal came to light. The burglary of the Democratic Party Headquarters by the aptly named CREEP—Committee to Re-Elect the President—and the subsequent cover-up led to Nixon's resignation and brought the legitimacy of governmental authority into further doubt.

In response to the war's continuation, activists adopted a number of strategies for subverting the dominant social order, or "the system" as it became known. Radical left factions argued for assaults on the U.S. system that, in the view of those inside it, bordered on treason. Some of these planned offensives were also explicitly aimed at bringing an end to White power.

In an attempt to identify themselves with those who were subjugated by U.S. policy at home or abroad, some White counterculturalists styled themselves "Americong." They affronted the mainstream by donning elements of U.S. military dress but mixing it with the enemy's symbols or signs of the racial "other." Engelhardt records that the images they elevated were often ironic, mainly an enemy-ness recognizable from Western films, the genre that had invested nineteenth-century imperialism with its iconicity.

Counterculturalists took to the streets costumed in elements of Native American dress—headbands, moccasins, and beads. They painted their faces, grew their hair long, and smoked peace pipes. They refused to follow in the footsteps of their suburban parents; instead, they established communal families, sometimes designating themselves as tribes and taking Native American names (Engelhardt 244). Thus, one of the most striking features of radical left discourse in the 1970s is the way it attempts to shed symbolically the protective coloration of Whiteness. White counterculture activists could inspire even more fear over the long-term stability of the reigning political and social system than Black resistance, for they were the enemy within Whiteness itself.

White Absurdities: Edward Albee's *The American Dream*

Edward Albee's *The American Dream* prefigures the way in which the edifice of Whiteness would be gradually shaken from within during the 1960s and '70s. First performed in New York in 1961, the play stages the underbelly of the American-way-of-life. Whereas Broadway at this time was dominated by musicals and lightweight comedies that catered to middle-class sensibilities, an increasing amount of work off-Broadway drew upon avant-garde European theory and practices to articulate an oppositional aesthetic and political viewpoint. With its touches of absurdism and expressionism and its scathing criticism of reigning values, *The American Dream* represents a radical new departure from earlier forms of U.S. theater.

In his preface, Albee describes the play as an antidote to the "fiction that everything in this slipping land of ours is peachy-keen." (21). Reacting to criticism that the play is "nihilist," "immoral," and "defeatist," he does not deny the charges; rather, he says "let me answer that *The American Dream* is a picture of our time." (22).

The prospect Albee stages is the effect of people's capitalism on the American character, especially its consumerist ethos and conformist mindset. The play urges resistance to the inner grip of capitalism's false values. Yet the play is a curious combination of a subversive attack on the conservative image of White middle-class family life in the early 1960s and a nostalgic yearning for a historic, and partly mythic, White model of personal and social relations.

Doubtless Albee intends to indict the established order; nevertheless, as Charles Marowitz writes in an introduction to the play, "at the end, one finds oneself liking it for things it *should* have said, and is almost deceived into thinking it *has* said them" (12). My aim is to explore what *The American Dream* actually ends up saying about U.S. national character in the 1960s, in particular its comment upon the relation between consumer capitalism and racialized identities.

Albee makes ironic use of a conventional theatrical setting, the living room, as the backdrop for his portrait of the American-way-of-life. The action takes place in a single scene. Only one of the cast of characters— Mrs. Barker—is named, the others being designated by their title roles: Mommy, Daddy, Grandma, and Young Man. The characters are emblematic of the White nuclear family unit, idealized in the 1950s as an unchanging, natural institution.

The opening dialogue between Mommy and Daddy involves swapping pointless comments about a dispute over the color of a hat that she has with some women. It points up the tragically absurd state of their lives, where individual identity is seen to derive from the acquisition of a one-of-a-kind piece of merchandise and communal relations are marred by an ugly competitiveness. Their exchange also illustrates how the use of language no longer results in actual communication, which is the first sign of the perverted nature of their relationship. Marriage and sexual relations have been reduced to a purely commercial form of exchange. Affection is absent from the character's lives; instead, the values informing family relations are self-interest and materialism. Mommy admits marrying Daddy for his money; she tells him: "I have a right to live off you because I married you, and because I used to let you get on top of me and bump your uglies" (Albee, *TAD* 31). Mommy wants to put Grandma in a nursing home so that she won't have to share any of Daddy's money when he dies, an event to which she obviously looks forward.

Because exchange values have replaced human values in U.S. life, Bigsby points out that the characters demand the same satisfaction of people that they do of their possessions (*Albee,* 32). This is reflected in the consumer attitude Mommy and Daddy bear toward their first adopted child, who critic Eric Sterling suggests they have acquired because a male child represents a social status symbol (35). Mrs. Barker is present because Mommy has complained about the poor quality of the child provided by her agency. Known only as the "bumble," the child has proved a disappointment because, among other things, it doesn't look like them.

In Albee's landscape, the family functions as the central institution mediating between the individual and the nation, and as the receptacle for dominant values. His grotesque description of the child's systematic destruction relays the way in which the White family has been transformed into a destructive agency that is decomposing from within. Mommy and Daddy cut out the bumble's tongue, sever its hands as well as its "you know what" when it shows too much interest in itself, until "for the last straw, it finally up and died; and you can imagine how that made them feel, their having paid for it, and all" (Albee, *TAD* 48). The correspondence drawn between the organization of family life and the modes of production and consumption prevalent in the 1960s suggests that the values governing family life have become spiritually corrosive, which, in turn, means that U.S. society is morally bankrupt.

The play poses the American Dream as false and base, as personified by the Young Man, who will do " almost anything for money." Those who live the dream, like Grandma's boxes (metaphors for the human environment), might be pleasant to look at, but they are empty on the inside. The Young Man describes himself as "incomplete": "I no longer have the capacity to feel anything. . . . I have been drained, torn asunder . . . disemboweled. I have, now, only my person . . . my body, my face. I use what I have . . . I let people love me . . . for while I know that I cannot relate . . . I know I must be related *to*" (Albee, *TAD* 55). The source of his spiritual death is the capitalist ethic that, according to Bigsby, "has spilled over into the area of personal relationships" (*Albee* 32). The status of the Young Man as commodity is cemented when Mrs. Barker sells him to Mommy and Daddy as a replacement for their broken child and with the implication that he will prostitute himself to Mommy.

Albee represents Mommy as an egoistic virago and Daddy as subjugated to the point where he is completely impotent in all senses of the term. The figure of woman does not appear to advantage here, being depicted as the source of the family cancer diagnosed, and critics have faulted the play for its sexism. Mickey Pearlman, for example, considers Mommy, Grandma, and Mrs. Barker to be part of an "odious triumvirate" of women that Albee poses against two innocent male victims (188).

To the contrary, I would argue that the play escapes being misogynistic, for Albee invests Grandma with a rare humanity. I accept the extent to which the playwright places some of the blame for the ills in U.S. society on the conventional construction of Woman. At the same time, to place Grandma in the same light as Mommy and Mrs. Barker is to ignore the contrast between the values governing contemporary U.S. life and the idealized earlier lifestyle that forms a critical part of the play's design.[64] Grandma functions as the voice of reason, directly communicating to the audience her disapproval of Mommy's selfish dissipation.

Ronald Hayman reads Grandma as "an incarnation of . . . American nineteenth-century liberal values" (26). It is via her character that the play laments the elapse of the arguably more humane moral standards that characterized nineteenth-century family and national life, but herein lies the problem and the source of the play's ideological tension surrounding its construction of White identity.

What Fredric Jameson has termed the "repressed and buried reality" of a text proves in this case to be the Victorian family (20), which makes the values mourned in the play decidedly White. Steven Mintz states that the nineteenth-century home was idealized as an oasis from the materialist corruption of the outside world (12). Marriage was envisioned as a spiritual contract, free from associations with carnality and dominion and subservience and thus mutually emotionally fulfilling (135). The family consisted of a patriarchal figure, who, besides providing financial support, embodied intellectual and moral authority, and a mother who represented an image of pure selflessness. Both were idealized as guardians of their innocent and impressionable children, and all were unquestionably racialized as White.

The values Grandma symbolizes are saturated with the presence of the racialized other. Morrison contends that "Even, and especially, when American texts are not 'about' Africanist presences or characters or narrative or idiom, the shadow hovers in implication, in sign, in line of demarcation." Race, she argues, has come to function as a metaphor so necessary to the construction of American-ness that it rivals the old pseudoscientific racism (46–47). The historical and imaginative terrain shaping what Albee proffers as the real substance of Grandma's American-ness is, in fact, informed by the same relations of domination as the absurdist reality inhabited by the other characters.

Bigsby considers the play's "fundamental theme to be the collapse of communality, the Other as threat" (*Modern American Drama* 125). On the surface, the "other" resides within the anti-type family model presided over by Mommy—the castrating female. However, within the interpretive master code of U.S. racial discourse, the peril to both the nineteenth century and the contemporary all-American way of life comes from a set of Black anti-types to the idealized mother, father, and child of Victorian domestic mythology.

Robert M. Young argues that humanism is itself already antihumanist because it necessarily produces the nonhuman in setting up its problematic boundaries (*White Mythologies* 125). Consequently, the liberal doctrine symbolized by Grandma, which Albee sets up as the basis for his criticism of the decadent and destructive 1960s family that generates and is produced by the institution of consumer capitalism, reproduces very similar social inequalities to those against which the play would set its face. Grandma represents family feeling, stability, and continuity, which translates into healthy community, but the worth of this community for Albee's oppositional politics is marred by its racially exclusive character.

Returning to Marowitz's point about the play's political unevenness, I argue that what *The American Dream* seems to be speaking to is the symbolic death of the dominant order and the erosion of the White subject's moral integrity and worth. However, its ideological underpinnings disable it from adequately resolving the fundamental questions it poses about the source of the insufficiency at the heart of U.S. society. Indeed, the contrast posed between the artificiality and baseness of modern society and the laudable, authentic foundation of previous generational principles in one and the same move negates and reinforces White hegemony. It temporarily dislocates the White subject through parody and satire, only to replace it with a recuperated historical figure.

It is essential to recall that Grandma's epoch represents an age where race instinct—in other words, the naturalization of White superiority—was at its height. Thus Albee's strategy for revealing the illegitimacy of 1960s American-ness, reliant as it is upon the historical process of othering Blackness, ends up reifying Whiteness. Rather than relegating the idea of the American Dream to the graveyard, the play inadvertently implies the existence of a more valid mode of White living that is worthy of being recovered.

This has the effect of buttressing the power of this myth for the U.S. psyche, and it renders the play complicit with aspects of reactionary politics. To be fair to Albee, his savage critique of White ways succeeds to a degree in tilting the spectator's position on White identity, for he does manage to portray some of its contradictions. Nevertheless, taken as a whole, like the soap-flakes that dominated 1960s advertisements, it ends up leaving the American Dream Whiter than White.

Castrating Whiteness: Amiri Baraka's *Dutchman*

The arts were considered an integral component of the Black power movement. Theater was viewed as a powerful agent for transmitting the new Black consciousness that would underpin community because it was the most social form of cultural production. Mike Sell records that the theory and practice of Black art, though it was led by a vanguard of radical intellectuals, struck a chord with a large segment of African American society (57).

In the 1960s there emerged a thriving subculture of Black theater. Productions ranging from short agit-prop sketches to soul musicals and Black reinscriptions of classic plays took place on college campuses and toured town halls and community centers in inner-city Black areas across the United States. New Black work did not go unnoticed by the mainstream either, with some plays garnering both commercial and critical success.

Amiri Baraka's *Dutchman* opened in New York in 1964 and won an Obie Award for best play of the season. Baraka was a leading voice in the Black arts movement, and he formulated the politics of Black theater in his poetic essay "The Revolutionary Theater" (1966). Holding ethics and aesthetics to be one, Baraka describes mainstream theater as reflecting the "unholy" values of White society. Against this, he presents the aims of the new Black theater. Firstly, it should deconstruct the fiction of Blackness and Whiteness propounded within dominant White ideology and, by looking "into black skulls," help root out internalized racism. Secondly, it should provoke the Black spectator into action outside the theater.

Larry Neal explains Baraka's meaning as a rejection of protest literature, which attempts to bring about change by appealing to White morality. In contrast, the motive behind the Black aesthetic is the destruction of the "White thing": White ideas and White ways of looking at things (Neal 56). Thus, while not shying away from actual violence, Baraka envisions the revolutionary theater as an instance of epistemic assault, part of the ongoing history of epistemic violence between Black and White discourses.

Dutchman expresses the core values Baraka elaborates in his treatise, which makes its success with the White establishment interesting to consider. One of the biggest challenges facing Black theater in the 1960s was how to avoid its cultural artifacts being co-opted and their revolutionary potential diluted. While I do comment on this dilemma, it is not the focus of my discussion here. My interest in the play stems from the way in which it illustrates how Whiteness was understood within Black culture at this time, how Whiteness was perceived to structure the world, and how these impressions were translated into dramatic representations. My aim is to demonstrate how *Dutchman* refuses the fixity of identity, restaging the social, cultural, and historical construction of Whiteness within the terms of Black discourse.

Dutchman provides an example of the profound new vision of racialized identities being constructed in the 1960s, exploring the formation and function of power in U.S. society. While the play touches on the dominance of White power as a process of suborning Black subjects, it is more concerned with foregrounding what Foucault terms "power/knowledge"— in this case, a violence done to the truth in which truth is made to appear as originally and ideally White. As Kimberly Benston phrases it, Baraka notes that "what is at stake in revolutionary action is precisely the power to define 'the real' itself: in the Barakan calculus, what one seeks is '*the* real world,' antidote to the stifling 'appearances' (codes) of '*this* real world'" (34).

Baraka frames the initial exchange of looks between his two main characters, Clay and Lula, before the action begins. Clay sees a woman's face staring at him through the window of a subway car; "when it realizes that the man has noticed the face, it begins very premeditatedly to smile" (Baraka, *Dutchman* 873). Their encounter has the appearance of routine; that is, their meeting symbolizes a long-standing social ritual between Blacks and Whites in the United States (an idea reinforced by the play's ending, which is really just another beginning of the same racial story).

Further, by depersonalizing Lula, referring to her as "it," Baraka makes her a symbol of the dominant White gaze. The sexually charged duel between Clay and Lula not only exemplifies but also enacts the clash between two diametrically opposed ways of seeing, and therefore knowing. The constitution of the characters' racialized forms of subjectivity are linked to the act of seeing—who possesses the cultural authority to look at or overlook the seen object, and the relation between seeing and knowing.[65]

Upon entering the subway car, Lula immediately begins her seductive game with Clay. Drawing on the mythology of Eve, Baraka shows her provocatively eating an apple, which she offers him. Baraka creates her as a crude *femme fatale,* wearing minimal clothing and "loud lipstick." At times he reduces her to a walking, talking vaginal orifice—the *vagina dentata*— that will devour Clay; this, read within the White/Black binary of U.S. discourse, stresses the historical castration of the Black male by the White fe/male subject.

Within the history of U.S. race relations, Lula herself is forbidden fruit for a Black man, and she plays on this fact. Her observation of Clay is based on her assumption that she knows what he desires—she believes him to be part of a collective type for whom the allure of the White woman is undeniable. Lula also subscribes to the myth of Black male bestiality. Violence and desire are imbricated in her attempts to stoke Clay's presumed natural urges; what she seeks is not a sexual encounter, though, but a display of her racial command.

Her salacious use of language and her body is designed to spark Clay's descent into the primitive, which is what the Black male basically figures as within White racist discourse. Toward the end of scene 1, she refutes Clay's right to wear ordinary dress, which she codes as White: "And why're you wearing a jacket and tie like that? Did your people ever burn witches or start revolutions over the price of tea? Boy, those narrow-shoulder clothes come from a tradition you ought to feel oppressed by. . . . Your grandfather was a slave, he didn't go to Harvard" (Baraka, *Dutchman* 876). Similarly, when Lula talks about Clay's manhood she uses the coarsest terms to describe the sexual act: making love, even having sex, is something reserved for White people, whereas Blacks screw, "rubs bellies," and do "the nasty."

Still, Lula possesses some allure for Clay, which facilitates her direction of his glance. Baraka does not represent him as an innocent victim. Rather, it is his desire for the signs of Whiteness, Lula being the most privileged among them, that places him at risk in the first place. As Bigsby points out, it is his willingness to be assimilated that makes Clay a target for Lula (*Confrontation and Commitment* 146).

However, Clay is not the irremediable Uncle Tom Lula believes him to be, and when she tries to make a spectacle of him in front of the other White occupants, she meets with stiff resistance. When he refuses to simulate intercourse with her, Lula resorts to vile racist taunts in an effort to bully and embarrass him into complying, if only to silence her. Yet if Clay is deluded that his veneer of bourgeois respectability offers a kind of social insulation, Lula also suffers from the delusion that her game with Clay is risk free. Wearing her Whiteness like armor, she allows Clay the *privilege* of staring at her ass and legs only because she believes that her understanding of him can keep him easily under control. Instead, Clay stuns her by physically retaliating.

His action enables him to momentarily take control of events, and he uses his moment to place Whiteness in the spotlight. Whereas Blacks have always endured the gaze of White dominance, Whiteness has operated on the assumption that it is invisible to those it subordinates. Critic bell hooks recalls why slaves were punished for meeting the eyes of their White masters, by "appearing to observe the whites they were serving as only a subject can observe or see" (340), and thereby reconfiguring the White master-subject in terms of the known object. In the same way, Clay reverses the normal order of things. He forces the White occupants to avert their eyes. The drunk who comes to Lula's aid but is beaten off by Clay now "shuts up when he sees Clay watching him" (Baraka, *Dutchman* 879).

Clay's switch to anti-type silences Lula long enough for him to deliver a climactic speech refuting the authority of the White gaze and the reliability of White knowingness. Neal points out that in Black aesthetics poetry is understood as having a concrete function (58). Clay's dramatic speech then represents an action—it is as much a violent assault upon Lula and the White order as is his physical rebellion. It is a moment of performative Blackness in which Clay transforms on stage from a fantasy figure of the White imagination—the polite, assimilated, middle-class, but still *Black boy*—into a man, angry and alienated, who sits "here in this buttoned-up suit, to keep myself from cutting all your throats" (Baraka, *Dutchman* 879).

Black discourse in the 1960s attempted to effect a deep transformation in how both Black and White societies conceived of racialized identities. *Dutchman,* as a part of this project, forwards concepts of Whiteness and Blackness that represent radical departures from their dominant historical configurations. George Piggford identifies how the play inverts some of the typical significations of the tropes of Whiteness and Blackness in White American culture, with Blackness signifying virtue and naiveté and White-ness vice and disingenuousness (82). By speaking publicly the alternative and negative meanings that Black culture historically placed on Whiteness, Clay's discourse critically intervenes in the White regime of truth.

Baraka recasts Whiteness as a terrorizing, murderous discourse. Clay's apocalyptic vision of Whites with their throats cut, being dragged out to the edge of their own cities so the flesh can fall away from their bones in sanitary isolation, allies U.S. racial practices to the ideology of racial supe-riority that only two decades previously gave rise to Nazi atrocities. He warns Lula against promoting among Blacks this "great intellectual legacy of the white man, or maybe one day they'll begin to listen."

And on that day, as sure as shit, when you really believe you can "accept" them into your fold. . . . With no more blues, except the very old ones, and not a watermelon in sight, the great missionary heart will have triumphed, and all of those ex-coons will be stand-up Western men . . . and they'll murder you. They'll murder you, and have very rational explanations. Very like your own. (Baraka, *Dutchman* 880)

Clay's violent outburst reflects one of the most significant aims of Black power; that is, to expose Whiteness to view and thereby reveal and undermine the unstated assumptions about race that support Whiteness as a major idea system to explain and order U.S. life.

In addition, Clay reverses the historical position whereby Whites defined themselves and everyone else, thus initiating a process of "othering" Whiteness. His reference to Whites as "old bald-headed four-eyed ofays" mirrors the way in which radical Black discourse was redefining Whites in its own terms, as "blue-eyed devils" and "honkies." Clay's speech also functions as a corrective to White concepts of Blackness.

The Black movement aimed to force Whites to acknowledge Blacks according to the terms in which they perceived themselves. Thus Clay ridicules Lula's claim that she enjoys Black music, because White fascination for Black cultural forms is based on a fundamental misunderstanding of them. Jochen Achilles describes the theory of Black art put forward in *Dutchman* as "sublimated carnage" (225); Clay makes it clear that Whites would not love Bessie Smith if they understood that what she was really saying is "kiss my black unruly ass" (Baraka, *Dutchman* 879).[66]

His assault on the White discursive framework of assumptions about Blackness works not only to revalue Blackness but also to further jar Whiteness out of its position of unseen safety. By openly questioning and condemning White practices, Clay places Lula in the unusual position of having to react rather than act, and from a morally defensive standpoint. Having rebutted the lies that she admits allow her to control the world, Clay leaves the White subject with no place to hide, and she kills him for it.

Most significantly, Lula's reaction to Clay's speech authorizes the Black system of knowledge about Whiteness to which he has just given voice, for by murdering Clay, Lula performs his version of Whiteness. In previous chapters I have demonstrated how the dominant White logic posits Whiteness to be amorphous, and Whiteness as a discursive category derives its cultural authority from this ostensible formlessness. Therefore, through her role as White avenger bringing destruction and death, Lula visually and undeniably disrupts this logic and undermines one of the bases of White cultural authority.

Dutchman's great strength as an oppositional play resides in its othering of Whiteness and in the way it makes the Black perspective on Whiteness visible. In Baraka's original version, the play ends with a scene of recognition between a Black conductor and the young man whom Lula is eying as her next prey, an occurrence that is omitted from the first director's edition.[67] The sign of solidarity that passes between the two Black men breaks the exchange of looks between Lula and her intended victim as her gaze is drawn to the conductor while he moves through the car. After greeting the young man, the conductor gives Lula a nod of recognition, as if to say, in seeing you, *I know you.* This tripartite exchange of looks leaves spectators with some hope that the racial narrative they have watched transpire, which has been unfolding throughout the course of U.S. history, is not bound to be repeated and may yet be rewritten within the terms of a new racial order.

Whiteness as a Simulacrum of Death: David Rabe's *Sticks and Bones*

New left views about the oppressiveness and spiritual emptiness of White middle-class life found expression in 1970s theater in the early plays of David Rabe. Rabe explores the 1960s and '70s as a vital psychological moment. Often characterized as a Vietnam playwright, Rabe does address the war in his work, but the conflict itself is often lateral to the plot.

According to Janet Hertzbach, Rabe transmutes this turbulent era of the Vietnam war, "racial conflict, the Manson murders, the generation gap, and the sexual revolution into a dramatic world of irreconcilable conflict." Rabe's characters lie in the midst of a metaphorical battlefield. It is in this sense that his plays are war plays (173).

In *Sticks and Bones,* produced in 1971 at the New York Shakespeare Public Theater Festival, Rabe addresses how the Vietnam conflict is the terrible but logical outcome of the way in which modern U.S. society organizes itself. [68] The war is an allegory for deconstructing idealized notions of White family life and community. Like Albee, Rabe locates the sickness at the heart of U.S. society in the relation between the nuclear family unit and consumer capitalism, yet he is more successful at making the connection between the myth of the American Dream, the family's reproduction of Whiteness as social capital, and individual/social degeneration.

Set in 1968, the play involves why a returning soldier, David, finds himself unable to reintegrate into his family. Rabe provides him with the perfect All-American family—Ozzie, Harriet, and Ricky Nelson, characters drawn from a popular 1950s TV sitcom *The Adventures of Ozzie and Harriet.* Hertzbach considers this choice to indicate that the ritual matter emanates from what the playwright considers the emblems of modern American culture: television and racism. Both, she argues, preclude communication and, as such, indicate the mutual alienation of David and his family. Whereas TV offers a fantasy life vastly preferable to reality, and commercials reflect middle-class America's obsession with money and material possessions, racism answers the White need to feel superior to some groups (176).

At first David's family seems welcoming, if shocked at having to deal with their returning son's blindness. Very quickly, though, he becomes a canker in the home, as he relentlessly discloses the reality of his experiences in Vietnam and the new vision of his family and nation to which his sightless eyes have been ironically opened. When the Sergeant first deposits him at home, David insists that "It doesn't feel right," and later, "I don't know these people" (Rabe 105, 107).

He tries to figure out just what it is he has lost in the war. The answer Rabe provides is equivocal, because David's inability to fit back into his family, and through them, his community, also amounts to a gain—the valuable awareness that the truisms of White culture to which he once unthinkingly subscribed are the very things that condemned him to the hellishness of Vietnam. Most importantly, he is able to perceive his family's complicity, for it is his family that schooled him in these maxims.

Rick Berg and John Carlos Rowe interpret the play as illuminating how the "typical American family" was one of the contributing factors in the war (3). Rabe foregrounds how the values being expressed in the villages-cum-battlefields of Vietnam are also played out within the White nuclear family. After an argument between Ozzie and his wife, Ozzie flies into a rage and reveals to the spectator the feelings usually suppressed beneath his façade of the model patriarch: "They think they know me and they know nothing. . . . How I'd like to beat Ricky with my fists till his face is ugly. How I'd like to banish David to the streets. How I'd like to cut her tongue from her mouth" (Rabe 125–26).

Through such invectives, Pamela Cooper argues, the play posits a "moral kinship between Ozzie, the apparently bland and boring "typical father," and the GIs capable of flinging razor-lined caps and fifty-pound bags of cement at civilians in Vietnam" (620). Ozzie blames the family for the erosion of self, lamenting the loss of a time when he was "nobody's goddamn father and nobody's goddamn husband! I was myself!" (Rabe 126). Rabe extrapolates these individual emotions to the wider community by casting the audience as Ozzie's "friends, his buddies."[69]

Ozzie's perspective on the family as an institution that smothers personal freedom is expanded by David to include the stifling of civil freedom for U.S. citizens and those who feature as targets of imperialism. *Sticks and Bones* asserts that the White family and the consumerist fantasy it represents make possible the carnage in Vietnam because the family has been rendered blind to it. David compares his family to murderers who "don't even know that murders happen" (Rabe 135). Thus, he determines to bring the nightmare of the war into the suburban landscape of his childhood.

In one episode, David stands above his father while he sleeps and whispers into his ear: "I think you should know I've begun to hate you. I don't think you can tell me any more. I must tell you. . . . If I had been an orphan with no one to count on me, I would have stayed there. Restless are you? You think us good, and yet we steal all we have" (144). Ozzie awakes screaming in fright, but unlike the TV screen that so often flickers in the background, the picture that David keeps exposing cannot be turned off.

David's family members employ numerous protective strategies to shield themselves from the reality he insists on revealing, from their excessive consumption of TV and food to Ricky's constant photographing of normative family images. One of the family's most potent shields, however, is the dehumanization of the Vietnamese. Berg and Rowe hold the racism and ethnocentrism that took the United States to war in Vietnam to be part of the "psychological equipment of the decent American citizen" (7). This equipment allows David's "decent" relations to project their own flaws onto the Vietnamese, for, as Bigsby comments, "What happened in Vietnam is so at odds with American self-images that it must be denied and suppressed" (Introduction xvii).

When David presents a graphic description of the action he witnessed instead of providing Ozzie and Harriet with the expected slides of yet more family images, his parents evade the issue by automatically characterizing the Vietnamese as responsible for atrocities: "It's so awful the things those yellow people do to one another. Yellow people hanging yellow people. Isn't that right? Ozzie, I told you—animals—Christ burn them" (Rabe 143). They cannot, though, ignore forever the presence of the Vietnamese "other" whom David has introduced into the family home. The fantasy figure of Zung, a young Vietnamese girl whom David loves, yet has abandoned, haunts him. She proves the determining factor in the final break between him and his family, as Ozzie's rant attests:

I MEAN, I JUST CAN'T STOP THINKING ABOUT IT. I JUST CAN'T STOP THINKING ABOUT IT. LITTLE BITTY CHINKY KIDS YOU WANTED TO HAVE! LITTLE BITTY CHINKY YELLOW KIDS! DIDN'T YOU! FOR OUR GRANDCHILDREN! (AND HE SLAPS DAVID WITH ONE HAND.) LITTLE BITTY YELLOW PUFFY . . . CREATURES! (Rabe 146)

The family members' assessment of the Vietnamese as monstrous in actuality parallels their own psychological make-up. Like Albee's model White family, there is no affection or real communication among them.

Rather, they repeat a set of clichés from family sitcoms that speak only their consumerist values. Ultimately, they resort to murder in order to preserve the façade of their happy family life, excising David from the family by actively promoting his suicide. In this way, the kind of things White people will do even to other White people is shown to lead inevitably to a fracturing of human bonds, both familial and social.

David's struggle in the play to shed his Vietnam experience should be seen in terms of a struggle to shed also his White inheritance. The two are connected most closely in the figure of Zung. Christoph Houswitschka describes Zung as David's potential savior, from whom he hopes to find "redemption from his and his family's racist, sexist or imperialistic guilt," as opposed to Father Donald, who represents the hypocrisy of Christian ideology by defending the war (123). David describes her as possibly the most valuable thing in his life; paradoxically, he sometimes sees her as "garbage" and "filth," reflecting his fear of shedding entirely his inheritance of his parent's values because of the immense subjective loss this might entail.

This conflict, which precipitates David's drive toward suicide, suggests that Whiteness is in the process of breaking down. The link between capital and death theorized within countercultural discourse is shown turning its machinery toward its producer. In one of David's most poignant descriptions of Zung, uttered in response to Harriet's expressed repugnance of her yellow skin, he says: "She was the color of the earth . . . and what is white but winter with the earth under it like a suicide!" (Rabe 120).

Minnie Bruce Pratt describes the feelings of fear that may be provoked when an individual attempts to shed his/her culture's racist baggage: "As I try to strip away the layers of deceit that I have been taught, it is hard not to be afraid that these are like wrappings of a shroud and that what I will ultimately come to in myself is a disintegrating, rotting nothing: that the values that I have at my core, from my culture, will only be those of negativity, exclusion, fear, death" (39). David finds himself in a place of rot and nothingness after his attempt to shed the cultural values that formed his identity. David's response to his mother represents Whiteness as an identity bereft of positive value, of hope, and his quest to deserve Zung by reforming not only himself but also his family results in his loss of his social and psychic bearings. At the same time, however, like Clay in *Dutchman*, David denies White identity the security of its own self-penned narrative, reformulating it as the effect of a social and cultural history that carries with it desolation and death.

Post-Vietnam, Rabe suggests, "decent" White Americans will never be quite at ease with themselves again: a new tension has surfaced within

White identity, a new suspicion of Whiteness as destitute of cohesion, social and otherwise, a fracture that henceforth will require greater ideological
work to cover over. *Sticks and Bones* presents the spectator with a construction of Whiteness in the process of being radically recast by its encounter with the racialized "other," but even more significant is the way that
it is shown being reworked through the reflection of its own altered face.

The U.S. Women's Movement and Black Feminist Subculture

In the 1970s White male hegemony in the United States faced attacks
from not only Black and counterculture activism but also feminist movements that were growing in momentum. In an early analysis of U.S. feminism, William H. Chafe argues that the second wave of the women's movement gained the energy it did during the 1960s because the country was
already engaged with the demand to eliminate prejudice and discrimination. Although the civil rights movement did not create the revival of feminism, it did help to produce a favorable set of circumstances in which it
could flourish (232–33).

Many feminists adopted and adapted the language of Black rights in
order to forward their own case for gender equality, yet in the process of its
adaptation this model of resistance was Whitened.[70] There have always
been several strands of feminist thought within the U.S. movement; however, many of the mainstream movement's goals, as expressed, for example,
in Betty Friedan's seminal text *The Feminine Mystique* (1963), are based on
the experience of living as a White middle-class housewife/mother in sub-
urbia.[71] This personal-political connection explains the movement's central
focus in the 1970s on White women and the goal of finding a solution to
the "housewife syndrome" that they experienced in relation to their social
condition in the postwar era, a condition that was mediated through their
relation to the White patriarchy.[72]

Hence, it accounts also for why Black women could not identify easily
with mainstream feminism. Few feminist writers in the 1970s took account
of the way that capital manipulates White and Black women in different
ways. The Black middle class was small relative to the mainstream, and thus
Black women's roles and images in U.S. society remained markedly different from White women's. Also, Black and White women historically shared
very different relations to White men.

Despite these material differences, White feminist theorists like Kate
Millett, who came to feminism via the civil rights and peace movements,

posited sexual dominion as the "most pervasive ideology of our culture," the foundation for "its most fundamental concept of power" (25). Millett describes racism as one of the "final variables in sexual politics"; therefore, "it is pertinent . . . to devote *a few words to it as well*" (38–39, italics mine). This approach reduces race to a remainder, suggesting that racism will dissipate once a cure for sexism is achieved, and it removes White women from the narrative of racial oppression.

To be fair to Millett and the White feminists of her generation, their accounts of sexism and racism rarely intended to exclude Black women. Notwithstanding, mainstream feminist thought failed to adequately address racial concerns: it either reduced racism to an after-effect of sexism, or it completely overlooked the dissimilarities between White and Black women's experiences in society and, more importantly, the *similarities* between White women's and White men's social positions.

Vivian Gordon explains the differences between U.S. society's discriminations against White and Black women as one of relative versus abject deprivation. "Blacks have been victims of a racism which defined them as less than human, whereas white women have been defined as having limitations or unique roles appropriate to their gender within the human species" (53). Therefore, if they wanted to participate in the mainstream movement, its implicit class and race bias meant that Black women had to "compartmentalize themselves into segments of race versus gender" (46).

Refusing such fragmentation, Black women worked toward creating a social and philosophical movement that would express their needs in U.S. society and offer viable solutions to their problems. While White women focused their energies on the Equal Rights Amendment, a proposed change to the U.S. Constitution stipulating gender equality in the public sphere, Black women, sharing a commitment to full employment rights, needed to address other issues, such as housing, health care, education, crime, and police harassment, that were not urgent problems for the majority of middle-class White women.

Barbara Omalade identifies why the equation White feminists drew between the liberation of women and employment opportunities and changing sex roles is problematic. First, it ignores the history of Black women as workers in Africa and the United States, where economic independence from men has not led to liberation. Even more striking, most of these Black women's work has been as domestics or office workers under the direct supervision of White women, many of whom were racist (255).

Moreover, Black feminists needed to combat sexist practices among Black men while at the same time working with them against racism in the larger society. This necessitated contesting the claims of patriarchy, both White and Black, as well as the racial privileges of White women, for White skin privilege enabled White women to exercise a share of power over both Black women and men. The triple objective of Black feminism led to the development of a methodology that challenged the notion of homogeneous sisterhood and the idea of patriarchy as a fundamental system of domination independent of other social structures. I would not deny that the pressure White feminism brought to bear on the form and function of masculine authority in U.S. society considerably troubled men's position in the social order. However, in the 1970s Black feminist thought provided a far more radical critique of the masculine subject by virtue of its demonstration of the relation between U.S. Man's gender and race and his dependence on White womanhood for the maintenance of his power.

White Talking Black: Adrienne Kennedy's *A Movie Star Has to Star in Black and White*

Writing in 1970, Margaret Wilkerson speaks of the rarity in U.S. performance of a "mirror of self" for Black people. Blacks are expected to "filter their self-perceptions through stereotyped images . . . or through a blind identification with white characters" ("Critics, Standards and Black Theater" 122).[73] This was especially true for Black women, but not only in relation to White cultural practices. Playwright Aisha Rahman talks about the way that most of the overwhelmingly male Black arts writers "painted worse pictures of black women than ever before. I say worse, because, in their reflection of how our *brothers* saw us, the images were much more damaging to the black woman's psyche than their precursors had been" (258).

Black feminists used theater as one vehicle for disseminating their position, one that was distinct from both White mainstream feminism and the Black arts movement. Keanne-Marie Miller characterizes Black feminist theater work as attempting to present positive images of dynamic and strong Black female characters (289). The work of Adrienne Kennedy exemplifies theater that reflects a Black woman's vision of reality; however, the private and public consciousness reflected through her aesthetic is rarely straightforwardly reaffirming.

More often than not, "my plays make people uncomfortable," Kennedy admits (Diamond, "Adrienne Kennedy" 137). This sense of disturbance arises from her brutally honest depiction of Black women's self-contradictory and often unconscious participation in their own subordination. Despite a frequent awfulness of vision, though, Kennedy's plays are not pessimistic. In reflecting Black women's fraught relation to self, they reveal the internal conditions informing the special character of Black female experience in U.S. society, and thereby lay some of the groundwork for freeing women from these constraints.

Margaret Wilkerson identifies "metaphor, image, and symbol" as the main elements in Kennedy's work ("Diverse Angles" 70). Kennedy refuses the ordered structure of the well-made play, instead offering a symbolic theater language that is a rich mix of expressionist and surrealist practices, the devices of which are used to pose fundamental questions about race-gendered identity. *A Movie Star Has to Star in Black and White,* which premiered at the New York Shakespeare Festival in 1976, lacks a conventional plot, though it does have a center—Clara and her family. However, although Clara and her husband, mother, and father provide the material for the events, they are granted only supporting roles in its presentation. Different episodes in the family's history are staged by a cast of actors made up to closely resemble White Hollywood film stars: Shelley Winters and Montgomery Clift, Bette Davis and Paul Henreid, Marlon Brando and Jean Peters. Each couple is framed within a film narrative: *A Place in the Sun, Now Voyager,* and *Viva Zapata* respectively.

Most studies of the play address the way in which it highlights the complex and contradictory nature of Black feminine identity, making reference also to the intersection of Black and White femininity. Scant attention has been given to the play's representation of masculinity, in particular its three White male figures: Brando, Henreid, and Clift. Yet the play elaborates a complex triangular relationship between Black and White femininity and Black/White femininity and White masculinity, which imbricates all three in the production and maintenance of White power. Hence, I want to examine the play from the angle of its White masculine "other."

A reading that focuses on White men may seem to set its face against the play's Black feminist thrust, unless one considers that its White masculine symbolic characterizations (in place of characters) function as vehicles for narrating different aspects of Black femininity just as much as the White female figures do. Because the Black female subject attempts to make sense of herself within a race-gendered system where the terms favor the White fe/male dyad, articulating her experience necessarily entails a reading of White masculinity as well as femininity. Thus, the focus of my analysis is not on how White masculinist discourse writes or reads Black women; rather, I explore the way in which Kennedy's discursive reinscriptions of

White masculinity might effect the meanings attached to Whiteness and the security of the dominant White subject's position.

Kennedy's stage notes describe Clara as passive and preoccupied: "Her movie stars speak for her." They "star in her life" (87). However, only the female stars actively voice her experience. Another stage note describes Clift, Brando, and Henreid as mute. Elin Diamond points out that when the White female characters speak the life of the *visible* black woman the Whiteness of the performers enters into consciousness (*Unmaking Mimesis* 128). Does, then, Kennedy's silencing of the White male enable the operations of White masculinity to escape the spectator's notice?

To understand how Kennedy dispossesses White masculine identity of its privileged position in the racial hierarchy, as well as the position of White femininity, it is essential first to trace the process through which the White feminine is made to reveal itself through its performance of Blackness. Ross Chambers, describing the mechanism through which Whiteness produces and reproduces itself as racially unmarked, asserts that the structures of power mediating social relations endow Whiteness with the quality of unmarkedness through a process of examining the "other."[74] What all cases of examination have in common, he writes, is the White subject's desire not to be associated with those who, because of their examinability, are its objects, a desire that in fact acknowledges their connection.

That the White female stars fulfill the role of translating Clara's emotions for the spectator establishes a relation between Black and White femininity, one that allows the Black feminine to colonize the White voice. The effect of this colonizing move is twofold. Firstly, Whiteness gets displaced from its normative narrative structural position; in turn, Whiteness as the locale of the seeing subject shifts to the same level of Blackness— that of the seen object.[75]

White and Black racialized femininity still appear as asymmetrical categories but no longer, because of the marking of the White feminine, as pure opposites. *Movie Star* illustrates that each depends on the other for its meaning-fullness. In other words, the presence and effectiveness of Whiteness on stage relies on the materiality of Black experience, and Blackness, in order to be heard above the violent din with which White racial discourse obfuscates the hierarchy of race-gendered identities, must utilize Whiteness to bring its message into being.[76] As a result, Savas Patsalidis makes clear, the stage across which Kennedy's feminine signs move is so slippery that no one can hold on to her position for long (305).

This inability to remain in a stable race-gendered location denies a continuity of self to the Black and White female subject, (dis)allowing the occupation of a privileged space to each at different times. The play applies a similar tactic for destabilizing normative White masculine significations, for the verbal passivity of the White male trio suggests a closer resemblance between White masculinity and Black femininity than is normally allowed or admitted in dominant racial discourse, Clara, of course, also representing passivity and impoverished speech.

Clara's husband complains that her diaries consume her: "my diaries make me a spectator watching my life like watching a black and white movie" (99). In the same way, Brando, Clift, and Henreid are reduced to watchers, passive and quiet reactors in relation to the stories in which they are performed. The White female stars always take the lead within the narratives they inhabit, which, because they signify Black feminine experience, implies another destabilizing connection between White masculinity and Black femininity.

Peggy Phelan argues a point similar to Chambers's when she asserts that the "unremarked is more powerful than the marked." She contends that to gain visibility for the politically underrepresented without scrutinizing the power of who is required to display what to whom amounts to a politically impoverished agenda (26). Therefore, Kennedy's coloring in of the White masculine subject, like his feminine counterpart, is crucial to the play's political efficacy.

The silence of the three male characters renders White masculinity available for scrutiny. Chambers attributes the blankness of Whiteness as a category to a denial of its own dividedness, which is accomplished through the production of its "other" as split (196). By this, he means that Blacks are perceived as a function of their group belongingness (for example, stereotyped as all the same), and at the same time Blackness as a category is pluralized by being made to stand for a plethora of racialized types, whereas Whiteness denotes unmixedness and invisibility. Kennedy rearranges the order through which Whiteness knows itself. The play disables the White masculine subject by splitting him off from his normative functions and aligning him with different forms of racialized femininity.

Once thus split, he must play an alternative passive role. In this way, his claim to priority is subverted. The terms upon which the White male figures engage with the White female stars are set by the women, but they are also always Clara's terms. So they represent a Black female political aesthetic. Thus, the White masculine subject, like his White female counterpart, slides between one racial discursive reality and another, which makes him unable to operate with his customary degree of control.

Clara serves as both link and lever between Black femininity and White gendered identities. As a linking device, she challenges the presumed un-examinability of both White femininity and masculinity. By virtue of meta-phorically inscribing on the White female body her own imagination, she acts as a wedge between White masculinity and femininity, each of which acts as a prop for the consolidation of the other's authority.

Her occupation of the White female voice also denudes this prop for White masculine authority of some of its value. A compromised White femininity, one made remarkable due to its close proximity to Blackness, cannot perform its usual function: confirming White masculine difference and superiority. At the end of the play, all the signs of racialized identities that move across Kennedy's stage have been corrupted. In this way, the sys-tem of race-gender binaries breaks down, and Whiteness is made apparent in a new, fractured form.

chapter 6

Undigestible Difference: Powellism and New White Racism

n the 1960s and '70s, British society was deeply concerned with questions of national identity. Harry Goulbourne traces the shifts in the definitions of a British national through the passage of immigration laws. Before the major waves of commonwealth immigration, one could be British if one bore allegiance to the Crown, without regard to geographical location or ethnicity (*Ethnicity and Nationalism* 92).[77] As the number of immigrants entering Britain rose in the mid-1950s there was a gradual mingling of traditional forms of nationalism (based on shared language, religion, social customs, and so on) and ethnic-based nationalism (*Ethnicity and Nationalism* 87).

The idea that all British nationals are equal under the Crown is in reality nominal. Historically, this myth served the purpose of making it appear that common interest bound everyone together in the empire and later the commonwealth, and thus it has functioned as a mechanism for maintaining White control over a host of different ethnic peoples. White ethnicity has always been part and parcel of what it means to be British. What changed in the 1960s was the kind of conceptual maneuvers used to sustain the integral connection between Britishness and Whiteness, a link whose concretized form may be read through the series of immigration laws passed in the 1960s and '70s.

John Solomos compares the way that Black and White migration was politically perceived in the post-1945 conjuncture. After the war, migrants from European countries arrived in the hundreds of thousands in response to the labor shortage. Far from discouraging their entry, the government encouraged immigrants from Poland, Austria, and other Euro-nations (44–46). Even though many had languages and religions different from the host population, European migrants were preferred. Because they could be absorbed into the category of Whiteness, these groups were viewed as more compatible with British society, including even the Irish, who had once been compared to Blacks.

However, as long as the number of Black migrants was relatively small, there was still some elasticity in the construction of Britishness. Shortly after the *Empire Windrush* landed, the Labour Home Secretary stated that his government recognized the rights of "colonial peoples to be treated as men and brothers with the people of this country" (Brooke 126). In the initial postwar period, it was hoped that Blacks might eventually blend into British society in spite of their obvious color difference.

As the influx of migrants from former colonies increased, so too did the fears about how their presence would alter society, and the construction of national identity became less elastic. An important development in 1960s racial discourse, Paul Gilroy suggests, was making immigrant synonymous with Blackness (*There Ain't No Black* 46). Immigration came to be perceived primarily as a racial (read Black) question. Conceptualizing migrants as the racial "other" both reflected and exacerbated public concern and opposition.

As Goulbourne notes, there was a remarkably unified response by political leaders to the perceived threat and growing unpopularity of non-White immigration (*Race Relations in Britain* 57). Both Labour and Conservative governments issued similar and increasingly discriminatory legislation, suggesting that both left and right viewed non-White immigrants as a serious social threat, even if Labour used less inflammatory rhetoric.

The 1962 Commonwealth Immigration Act and the 1971 Immigration Act ended the free entry of non-White commonwealth citizens and scripted a "grandfather" clause stipulating that only people able to claim close contact with the U.K. by virtue of having a grandfather born in the country could gain entry. This excluded Blacks while allowing Whites whose ancestors went to the colonies the right of return. In a sense, the legal discourse surrounding immigration may be considered fundamental to the process of writing modern British history in a way intended to reestablish and justify Britain as a White nation.

The perception of Black migrants as a threat to White privilege led to a hardening of racial identities. Blackness came to signify an undigestible form of difference. Many of the crude stereotypes that predominated at the turn of the twentieth century reappeared. Journalist Chris Mullard quotes from a letter he received in response to an article in *The Times* (1967), warning him that "Black rubbish" could never be English: "We shall always hate you, because blacks are lazy, immoral, savage. . . . How dare you presume to call yourself English—Black Apes and Cannibals not so long ago" (17).[78]

Note the emphasis on Englishness rather than Britishness. The changes in representations of White British identity were brought about in part by a revision of imperial history that altered the prestige attached to identities forged during the empire. In a 1964 speech the Conservative Member of Parliament Enoch Powell described the British Empire as "self-deception," and a "delusion," and a "hallucination." He reconstructed British national identity in terms of a romanticized pastoral idyll. The identity of the nation was said to have been forged in the days of Elizabeth I, where Powell's imaginary White "Englishman" lived out his days in a "marvelous land, so sweetly mixed of opposites in climate that all seasons of the year appear there in their greatest perfection; of the fields amid which they built their halls, their cottages, their churches, and where the same blackthorn showered its petals upon them as upon us" (Rutherford 124–25).

In this context empire becomes a break in the historical continuity of a White Anglo-Saxon English identity. Powell declares that from "this continuous life of a united people in its island home spring, as from the soil of England, all that is peculiar in the gifts and achievements of the English nation."[79] This is an unalterable truth that "no Hanoverian" or "Headships of Commonwealths" can undermine (Rutherford 124–25). By naturalizing the evolution of English identity, Powell presents the colonial rupture in racialized terms, harnessing national continuity and stability to English White racial homogeneity.

In the 1960s White domestic ideology was used to argue for the natural dominance of White Englishness on the British homeland. Black migrants were cast as illegitimate heirs to British identity. In his most notorious statement, Powell compared immigration to "watching a nation busily engaged in heaping up its own funeral pyre." Labelled the "rivers of blood speech"[80] because of its most famous image, the "River Tiber flowing with much blood"—his vision of a multiracial British future—the speech radically rechristens White English people as a persecuted minority in their own homeland. Powell attempted to mask the racism of his speech with the language of culturalism, but his most emotive symbol, the harried White grandmother, makes clear that the speech is motivated by fears that the Anglo family will be contaminated by Black racial difference.

He tells the story of a White woman who only eight years previously had lived on a "respectable street." Respectable means White, because the sale of one house to a "Negro" precipitated a flood of immigrants, with the result that her once decent street declined to a "place of noise and confusion": "She is becoming afraid to go out. Windows are broken. She finds excreta pushed through her letterbox. When she goes to the shops, she is followed by children, charming, wide-grinned piccaninnies."[81] Whereas in the nineteenth century the monarch was represented as reigning supreme over her many-colored colonial children, according to Powell the very existence of her descendant—the modern White maternal figure—is threatened by the racial detritus of empire.

Many in the broadsheet press condemned the speech, and Powell lost his shadow cabinet position as a result of it. Nevertheless, he struck a chord with a broad cross-section of the public. His claim to speak on behalf of White people who could no longer voice their true feelings in case of a Black backlash is supported by the more than 100,000 supportive letters he received within days of his speech (Rutherford 131). He also enjoyed the endorsement of many in the tabloid press, as well as some union members, who staged pro-Powell marches.

The "rivers of blood" speech reflects how in the 1960s and '70s the British family continued to constitute one of the principal institutions that was felt to be threatened by Black racial difference. British racial exclusivity depended quite heavily on representing both Asian and Afro-Caribbean families as pathological. Asian families were portrayed as autocratic and backward in their treatment of women, which rendered them unable to be assimilated. Afro-Caribbean families, in contrast, were represented as unstable, as wellsprings of criminality. These constructions both contributed toward shaping the White family as the only healthy, productive social unit in British society.

Both Asians and Afro-Caribbeans were considered causes of the decline of British communities. Asians changed the face of neighborhoods by taking over all of the local shops; Afro-Caribbeans destroyed them by draining social resources, using up an undue share of housing and unemployment benefits. These constructions tie national stability and prosperity to a homogenous White socio-racial landscape.

Though disqualified from British identity for different reasons, the net effect of the way in which domestic ideology is explained in racialized terms is similar for all migrant groups—exclusion, scapegoating, stigmatization. John Solomos, Bob Findlay, Simon Jones, and Paul Gilroy argue that the "battle lines between 'society' and its 'enemies' were more clearly drawn by the end of the seventies than they had been for decades," and by the mid-1970s Blacks were being presented as the main enemies of British society (26). This left communities made up of White families in the position of natural owner-occupiers of Britishness.

Within a master narrative where the object of racialized discourse is non-White people, the cultural force of White identity that enables a monopoly on British national identity derives from the amorphous nature of Whiteness. However, with increased levels of xenophobia in the late 1960s and '70s, Whiteness shifted toward the center of racial analyses, and the White subject gradually became the object of its own racial stories and analysis by those whom it designated as its "other." This move signified a change in the way that White people in Britain experienced their identity and standing in the nation-state, changes that were generated by continuing fears over the loss of imperial status, the concomitant influx of Black immigrants, and an increasingly vocal set of immigrant communities. Yet, the rhetoric chosen to reproduce Whites as the dominant group often worked against itself.

Speaking as a Member of Parliament, Powell helped make the White racist fringe appear more respectable.[82] Extremist groups such as the National Front, by aligning themselves with Powellite ideas (for example, ending immigration, repatriation), increased their membership and success at the polls. In addition, Dilip Hiro suggests that once the taboo against uninhibited public discussions of race had been broken, people felt licensed to vocalize racist opinions: "Whites discussed immigration and blacks and Asians openly in buses, pubs, and work canteens, without regard for the feelings of the coloured people present" (248).

The growth of the racist right, and its coverage by the media, provided a wide platform from which to disseminate the developing language of White rights. However, this new language represented a significant departure from the imperial codes that had shaped the White British subject as all-powerful, capable of subduing three-quarters of the globe. The idea of a still superior but now battered White English community that needed to fight for a corner in their home country signifies the emergence of a fundamentally new conception of the White British subject.

Furthermore, the attempt to reconstitute White Englishness over Britishness blurred the boundary between the White subject, whether designated English or British, and its racial "other" by virtue of opening Whiteness to greater examination. This breach in the opaque façade of Whiteness offered opportunities for new ways of negotiating raced identities on the part of those stigmatized by White racist discourse.

Therefore, while the new public discourse on race fostered an environment in which White interests could be aggressively reasserted, it also helped to consolidate Black resistance.

Unlike in the United States, where African Americans had developed a cohesive community identity, commonwealth immigrants had very diverse cultures. The colonial experience of West Indians had created an English-speaking, Christian, and British-orientated subculture, which meant that they had high expectations of acceptance by Mother England. Indians and Pakistanis, to the contrary, had entirely distinctive cultures with their own religions and languages. This made assimilation less desirable as well as more unlikely (Patterson 6–11).

When Powell opened Britain's racial can of worms on the national stage, one of the unintended progressive effects was the inspiration it provided commonwealth groups to work together against racism, despite real tensions among them. The U.S. Black power movement also acted as an important influence on Black resistance in the U.K. and the new definitions of racialized identities to which it would give rise. Previous chapters have shown how racism takes distinct forms in British and U.S. society, but it is clear as well that in many instances Black Britons have held analogous social positions to African Americans.

Black people in both nations have been positioned on the bottom rung of society, relegated to the lowest-paid unskilled jobs even when their education and skills fitted them for other types of work. Well into the 1970s many Blacks in Britain endured the worst housing conditions, in areas where public services were inadequate. Black children had to learn a curriculum from which positive Black models were absent or, worse, in which Blacks were represented through imperial stereotypes. There was consonance too in the way that new stereotypes of Blacks were developing in both countries, with images of the Black criminal, drug addict, and "welfare scrounger" being prime examples.

For the children of West African and Caribbean immigrants, cross-cultural exchanges with other diasporic groups began to give rise to an Afrocentric identity. Like their Asian counterparts, these immigrant communities came to realize that assimilation was not the answer to the problems they faced. Instead, progress depended on a unified Black subculture that could offer a base for resistance and psychological sustenance to its members. The British discourse of Black pride had many cultural expressions, from demonstrations in major cities protesting police harassment to Black consciousness meetings featuring poetry and history discussions. The growth of Rastafarianism, with its Black messiah Haile Selassie, and reggae are other prominent examples.

Afrocentric Black racial discourse in Britain came to resemble its U.S. counterpart in the way it was reconceptualizing White values and identity. By the 1970s it was the White Man who was increasingly perceived to be responsible for any gulf that existed among Blacks and Asians in Britain, and to be the source of most of their troubles (Hiro 64–67). However, some Black and White British people joined forces to fight racism through groups such as the Anti-Nazi League, and youth subculture in particular sought to create a revisionist concept of Blackness and Whiteness to counter the dominant White representation of race.

These activities combined to exert great stress on both historical and emergent definitions of White identity. The strategy to consolidate racial boundaries by articulating emphatically the attributes of the "real" British or English national must be understood as arising in part from extra-White social pressures that were working to bring the operations of White power into sharper focus as much as from self-reflexive modifications. The quotes by Powell suggest that Whites were contemplating their own image and interpreting the material changes in their daily lives in new ways, alterations that they were attributing to the presence of Black immigrants. As a result, the White British subject that emerges at the end of the 1970s represents the product of the attempts at replacing the mixed-ness of imperial British identity with a renewed quasihistorical White Englishness and the negotiations this engendered between subcultural racial groups and the hegemonic White culture.

Whiteness Made Flesh: Edward Bond's *Early Morning*

In the theater, the question of identity after empire continued to exercise the artistic imagination as much as the political in the 1960s. A new generation of playwrights was building on the radical work of the 1950s to criticize established society. While Powell was engaged in wishing away imperial vestiges, radical playwrights refused any such forgetting; rather, they continued to recontextualize and refigure imperial history in order to disrupt its hold upon contemporary cultural practices.

Edward Bond is one of the most controversial and innovative White writers to come to prominence in the 1960s. His second play, *Early Morning* (1968), intervenes critically in contemporary debates surrounding British national identity.[83] *Early Morning* is best described as an episodic tragicomedy. In brief, Bond offers a revised Victorian age, one ruled over by a lesbian queen who rapes her son's wife, Florence Nightingale. Victoria's consort, Albert, is planning to assassinate her, and for this he seeks the help of their two sons, George and Arthur, who are Siamese twins. The politicians Gladstone and Disraeli make appearances, the former as a brutal trades union official, the latter as a conspirator, and Bond brings in the character of Len from his first play, *Saved,* here cast as Gladstone's murderous son. Most of the characters end up being killed by Arthur in a second "final solution" before ascending to a heaven where, unusually, White people are represented cannibalizing each other. The play ends with a parody of Christ's Last Supper and the resurrection of the murderer par excellence Arthur.

Aesthetically, the play was not well received.[84] It caused a storm of political controversy as well that began even before its premiere. The sexual metaphors relating to Florence and Victoria and the imagery of the scenes set in heaven provoked the strongest criticism.

Early Morning was banned by the Lord Chamberlain for showing in an unfavorable light two classes of persons about whom he was particularly sensitive: politicians and the royal family. The Royal Court attempted to get around the ban by billing the work as a club production, but when the play's premier attracted police attendance they cancelled the second, substituting instead a critic's dress rehearsal at no charge and by invitation only (Hewison 196).[85] Despite the brevity of its run, the play's startling content, combined with Bond's stature as a playwright, has assured it a good deal of commentary. Critics are divided over its interpretation: should it be read as a dream image, divorced from real social practices, or as a fantasy of Oedipal conflicts?[86]

Christopher Innes relates Bond's rejection of an apolitical/Freudian reading, quoting him as saying: "I am writing about the pressures of the past that are mis-forming our present time, and that's where it received its public image and its normative values" ("The Political Spectrum of Edward Bond" 85) Bond's keynote to the play states that "The events of this play are true," and the furor it provoked lends credence to his assertion that he is presenting a form of social realism.[87]

Innes analyzes the play as "a realistic demonstration of the psychology that perpetuates and justifies political power structures" ("The Political Spectrum" 85). In other words, Bond sets the play in Victorian England in order to illustrate how contemporary British society is governed by an antiquated and absurd system of psychosocial values. In Bond's sense of social realism, normative institutions foster a delusional state of affairs: "What we perceive really isn't a straight transcription of reality, and because people do live in fantasy worlds that is part of social reality. If we could understand our problems, we wouldn't have any need of mythologies and absurd religions to close that gap" ("The Political Spectrum" 85).

For Bond, Britain's contemporary social hallucinations can be located most precisely in its nineteenth-century imperial heritage. What I want to address is how the play opens to scrutiny some incoherencies in the imperial mythology of White British identity while papering over other gaps. Firstly, I consider how *Early Morning* exposes the function of White domestic ideology in masking the openings through which people might glimpse the irrationality of what passes for social order, a unified self, and a coherent national White identity.

Bond identifies the nuclear family as instrumental in determining social relations because it is the basic transmitter of cultural values in advanced capitalist societies. The common perception of the Victorian royal family, which has been passed down from historical self-portraits, makes them symbols of the solid virtues of home and fireside. Margaret Drabble writes about the way that the Victorian middle class identified with Victoria and Albert as role models: they were viewed as sober and hardworking, and enjoying only innocent pursuits (16–17), an image that the queen and her husband capitalized on to bolster her popularity.

Thus it was during her reign that the institution of marriage took on its connotations of sanctity, and the walls of the home became associated with protective boundaries that shut out materialistic, corruptive influences. Tony Coult describes Victoria's family and her society as mirror images of each other that also reflected modern Britain's optimization of the family as a unit of isolated consumption so that capitalism might run more efficiently (64). Bond invests the dog-eat-dog mentality of capitalist relations into the plotting and counterplotting that punctuate Victoria's family life, then makes this literal by having the family and court cannibalize each other.

He renders Victoria's iconographic status the product of Victorian "spin." By contrast, he represents the walls of her household as porous. *Early Morning* shows the chaos at Windsor Castle matching, and often bettering, the disorder that prevails outside its boundaries.

According to Richard Scharine, the play's central question concerns how the individual may preserve his/her humanity in a society that is alien to the human condition (92). This query is addressed through the figure of Arthur, whose eyes guide us through the play's events. For most of the play, however, Arthur appears as Arthur-George.[88] George represents the social self, the heir apparent of Victoria and the values she embodies. Arthur represents man or woman in an innocent state. He possesses the pair's heart and has the potential to be fully human.

Arthur's unsocialized self is seen at the least as troublesome by his family, and ultimately as dangerous. Albert can count on George to support his coup d'état because he is his mother's political tool, but Arthur, whose participation is needed for the appearance of legality, makes difficulties over the planned violence.

Arthur must find a way to function in a family/society where a father can describe his son as "peculiar about his mother" because he objects to her assassination (Bond, *EM* 147). Showing how Victoria's sons are being shaped for ill, which is already mirrored in their literal misshaping as Siamese twins, locates the opponents of morality and stability within the institutions of family and home. The hypocrisy and violence shown at the heart of this iconic couple's affairs corresponds to an assault also on family and home's modern progeny, the play's anachronistic references indicating an intimate connection between historical and contemporary understandings and functions of family life. Bond reevaluates Britain's Victorian legacy as the "muck of ages" in an attempt to expose and make fragile the reliance of modern constructions of British identity upon Victorian cultural ideologies. He does this most successfully by querying the inconsistencies in the meaning and possibilities of Victorian femininity as they are captured in the figures of Victoria and Florence.

Of the two figures, it was much easier for the Victorians to perceive Florence Nightingale within the terms of conventional femininity. Even though reservations about her presence among military men were expressed, as a nurse she fit neatly into the model of woman as nurturer/caretaker. Turning Victoria into an ideal of womanhood was a more complicated task, one that required a good deal of ideological manipulation, for her position as monarch made her a highly ambivalent feminine figure.

Even though in the domestic sphere she was portrayed as adhering to the narrow strictures of womanhood, as queen she regularly engaged in public displays of power that challenged those same conventional codes of gender. This required a carefully balanced double act on her part, the assumption of an identity that would enable her to exceed the proper boundaries of female behavior without overtaxing Victorian anxieties about female authority. *Early Morning* maps the discursive intertextuality of Victorian domestic codes, imperialism, and the signifying practices of White racial ideology by demonstrating how each extends into the discourse of femininity.

The play turns the idea of Victoria and Florence as models of White womanhood upside down in a number of ways. Florence is shown prostituting herself for empire—she aids the soldiers by having sex with them. Victoria's sexual morals and maternal instincts are compromised through her marital infidelity with a cross-dressed Florence, her manipulation of her husband and children, and her participation in their deaths.

Most importantly in Victoria's case, though, is the way that the White woman's social role as mother is tied to the brutality of imperial expansion. Not everyone in Victorian England was sitting cozily in front of the family hearth; explorers were busy taking advantage of the "primitive" peoples of the Indian subcontinent and Africa in the regal White mother's name. Albert's coup is motivated by a desire to wrest Victoria's empire from her: "I want to build. The people are strong. They want to be used—to build empires." (Bond, *EM* 141).

There exists an inextricable link between Victoria as an idealized model of White maternal femininity and Victoria as head of state or Empress of India. Elizabeth Langland refers to John Ruskin's comparison of Victorian women to "gardeners," whose tasks involved cultivating human plants not only at home as wives and mothers but also in the community to remedy social ills (77). As female ruler of a rapidly expanding empire, Victoria had a dual maternal function: to nurture domestic wellbeing within her own family sphere as well as the interests of the British people at home and abroad. The growth of empire during her reign contributed toward the material well-being of the nation, and in addition it created a heightened sense of complacency and condescension in society, especially around the meaning and representation of Whiteness.

The material abundance of Victoria's reign rested on a repressive raced-based system. Racial difference and Victorian domestic ideology came together in the language of the family. Catherine Hall describes how missionaries, for example, spoke of Blacks as "babes in Christ," children who must be led to freedom (237). As mother of the empire, Victoria stood as the White parental figure who would lead the "savage," by example and reproof, into a civilized way of life. Therefore, her motherly identity, insofar as it encompasses her as the mother of colonialism, represents an ideological strategy that relies upon maternal language to shroud economically motivated nationalism.

In *Early Morning* the image of Victoria knitting a union jack (scene 9), the banner of colonial enterprise, is a damaging discursive formation because it reveals how the aggressive impulse of Victorian, and modern, British society runs through and connects the family to the rapacity of national politics. The truth about the regime that molds White British identity is glimpsed through the opaque walls of the house over which Victoria presides as "angel," for like the heaven to which Bond sends her it is characterized by grasping self-interest, expressed most effectively through the motif of cannibalism.

The ultimate form of social aggression so often used to stigmatize Black cultures, the trope of cannibalism in *Early Morning* is used to interrogate racial stereotypes. In scene 4, where Victoria presides over the trial of Len and Joyce for killing and eating a man who broke the queue at the cinema, the practice is shown to issue from the highest level of White society. Arthur notices an affinity between the couple and his Siamese self; this leads him to become aware that the only thing proved in the trial is how the pair has ingested dominant social values. The difference between Len and Joyce and the royal family is one of class, not morality; the royals' higher status gives them the power to feed off others and get away with it.

This episode, in which the characters speak in modern idiom, illustrates how the postwar legacy of imperial identity is central to the play's meaning. The past and present are only slight variations of the same themes, according to Bond. The network of power relations in White-dominated society is shown to be structured in such a way that who can eat and who can be eaten, and within which social relationships, reproduces a number of imperial axioms within modern British culture.

Early Morning launches a damaging attack on the sanctified portrait of the White family encapsulated in Powell's discourse by placing a question mark after the humanity of the White subject. As I showed in chapter 1, before their encounters with White society Africans were deemed savage, culture being one of Britain's gifts to the "dark continent." According to Bond, however, these gifts must be seen to include the inhumanity capable of producing the ferocious destruction of Hiroshima and Auschwitz, symbolized by Arthur's wholesale act of killing in scene 14.

Bond magnifies the madness of a social order able to produce such tragedy in his version of heaven (113). It is structured according to the pernicious values he equates with consumer capitalism, and the characters, except for Arthur, are content in heaven because it reproduces the conditions with which they are familiar. These include the racial character of society.

The sign on the gates of Bond's heaven might well read "Whites only." Similar to the trial scene, cannibalism as a trope of British racial discourse once again gets used in heaven against itself. Before dining, Joyce inquires of Victoria the provenance of some meat. She is assured that it is "person," but Griss makes clear that what they are concerned about is the race of the meat. He wants a guarantee that it is English, that is, White, person: "I wouldn't fancy no black and yeller imported muck" (Bond, *EM* 203). Ironically, the perceived superiority of Whiteness creates a proclivity in the

White subject to feed on itself. Victoria can assure Griss only that it is British freedman, but because one's hunger to consume is never assuaged in heaven, as on earth, they devour the flesh despite the possibility that it is racially impure.

The incidents of feeding that take place in heaven, including the consumption of Victoria's son, point up the shared and conflicting ideological economies that inform the discursive formation of Whiteness. *Early Morning* displays White British identity in the modern age as an amalgam of several other ideologies: a domestic ideology regulating family life, a nationalist ideology with a self-justificatory narrative of citizenship designed to prevent incursions by the "other." and a capitalist ideology regulating class relations. However, while the links drawn between the values sustaining empire and those regulating domestic life reveal some of the disruptive tensions within the interacting sign systems of race, gender, and national identity, at the same time they combine to represent a regressive construction of female sexuality.

In the world of the play, the censor rightly considered that Victoria's lesbianism signified a "gross insult" to the historical queen (Kowalski 55). Modern critics have read it in the same way; Innes, for example, says that Victoria's lesbianism signifies the "perversion of personality by power" (*Modern British Drama* 166).

As mentioned, imperial versions of heterosexual femininity reside within a larger structure of binary oppositions that include Whiteness/Blackness, culture/nature, civilized/primitive, and so forth. In the Victorian era these binaries operated alongside a medico-moral discourse that related other binaries, such as clean/dirty and healthy/diseased, with the constructions hetero/homosexual. By leaving unchallenged the reasons why dominant logic theorizes lesbianism as a subversive agency, the lesbian subject remains aligned with the inferior part of the above binaries. In turn, this permits the act through which the Victorian hegemonic White subject, and its modern correspondent, validates itself as superior on the basis of its heterosexuality to proceed unseen.

This act involves locating Blackness on the periphery of the opposition between the normative construction of White womanhood and that of the female sexual deviant. Victorian race-gender discourse made a pejorative link between lesbianism and Black female sexuality. The connection was written through the medico-moral discourses on masturbation and the clitoris.

Ornella Moscucci relates that in nineteenth-century manuals of gynecology the clitoris in Black females was diagnosed as malformed because it was overdeveloped. This anomaly was read in several ways: as an emblem of the lascivious apelike sexual appetites of Black women and as an enabler of the practices of self-stimulation and sexual inversion (70–71).[89] Therefore, auto-arousal in White women was deemed unnatural to them because it was regarded as natural for "primitive" Black women. In so far as it was believed to cause hypertrophy of the clitoris which in turn could lead women into practicing an active sexuality with each other, masturbation among White women was deemed to threaten the whole process of evolution in White society.

Rosemary Jann notes that in Darwinian thought human sociability in the form of monogamous marriage was granted a monopoly on morality because it represented the conquest of one's natural, that is, bestial, sexual urges. Promiscuity, said to be common among "savages," was taken as a sign of inadequate moral development. Therefore, marriage and the construction of family relationships leading from marriage became central to defining human civilization for nineteenth-century social anthropology (81–82). In this formula, lesbianism threatens the basis of White civilization by endangering the institution of marriage as defined within patriarchy. Also, active female sexuality was believed literally to breed disease. For example, White prostitutes were held in the same low regard as Black women, both associated with a primitive, unrestrained sexuality that led to venereal infections.

Early Morning imitates this metaphor of female same-sex relations as a moral and physically contaminating force. The way it exploits transgressive female sexuality under capitalism in order to demystify the imperial social order closes a gap in the representation of White identity. The result of this closure is the stigmatization of the lesbian subject and the ability of the White hegemonic subject to double back and refigure its authority.

Consider how Florence imbibes Victoria's corrupted values through sexual contact: "I'm changed. Queen Victoria raped me. . . . George will know. I'll disgust him . . . I've started to have evil thoughts. Her legs are covered in shiny black hairs" (Bond, *EM* 154). The illness that lesbianism represents is marked upon Victoria's body in the form of shiny black leg hairs. Likewise, Florence physically mutates, taking on the appearance of masculinity: "She now walks and talks like John Brown" (Bond, *EM* 175). Florence violates further the natural order of things not only by turning to prostitution but also by usurping the rightful place of the patriarch in the family. As John Brown, she substitutes for Albert.

In scene 9, Chamberlain repeatedly asks Florence "What's up that kilt?" and then "Am I your type?" (Bond, *EM* 176). This could be read in two ways: is he asking whether Florence has been built for him or, given that she is cross-dressed, does he mean are you built like me? Chamberlain's confusion suggests that Florence's lesbianism destabilizes even presumed biological distinctions, and, as Moscucci notes, once these are rendered suspect the natural differences believed to separate the races, which served as the basis for the hierarchical ordering of society, could also be undermined (72).

However, this conceptual chain creates difficulties from the perspective of a progressive sexual politics, for it is only when she remains positioned as humanity perverted by the deluded values of capital does the lesbian subject possess the agency to disrupt the order that creates her. In this way the play replicates the silencing of both the Black and the lesbian subject that characterizes nineteenth- and twentieth-century race-gender discourse.

The play offers hope that after his resurrection even Arthur may become fully human. Florence and Victoria, however, are disqualified by their sexual perversion from full humanity. This representation of their sexual identity, by working in support of the White heterosexual subject's superior position, gives that subject a space in which it can repeat the terms of its Victorian history, including its fantasy of racial superiority, in modern White thought.

Bond gives us a double vision of Whiteness in *Early Morning*. The first representation reflects the way that those who aggressively and institutionally enforce its power would like it to be seen. The second, which is meant to undermine the first, shows us Whiteness in an almost irredeemably corrupted state. However, because the play's subversive presentation of White identity rests on reinforcing notions of naturalized sex-gender behavior, the substantial progress the play makes in subverting the White domestic and state order is compromised.

Legends of White Britannia: John Arden and Margaretta D'Arcy's *The Island of the Mighty*

The Island of the Mighty (1972) reflects the shift in the discursive construction of Whiteness that was taking place as a result of the loss of empire. The trilogy mirrors the debates about national identity that characterized the 1960s and '70s in Britain, and it captures the revolutionary spirit of counterhegemonic movements taking place across Europe in the early 1970s.[90]

Arden and D'Arcy named the conflict in Northern Ireland and their travels in India among the influences that shaped the writing. The way of life related in the plays, Arden comments, is "remarkably similar to that which exists today in the 'Third World'"—those parts of the globe that have been occupied and exploited by modern empires (49). Arden describes also being conscious, post-Suez, of the way that British imperialism in decline had much in common with that of its Roman predecessor (Arden, "Author's Preface" 12).

The trilogy comprises full-length plays, each involving between ten and thirteen scenes. Part 1, *Two Wild Young Noblemen,* features the tale of two brothers, Balin and Balan, who have been dispossessed of their property in an English raid and must now reestablish a place for themselves in the social order. Balin chooses to ally himself with Arthur; Balan, however, objects to Arthur's Romanized ways, perceiving him as an oppressor.

Balan leaves his brother's society, only to fall into the hands of the Picts, who make him their Year King in a pagan ceremony. As such, his function is to ensure the fruitfulness of the land by his death at the hands of the man who, one year later, will take his place. The brother's diverse experiences afford a number of comparisons and contrasts. Firstly, the spectator is given an unvarnished look at the similarities and differences between Arthur's Christian society and the Pict's customary tribal religious practices. Secondly, the top-down ordering of society in Arthur's world is contrasted to the Pict's communal ordering. Thirdly, as Javed Malick identifies, the brothers represent two different levels of political consciousness by exemplifying two distinct responses to oppression (164, 169).

In part 2, *Oh, The Cruel Winter,* the pagan foundations of Arthur's Romano-Christian world are shown to be still in force. Part 2 pits Arthur against his illegitimate and incestuous son, Medraut. Medraut has rejected the Roman culture in which he was raised. He aims to usurp his father's place and rule according to the revived native practices of his homeland. He leads a band of rebels called the "Hounds of Bran" in honor of a local deity.

Despite his allegiance to his native culture, however, Medraut should not be seen as a champion of his people, for he would make himself emperor, a title even Arthur declined. In any case, when Arthur and Medraut meet in battle, they end by killing each other, while the English, whose army has attacked them both, indiscriminately slaughter their men.

In part 3, *A Handful of Watercress,* Arden and D'Arcy explore in greater depth a theme that runs throughout the trilogy—the role of the poet in society. The three poets featured, Taliesin, Merlin, and Aneurin, each adopt a different position in relation to the political state. Taliesin appeals to tradition in support of the status quo. He is notable for his patriotism and Christian convictions. Merlin is Arthur's official poet and plays the role of a largely ineffectual diplomat until he is driven mad by the events surrounding his master's demise. His madness proves to be a blessing, however, for it is the means by which he is reconciled to his younger poetic self, the poet who was once connected to the people rather than to their oppressors. Aneurin represents the subversive poetic voice. He relates most directly to the people rather than to those in power. He may be considered to voice the playwrights' viewpoint, and he is the only member of the trio to survive at the end.

The plays are intended as a form of oppositional political action, which is reflected in their prefatory dedication "To Some Politicians of Our Day."

Kicking one another to the floor
(Year of 1974)
Neither Heath nor Wilson understand
Green fields of Britain were always someone else's land.
Eat the flesh of Irishman
And Welsh and Scot (and Englishman);
Remain eternally unsatisfied
Though for each dinner-time of power yet one more living creature died.
Hold up your extreme hands in moderation,
Usurpers of the imperium of this nation . . .

The reference to green fields and territorial occupation may be read as an implicit rejection of the belief that any one group is entitled to consider solely themselves to be full citizens of the British Isles and everyone else to be interlopers. The bracketing of "Englishman" in the poem signals how this class, despite also descending from a mix of earlier colonial powers, sets itself apart from Britain's internal colonized "others"—the Welsh, Scots, and Northern Irish—within contemporary nationalist discourse, even though these groups too are able to figure as White, at least in relation to Black immigrants. The naming of Wilson and Heath suggests that the desire to keep Britain for the British (really the White English) was not limited to an extreme fringe of society.

The poem prefaces also the way in which dominant discourse employs early British history to delegitimize the idea of the British nation-state as a racially and culturally homogenous entity. In an interview with Georg Gaston, Arden states: "I'm frightfully interested in the origins of everything that goes on. The origins are still with us. We are in history, we are part of it, we can't disconnect ourselves from it" (150).

The poem complements also Merlin's opening song in act 1 of *Two Wild Young Noblemen*, which sketches the exclusionary nature of imperial identities:

> O Christian men, are you aware
> How once an Emperor controlled
> The going-out and coming-in
> Of every man in all the civil world—
> So hard he toiled?
> Around his boundaries he set
> A ditch, a wall, a palisade.
> The wild men outside were kept . . .
> (Arden and D'Arcy 31–32)

Malick reads in the song the basic terms of the trilogy's overall structure: "Its opposition between inside and outside, identical to a certain notion of civilization vs. wildness, indicates the main theme and points to the conflict between the privileged rulers of the imperial 'civil world' and the 'wild' dispossessed masses" (150).

Similarly, Albert Hunt reads the trilogy as an attempt to "set the traditional heroic events firmly inside the framework of an oppressive social system": "King Arthur and his followers . . . go through their motions of heroism and chivalry against a background of peasant suffering and poverty. Their gestures need to be seen continually against this background" (158). *The Island of the Mighty* criticizes the extant social order "from a rocking and sinking post-imperial standpoint" by showing "how the early history of Britain foreshadows twentieth-century turbulences" (Hunt 49–50). I am particularly concerned with exploring the way in which the plays relate to the contested process of constructing White reality in post-imperial Britain, and the reciprocity they reveal between nationalism and racial, as well as class, difference.

The stories surrounding King Arthur make up Britain's national myth, hence their common reference as the "Matter of Britain." Essentially, Arthur's story refers to what happens in Britain after the decline of the Roman Empire forces the withdrawal of troops and administrators from the region. This is the matter of the trilogy, which tries to show the reality of life in sixth-century Britain. The overall perspective is Marxist; therefore, the plays are concerned most with the impact of post-imperialist economic conditions on the peasant class.

The trilogy works against conservative revisions of the Arthurian age, especially Victorian interpretations. Little is known about the historical Arthur who might have lived and reigned in Britain's "dark ages." Yet the influence of this figure in literature has been constant since the medieval period, and literary writers largely have constructed the modern conception of Arthur and his court.

Modern understandings of Arthur derive from the romanticized reinscriptions of material in early chronicles of British history, in which a figure taken to be Arthur is transformed from a military leader to an enlightened king and emperor.[91] The medieval French poet Chrétien de Troyes, and Sir Thomas Malory in *Le Morte d'Arthur,* add layers of courtly ritual and pageantry to the tales. The nineteenth-century poet laureate Alfred, Lord Tennyson, continues the use of the Arthur myth as a legitimizing device for monarchy in *Idylls of the King:* this had been begun by the Tudors, who traced their lineage to Arthur as the justification of their right to rule. Tennyson's version makes an explicit comparison between Arthur and the prince consort "Albert the Good." T. H. White's modern novels present a democratized version of the Arthurian world.

Though disparate on many counts, each of these versions has one significant element in common: it is directed toward a reader who represents the interests of the controlling social group at the time of writing. Tennyson, for instance, wrote for the Victorian bourgeoisie, and White's novels reproduce the political worldview of the modern democratic capitalist middle class. Hence, one way in which Arden and D'Arcy's version presents a subversive take on the national myth is by highlighting the effect of Rome's evacuation on those *excluded* from power.

Interrelated with this presentation of a history that reflects the concerns of the underdog is the reversal of history as an account of how order emerges out of chaos; instead, chaos is shown to result from the order of established indigenous cultures being disrupted by imperial practices. This is the Roman pattern continued by Arthur, a practice replicated as well throughout nineteenth- and twentieth-century British imperialism.

Commenting on Tennyson's interpretation of Arthurian legend, John Morris highlights its connection to nineteenth-century imperialist thought. Tennyson's knights are patterns of the Victorian hero, the man who is "just, benevolent, protective to his inferiors of any class or colour, *so long as they keep their station*" [italics mine]. Tennyson's version reflects his readers' predilections for admiring empire-builders as benevolent and chivalrous (119).

Arden and D'Arcy contest this view firstly by denying Arthur imperial stature. Reflecting his status in early chronicles as one of several warlords,

Merlin refers to Arthur as "general." Secondly, there is little to admire about this general. Arthur is portrayed as a vain, arrogant, grasping individual whose moral weakness is replicated in his physical lameness.

Depicting Arthur as a failed king instead of the nation's savior forms part of the trilogy's case for a new, socialist democratic world order. To those on the radical left, like Arden and D'Arcy, British capitalist democracy, despite the softer edges it achieved as a result of the postwar welfare state, is as inherently undemocratic as Arthur's monarchy. Aneurin champions the common people's cause when he states that:

The poet without the people is nothing. The people without the poet will still be the people . . .

. . . .

All we can do is to make loud and to make clear their own proper voice. They have so much to say . . .

(Arden and D'Arcy 232)

His words demonstrate the way that the trilogy reflects two seminal strands of British social thought in the 1970s—the perception that British society was falling apart, as well as the optimism among those on the left that the old social order would give way to a more equitable one. Its proclamation of insurrection echoes those being made by a host of progressive political movements in the late 1960s and the 1970s, when the country was experiencing a cultural revolution.

Arthur Marwick records the principal characteristics of what he terms the "high sixties," a period of large-scale social protests. Youth subculture becomes a significant force in this period. The children of the postwar baby boom were now the leading critics of the British establishment. They helped usher in a new level of social permissiveness in society, the "swinging sixties," which produced upheavals in the class system and in family relationships. They were also open to cultural exchange at home within a newly emerging multicultural Britain (*The Sixties* 16–20), the latter of which threatened to upset the nation's racial hegemony.

Alongside these progressive impulses, Marwick reminds us, reactionary elements continued to operate—for example, police forces, religious groups, the racist right (*The Sixties* 20)—and the early 1970s would be marked by clashes, sometimes violent, between regressive social elements and a plethora of oppositional subcultural movements. The trilogy reflects these conflicts, and it aims to replace the false but potent myth of England that characterizes conservative literary-historical representations of British history with an image that projects a radically amended future social order, one designed to appeal to the progressive social forces of the post-imperial age.

The way that Aneurin construes the Biblical Lazarus's resurrection at the end of *A Handful of Watercress* predicts an uprising by those excluded from the body politic whether because of class, race, or gender. While underground, Lazarus has witnessed the rotting corpses of those who were buried with "all the life inside." Cheated of freedom and a fair measure of prosperity, the people pledge to come back with a vengeance:

> And we are going to take hold
> So hideous and bloody greedy
> We take hold of the whole world!
> (Arden and D'Arcy 235)

Another way in which the trilogy unravels the conventional Arthurian legend is by restoring Arthur's Celtic ethnicity. By returning us to the Celtic roots of the legend, *The Island of the Mighty* critically intervenes in the myth's White racial narrative. The plays challenge the way that racial conservatives such as Powell were manipulating British history to legitimate White power and to exclude the racialized "other" from representations of modern British society.

It was not the case that the Tudors or the Victorians found in the history of the ancient Britons models of behavior and social structures to emulate; rather, they created Arthur's world *in their own images*. For the Victorians, this included their racial casting. In early British chronicles, Arthur was clearly identified as being of Celtic or Welsh origin. He was celebrated for defeating the Saxons, whom Geoffrey of Monmouth in his twelfth-century treatise describes as an "odious race" that were arriving in great numbers from abroad (Turville-Petre 90).

Stephanie Barczewski relates how in nineteenth-century Britain the Anglo-Saxons came to be placed at the top of a crude, biologically determined racial hierarchy, with the Welsh deemed a distinct and inferior race. This presented a problem for those who wanted to use Arthur as an example of the ideal monarch. If he were to function as a national hero, he had to be assimilated into prevailing ideas on race and national identity (124–25).

In the first instance, this was accomplished simply by ignoring his Celtic identity. Gradually, though, disregard of Arthur's ethnicity gave way to full-scale racial refashioning. By the second half of the nineteenth century, Barczewski notes, Arthur had been turned into a Saxon, taking on the fair hair, skin, and eye color associated with that race (153–57). The mythology of Whiteness here is used to buttress and at the same time veil a chauvinistic, xenophobic Anglo-Saxonism.

The trilogy resists Arthur's assimilation into Aryan racialist beliefs. It follows the early histories in positioning Arthur as a Welshman who defends the nation's borders against the English, northern invaders who are the ancestors of the Anglo-Saxons and who symbolize brutality and barbarity. However, Arthur's identity as a child of Bran is complicated by his identification with Rome.

Arthur shares the same ancestry as Balin and Balan, whose forebears were enslaved by the Roman conquerors, yet his assimilation as an imperial middleman means that he perceives them as aliens, as different from himself as the English. For example, he refers to Balin as a "stupid savage" (Arden and D'Arcy 55). Further, in the absence of the Roman rulers Arthur has risen to Chief Dragon on the back of his role as imperial go-between. His hold on power, therefore, necessitates that he decline Welsh allegiance. "We are a Roman army," he tells Merlin, and he wears the full dress of an imperial Roman general in battle (Arden and D'Arcy 33).

However, the truth of Arthur's family history cannot be suppressed indefinitely, and his liaison with his sister, the conception of their son, and Arthur's murder of all who know his secret comes out in part 2. We learn that, like Balan, Arthur has been made lame through a "strange ceremony" and not in battle as commonly assumed, but Arthur's saturation in Roman values, which amounts to an internalized xenophobia, makes him ashamed of his own people: "But by God I was a Christian and I knew at once I had done wrong. I remembered Constantine Emperor: he saw a sign in the sky, it was a Cross and he did conquer" (Arden and D'Arcy 168).

Arthur's rejection of his native culture leads him to become, as Medraut sees, a "butcher of his own blood" (163). It also highlights the relation between racism, nationalism, and class difference in Arthur's world. In the trilogy, conflict stems first from imperial social relations in which the tendency to articulate difference in racial or ethnic terms has been built upon the social divide constructed between colonizer and colonized.

The language of contempt used to characterize the Picts, Saxons, and English signifies the split within Celtic society that Roman imperialism instituted, wherein some, like Arthur, have been accepted as worthy to wield authority in the name of Rome while others are judged undeserving of privilege and thus relegated to the category of subhuman. In part 1, scene 3, Arthur and Taliesin discuss the threat posed by the Picts. Arthur assumes them to be harmless because they are "an enfeebled and poverty-stricken tribe" (Arden and D'Arcy 47).

Taliesin, on the other hand, argues that the danger lies in their cultural difference: "They are heathen. . . . And therefore by nature malignant." Their natural malignancy is proved by their "disgusting sexual customs," which "bring about the birth of a great number of children" (Arden and D'Arcy 47). Thus, they are to blame for their poverty: "we cannot ask our Christians to remove themselves from heathen territory! If they graze cattle, they also evangelize" (Arden and D'Arcy 51). In this way, the difference between the Christianized followers of Arthur and the other inhabitants of the island, which is constructed initially on class and national grounds, gets overlaid with inequalities represented as natural, racialized differences.

The derogatory terminology used by Arthur's adherents against everyone outside their ranks is similarly applied to those who would challenge him for domination of the island. The English invaders impose the name "Welshman" on Arthur's forces, which means foreigner or slave in their language. Ruth Frankenberg addresses how in the colonial context the naming of cultures and people was linked to the process of "othering" them, marking them as being less than the national selves who sought to dominate them. Those marked as "other" were named in terms that justified, at least in the minds of the marauding nations, the legitimacy of the colonial project ("Mirage of an Unmarked Whiteness" 74–75). To the English, the island's current Welsh occupants are not worth even preserving. In part 2, scene 6, Arthur interrogates a captured Englishman, who informs him that his people will be killed to make way for English settlement.

Arden and D'Arcy's trilogy illustrates how socio-racial identities in British history have been structured and revised as the result of multiple waves of settlement, forcible absorption, and assimilation. Its position opposes that of British racial discourse in the late 1960s and the 1970s, represented most notably in the racial language employed by Powell, which applied an explanatory framework to White identity that endowed English/British national identity with a historical and racial unity. In contrast, the trilogy refuses this retrospective construction of Whiteness, denying any identity status as a unique case—as self-constituted, insular, or whole unto itself.

The Island of the Mighty produces a kind of historiography that challenges what Dipesh Chakrabarty refers to as the "artifice of post-colonial history" by writing into "the history of modernity the ambivalences, contradtions, the use of force, and the tragedies and the ironies that attend it" (386). The plays negate the idea that there was ever a unitary racial or cultural impulse behind any identity that might form the basis of modern conceptions of White Britishness. On the contrary, the ancestors of modern Britons are portrayed as always having had intimate and complex connections to a wider imperial world, and external determinants have been as vital to the construction of British national identity as any ancient indigenous ones. In this way, the strategy to legitimate Whites' position and privilege in the modern social order through a nostalgic appeal to a collective historical White Englishness is undermined. In its place, the trilogy produces a conception of the modern British subject that would open the category of Britishness to a multiplicity of different socio-racial subjects.

Feminism in Britain: Black versus White Responses to Women's Subordination

The women's movement in Britain had several origins. It had links to the leftist peace movement, particularly anti-Vietnam and CND campaigns,[92] both of which provided models and theories of resistance, and it was influenced by the theory and practice of U.S. feminists. The movement also operated within a political environment where links with European socialist networks fostered debates about the relation between capitalism and women's roles in society.

Women frequently canvassed union support for feminist campaigns, but with uneven success, for like other minorities they were marginalized in most unions. Nevertheless, this connection meant that the concerns of working-class women received more attention in the British movement than in the U.S. movement. This is not to say that the movement was successful at bridging the class divide between women. If working-class women did have a greater voice, they were not necessarily speaking in tandem with middle-class activists. As Susan Bassnett records, the basic feature of British feminism was the local small group, which often focused on one issue (157).

This pattern of organization worked against the growth of interracial as well as interclass groups. Small groups tended to engage in dialogue with local authorities rather than centralized lobbying at a national level.[93] While this helped prevent the creation of bureaucratic and hierarchical organizations, it also made it difficult for women to liaise politically outside of a rather narrow local circle.

Even so, one can identify common concerns among British feminists in the 1970s. Movement activities focused on demands such as equal pay, free contraception and abortion on demand, free child care, and sexual equality for lesbians. The women's demands together reflected a belief that if their lives were to improve then the capitalist, patriarchal social order had to be transformed, while the emphasis on sexuality spoke to the recognition that women who identified as heterosexual held a relatively privileged position in society. Noticeably absent from the agenda was race or any hint that, like heterosexuality, it too conveyed relative privilege on some women.

Because Black communities in Britain were not able to marshal the resources for a unified social protest movement until the late 1960s, this meant that Black and feminist movements were developing side by side, yet discretely. The fragmented nature of British feminism, combined with the segregationist pattern of settlement common to most cities and the racism that was endemic in many unions in the 1970s, worked against Black and White feminists participating in the same local groups. Although many Black women's groups agreed with the White women's demands, they sought also to point out the problems they faced specifically as Black women.

While Black women supported the demand for free contraception and abortion, they pointed out that the implication of the slogan "a woman's right to choose" had a different meaning for them. The desire to limit the Black population meant that Black women might be sterilized without consent or offered an abortion only if they agreed to sterilization. Therefore, in its broadest sense the slogan needed to read as referring both to "a woman's right to choose *not* to have an abortion, as well as to have a safe and legal one" (OWAAD 145).

The authors of *The Heart of the Race* (1985) argue that it is impossible to separate an understanding of sexism in the Black community from its context in a racist society. Just as slavery in the United States impacted the way that Black women and men were able to live together, British imperialism distorted gender relations within its Black communities. The domestic arena became the only place where Black men could conform to the dominant male role (Bryan et al. 214). Therefore, Black women in Britain had to perform the same precarious balancing act as African American women, whereby they fought White racism with Black men while they also resisted conforming to Black male sexist expectations.

We can see, therefore, how the tendency for Black and White women to theorize and campaign separately led to the production of related but distinct feminist theories. However, because White feminist initiatives attracted more media coverage and interest from publishers, their ideas came to represent feminism with a capital F in the popular imagination. Consequently, Black women felt the need to mount an (ongoing) offensive against the exclusiveness of mainstream feminist ideas.

Razia Aziz defines the object as shifting the ground of feminist discourse: while "the adversary has at times appeared to be *white feminists* [it] is in fact, I would venture, white feminism—by which I expressly do *not* mean any feminism espoused by white feminists. I refer, rather, to any feminism which comes from a white perspective, *and* universalizes it" (70).

By treating White women's experience as universal, mainstream feminism in the 1970s produced a discourse that not only ignored the distinct problems Black women faced but also masked the role White women played in maintaining the subordination of people racialized as "other." Historically, White women in Britain have collaborated in the exploitation and subordination of Black women and men, both passively and actively, in a colonial context. In modern postcolonial Britain, White women's failure to acknowledge and act upon the way in which White patriarchal discourse addresses different groups of people in different ways meant that in some instances mainstream feminism actually worked in conjunction with these systems of domination. This complicated relations between female subjects racialized as White and as Black, and it contributed toward maintaining the system of racial hierarchy that afforded White women a more privileged position in modern British society.

Colonial Metaphors of Blackness and the Reality of White Racial Oppression: Caryl Churchill's *Cloud Nine*

Although Black theater would not gain a foothold until the early 1980s, White feminist theater-makers were successfully establishing themselves in the 1970s, at least on the fringes of performance. One notable exception, however, is Caryl Churchill, whose work had achieved a high profile by the end of the decade. Now accepted as part of the canon of modern British playwrights, Churchill began her career as a radio dramatist in the 1950s, and with the switch to stagework she quickly established herself as the leading socialist-feminist writer. Her work has been singled out by critics for the way it analyzes the intersection between class and sexual oppression, and the relationship it poses between social and theatrical roles and gender (Keyssar, *Feminist Theatre* 77, 94).

Cloud Nine, produced in 1979 at the Royal Court, was Churchill's second play for the Joint Stock Theatre Group. It developed out of a workshop about sexual politics in which the actors were chosen for their varied sexual backgrounds as much as their acting talent. Geraldine Cousin describes how the group used their own sexual experiences as the basis for examining sexual stereotypes and the relation between gender and social status (38).

In her introduction Churchill states that in writing the play one idea to which she returned was the parallel relation between colonial and sexual oppression, which "Genet calls 'the colonial or feminine mentality of interiorised repression'" (245). This perceived relation led her to place the first act in colonial Africa, where Clive, the great White Father, imposes his standards on his immediate family as well as the Africans. Act 1 explores the connection between the organization of Victorian family life and empire, or in other words how Victorian domestic ideologies of gender, race, and authority were translated in the colonial situation.

In the second half of the play, the action moves to London in 1979. Though taking a one-hundred-year leap into the future, the characters age only twenty-five years. The structure of act 2 is looser—there is no figure comparable to Clive around whom the action revolves. Also, here Churchill presents us with characters that are works in progress.

The characters in act 1 attempt to perform their familial and social roles according to dominant social mores. In the second act, they are in the process of rejecting society's view of how they should think and behave. Clive's family has broken apart, and each member is experimenting with new ways of living in the process of redefining him/herself. Clive's wife, Betty, has left him and gone out to work. Edward has come out, at least to himself, as gay and is living with Jerry. Victoria, though married, is having a lesbian affair.

Churchill explains that "having the historical first act wasn't so much to have a background scene saying 'this is how we came to be as we are'; it was more in order to show the sorts of changes that people even now felt they'd had to make."

When we discussed our backgrounds it occurred to us it was as if everyone felt they had been born almost in the Victorian age. Everyone had grown up with quite conventional and old-fashioned expectations about sex and marriage and felt that they themselves had had to make enormous break-aways and leaps to change their lives from that. (Fitzsimmons 47–48).

Cloud Nine has been celebrated for the way it takes on and revises conventional social expectations surrounding sex-gender identities. Critical attention has focused most intently on its progressive treatment of women and gays and lesbians, and particularly on how it uses the technique of cross-casting, both gender and racial, to disrupt stereotypes. Austin Quigley explains that by "setting the image of the actor against that of the role, [the play produces] a constant visual tension between a character's personal and public role" (33). For example, in act 1, Betty is played by a man to demonstrate how she is shaped in a patriarchal image.

Elin Diamond posits that the cross-casting enables the spectator to see what, "given racial and sexual politics, usually cannot be seen" ("(In)Visible Bodies in Churchill's Theatre" 266). Hence, having Joshua, the family's Black servant, played by a White actor enables the spectator to perceive the way in which he has interiorized the colonizer's view of Black and White identity. Despite generally noting them, however, critics have not addressed the play's racial politics in the same depth as its representation of sex-gender identities.

Clearly, the play illustrates that race, like gender, is a cultural construction, and it reveals some of the connections between dominant representations of femininity and Blackness that informed the application of colonial authority. Nevertheless, whether *Cloud Nine* undermines preconceptions about race with the same force that it undercuts stereotypes of gender and misconceptions about lesbian and gay identities is less clear cut. My reading will focus on the play's cross-racial casting of Joshua in order to explore the extent to which this theatrical device undermines or underwrites the dominance of White discourse.

In her seminal feminist statement "White Woman Listen!" written at the start of the 1980s, Hazel Carby argues that White women in the British women's movement are "extraordinarily reluctant to see themselves in the situation of being oppressors."

Consequently, the involvement of British women in imperialism and colonialism is repressed and the benefits that they—as whites—gained from the oppression of black people ignored. Forms of imperialism are simply identified as aspects of an all embracing patriarchy rather than sets of social relations in which white women hold positions of power by virtue of their race. (221)

She concludes that the "benefits of a white skin did not just apply to a handful of cotton, tea or sugar plantation mistresses; all women in Britain benefited—in varying degrees—from the economic exploitation of the colonies" (221–22).

By the time *Cloud Nine* premiered, Britain had shed direct control of almost all of its colonial holdings. However, it still benefited economically from commonwealth connections, and certainly the economic exploitation of immigrants from former colonies was in full swing at home. Therefore, Carby's observation about the social advantages afforded to White women is as valid for the British cultural climate in the 1970s as it is for earlier colonial periods.

However, the complicity of White women in the mechanisms of colonial exploitation, and the maintenance of White power in modern Britain, although implied, remains submerged in *Cloud Nine* by a feminist discourse that relies on a notion of universal patriarchy to illustrate women's objectification. While patriarchy is ubiquitous in both the domestic British and colonial settings, and there are clear parallels between the way women and colonized peoples are conceptualized in imperial discourse, there are also significant discontinuities between sexual and racial oppression. The discontinuities remain obscured in the play because the colonial setting is used as a metaphor for the way White patriarchy defines the role of White women and gays and lesbians. The position of Blacks in this setting is not addressed from their perspective but from one that relies on the materiality of Black oppression as a gauge for measuring that of White women and homosexuals.

In act 1, scene 1, Betty complains to her husband that Joshua does not obey her in his absence. The source of her displeasure is a crude remark he makes at her expense. Having asked him to fetch a book, she is told to "Fetch it yourself. You've got legs under that dress" (Churchill, *CN* 255). When confronted by Clive, Joshua insists that Betty misheard a joke he was making. Actually, he said "my legs were tired," which he explains as funny because the book was nearby and it would not have tired him to retrieve it.

Vron Ware discusses how the presence of White women in the colonial setting demanded that relations between Whites and Blacks be highly regulated. Within the dynamics of colonial oppression, the Englishwoman signified all that was most dear in British civilization (*Beyond the Pale* 37, 40). Nevertheless, even though Clive exacts an apology from Joshua for being impertinent, at the same time he accepts his account over Betty's, thereby casting doubt on the romantic conception of womanhood in colonial discourse. The episode ends with Clive winking at Joshua, unseen by Betty. Not only does this suggest that he is not very bothered by what occurred, but it also implies a false sense of sameness between the men. Their exchange of looks, which excludes Betty, makes her seem the victim of a patriarchal scheme in which a shared masculinity may somehow level racial inequality.[94] Clive and Joshua appear as two men united in their understanding that the "little woman" must be humored, and the act of pacifying her becomes a way of asserting their masculine superiority over Betty.

This scenario, in which Betty is positioned as the sole injured party of a male jest, is, of course, a patently false one. As the wife of the colonial chief, Betty is as much a White victimizer of the Africans as she is a victim of her husband's sexism. After all, despite his wink Clive confirms her White right to give orders to Joshua, as if he were indeed her boy-child, but the play fails to acknowledge that Betty is able to spend her days swinging in a hammock and playing the piano only because she exploits Black labor as much as her husband.

Sharing a joke with his White master does not produce any concrete benefits for Joshua. The reality of his location in the colonial scheme of things, of which Clive reminds him ("You know your place"), means that he must comply with any White person's demands. He is subservient even to the White children. Thus, in the end the joke is really on him.

Michael Swanson reads the intent in *Cloud Nine* as exposing the "dehumanizing despair of societally-enforced male oppression of women" (66). I would agree, but I would also point out that by ignoring the role of White women in the dehumanization of Blacks, the connection drawn between sexual and colonial oppression privileges White femininity. As Apollo Amoko points out, we are introduced to no other Black characters, male or female, although we are told that somewhere offstage other Africans are rebelling against the system (49). This absence creates sympathy for Betty's position at the expense of arousing an unjust amount of distaste for the sole representative of Blackness—Joshua—and thus Blackness itself. Admittedly, he shares Clive's objectionable attitude toward women and, therefore, he would be a hard figure to admire. At the same time, Betty and Joshua's relative positions in the race-gender system, whereby he is relegated to a negative passive mirror of White femininity, go some way toward explaining Joshua's hostility toward his White mistress.[95]

The way in which Churchill historicizes in act 1 the events that take place in act 2 exemplifies the way that nineteenth-century gender definitions and attitudes toward sexuality resemble contemporary constructions. The same cannot be said about the play's representation of race, though, for Blackness disappears from the play along with Joshua's character at the end of the first act.[96]

In scene 4, a break occurs between Clive and Joshua. Throughout, Joshua plays the role of informer as well as house servant, but this time the information he imparts about Ellen kissing Betty is too unpalatable and dangerous for Clive to admit in front of him: "Joshua, you go too far. Get out of my sight" (Churchill, *CN* 285). His ejection from Clive's immediate world means that he can no longer conceal from himself the hopelessness of his White aspirations.

I have already addressed how imperial ideology entailed the notion of an extended family that stretched across racial boundaries, one defined by common ties to the queen. This discursive link did not permit entry into the White microfamily in the colonial context, which continued to be represented as racially sacrosanct. Joshua, however, has completely bought into the myth, which is revealed when Clive's responsibility for the deaths of his parents during a raid on a local village fails to create a ripple in his loyalty.

Joshua's investment in imperial ideology stems from his desire to resemble the figure of the White patriarch. Although he accedes to Harry's request for gay sex, there is no suggestion that same-sex desire forms his persona in the way it shapes Harry's or Edward's development. To the contrary, he subjectively adopts a patriarchal White man's attitude patterned on Clive's behavior, and not on that of the homosexual Harry.

Except for the one instance with Harry, Joshua's behavior, especially his mocking of Edward as effeminate, matches traditional constructions of White heterosexual masculinity. This is due to the fact that Joshua wishes to attain what White masculinity represents in colonial society, to occupy a secure social position rather than one that might be compromised by homosexuality. His desire for White patriarchal authority, however, will be thwarted by his banishment. His separation from his subject of mimicry, Clive, re-places him among the "many bad men" considered to comprise the indigenous Black population, and his reaction is a new desire to destroy the order that he cannot join. By shooting Clive, Amelia Kritzer contends, Joshua signals the imminence of the end of the Victorian way of life (129), but an end that he will play only an inadvertent and brief role in instigating.

By having the actors double roles, Churchill enables the comparison between patriarchal and sex-gender oppression in Victorian and modern Britain to be made. However, because Joshua is played by a White actor who then appears in the role of a White gay man, the play does not contribute as much toward an understanding of how the repercussions of the masculinist order witnessed in act 1 extend far beyond the Victorian era for Blacks as well.[97] Modern representations of Black identity in White discourse can no more be divorced from past ones than representations of White womanhood or homosexuality, and without a clear and active presence of Blackness beyond act 1, an erroneous impression is created.

The disappearance of Blackness suggests that the relation between patriarchy and race in the nineteenth and twentieth centuries is somehow a discontinuous one. Also, it leaves the spectator with the disturbing sense that the presence of Blacks is natural only within an African setting, and thus it may feed into the idea that the modern British landscape is naturally a White only space. Furthermore, the lack of any character representing Blackness in the second act means that the contribution of Black subculture to the social progress charted in the play is not acknowledged. Only White women and homosexuals are shown as active agents of change.

Moreover, Frances Gray writes that cross-casting in the first act prevents the audience from treating characters as sexual objects, while in act 2 it leads the audience toward accepting them as sexual subjects, their subjectivity being achieved while they are still struggling with their oppressive heritage (54). The failure to continue Joshua's character means that he remains defined as an object, forever sealed in a White-defined Blackness. Lisa Merrill describes *Cloud Nine* as dramatizing the "evolution from repression to freedom" (94). However, because Blackness enjoys no presence in the representation of modern British reality, at the end of the play Blacks remain positioned simply as victims of an amorphous White racism, figures who never graduate to subjecthood, or, in the terms of the play, reach cloud nine.[98]

The presentation of race as a decidedly theatrical device in act 1 sets up the conditions by which the audience might critically contemplate the private and public meanings of Whiteness. However, this potential is never fully realized, because there is no correspondent demonstration in act 2 of the way in which modern cultural practices, both dominant and oppositional, also reinscribe White supremacy. Consequently, the manner in which the relation between colonial and sexual oppression is represented in the play only partially deconstructs the position of the White subject. I say *partially* because the absence of Blackness in act 2 leaves unchallenged the idea that the White woman and homosexual are as oppressed by the White patriarchy as the Black colonial subject, and therefore these White subjects appear somehow abstracted from the implementation of White power. Their abstraction works in favor of White hegemony, helping both White masculinity and femininity to maintain its centeredness, its universalist character. In turn, this enables the White self to reproduce the stable position it holds in dominant discourse—its protected cover of invisibility. Thus, *Cloud Nine* replicates the tendency of mainstream feminist theory in the 1970s to critically inspect sex-gendered identities while, however, reproducing Whiteness as an identity that is both everywhere and nowhere.

chapter 7

The White Backlash: A Second U.S. Revolution

The rise of neoconservatism in the United States in the 1980s entailed a White backlash. There was a feeling that White hegemony, especially masculine privilege, was at risk as a result of the social changes that had taken place in the 1960s and '70s and the development of identity politics among subcultural groups. Anthony Walton contends that many White Americans sincerely believed they had lost ground. Many thought that the American Dream was failing them, and they needed someone to blame: "If this country was once perceived as being rich, powerful, with limitless horizons, whose fault is it if none of that seems true any longer? Who has been the problem from the beginning?" (252). His implied answer—African Americans.

However, in the 1980s women and homosexuals joined Blacks as scapegoats, with the dominant group moving to contain these subcultural groups in an effort to resolve the White masculine identity crisis. The discourse of Reaganism played a key role in the reconstruction of White masculinity, in restoring, to use David Wellman's phrase, the "historic premium" paid to Whiteness and maleness (323). Ronald Reagan's rhetoric on the American-way-of-life, in particular, played a key role in refashioning racialized identities.

Political mythology in the 1980s recalls the Puritan mindset explored in chapter 2, in which Americans are conceived to be singled out by God. James Combs describes sacred and secular power as welded in the elaborate fantasy that developed about recreating a "Christian America," with an agenda to redeem U.S. society as well as the rest of the world (126). This power is envisioned as rightly belonging to White people.

Polls from this period suggest that a majority of White Americans accepted that racial inequalities still existed; nevertheless, they opposed government intervention to correct social biases. Walton reads this as indicating support for racial preference among White Americans—for Whites—

and he points out that the reigning political climate in the 1980s made it more acceptable for Whites once again to say these things plainly (256).

The philosophical engine that drove neoconservatism was an updated version of Social Darwinism. In his first inaugural speech (1981), Reagan stated: "We hear much of special interest groups. Well, our concern must be for a special interest group that has been too long neglected. It knows no sectional boundaries or ethnic and racial divisions, and it crosses political party lines" (Erickson 140).

Reagan echoes the ostensible collective voice that speaks in the nation's founding documents, the Declaration of Independence and the Constitution. However, as Angela Harris remarks, despite its claims "the voice of 'We the people' does not speak for everyone, but for a political faction trying to constitute itself as a unit of many disparate voices; its power lasts only as long as the contradictory voices remain silenced" (107–8). In keeping with White sentiment, Reagan refused to acknowledge that U.S. society in fact offers no level playing field upon which people of different ethnic/racial or gender divisions might compete equally.

Together with the religious right, Reagan aimed to return the country to a prelapsarian condition, what White conservatives imagined life to be like in the United States before the changes wrought by the 1960s cultural revolution. In his second inaugural address (1985), Reagan stated: "Let history say of us, these were golden years—when the American Revolution was reborn" (J. K. Smith 820). John Kares Smith reads Reagan's discourse as identifying a need for the restoration of a simpler life, but one that, in fact, people never had; as he notes, Reagan was oblivious to the history of slavery, anti-immigrant feeling, and the exploitation of women, among other institutional inequalities (822).

The new conservative ideology that would marry fiscal conservatism to fundamentalist Protestant morality was, like its reigning presidential symbol, riddled with contradictions. Reagan cultivated the appearance of a highly religious person, a man of compassion who was deeply committed to the values of family and community. In reality, Leslie Feldman points out, he was divorced, had a history of being a womanizer in Hollywood, rarely attended church, and gave little to charity (807).

No less ironic is the fact that many of the social changes against which Reagan and the religious right were reacting could be traced back to the overwhelming success of U.S. capitalism in the 1960s and its effects on the lifestyle of its principal beneficiaries, the White middle class. Reagan, however, seemed blissfully unaware of the inherent contradiction between the way free-market capitalism functions and the religious ideals he espoused.

Garry Wills notes that there is nothing less conservative than capitalism, so itchy for the new, which must raze in order to rebuild and which is detached from any moral imperative (452–53). Therefore, Reagan's social drive to re-create what was in the first place a mythic idyll of small-town Americana was actually hindered by his economic policies. For instance, Reaganomics worked against a return to traditional ways of organizing domestic life by making women's labor more essential than ever for the average family to survive and economic growth to continue.

In the short term, Reagan's supply-side economics created an environment in which a culture of rampant individualism could flourish.[99] In 1982 the United States began its longest sustained period of economic growth (ninety-six months), which produced nineteen million new jobs, most of them lucrative professional ones for White middle-class workers (Martin Anderson 38). It was never so good to be obviously rich in U.S. history as it was in the 1980s, the decade of the conspicuously consuming "yuppie."

However, for those who did not share in the newly created wealth, life was precarious. Reagan accounted for the discrepancy between the lives of the "haves" and the "have-nots," which might have undercut his claim that the American Dream was alive and well, by stressing that the United States lived in continual risk of jeopardizing its chance at the dream by straying from the righteous path—set by God and the founding White fathers. In his Manichean philosophy, U.S. Man was pitted against a host of internal and external enemies. Subcultural groups were stigmatized as culpable for a perceived decline in U.S. greatness. The old specter of communism was resurrected too, with the threat to the American-way-of-life posed by the Soviet Union, or "evil empire," as Reagan styled it, used to justify unprecedented U.S. military expansion and interference in the internal politics of other nations.[100]

Paul Erickson contends that Reagan drew on the Puritan vision of a jeremiad to account for U.S. troubles since the 1970s, in particular the loss of national confidence brought on by Vietnam and the Iran hostage crisis in 1979. This way Reagan was able to admit a moral malaise in U.S. society while portraying the United States as the greatest nation on earth. His talk of a jeremiad allowed him to locate the source of any sickness in modern culture outside the boundaries of U.S. Man, in other words, by scapegoating a string of "others"—women, Blacks, and homosexuals.[101]

The social identity at the heart of the self-styled "Reagan revolution" was unequivocally male, White, and heterosexual. His policies moved the nation away from the model of social inclusiveness that showed promise in the late 1970s and toward an exclusive concept of U.S. identity. An essential component of neoconservative policy in the 1980s was concerned with returning White women to the domestic sphere. Accordingly, programs like affirmative action that were aimed at assisting people to overcome historical inequalities to opportunity due to gender or race exploitation were redefined as social evils.

Equal opportunities legislation had enabled women to make tremendous gains in education and employment since the 1960s. As part of the project to roll back the clock on feminism, an image of ideal womanhood rooted in 1950s White middle-class America was promoted, along with a number of scare tactics to dissuade White women from pursuing a career. Susan Faludi explains how the mainstream media encouraged biased and frequently bogus social science and medical research in an effort to reverse the achievements of the feminist movement.[102] A "man shortage" was declared, and it was suggested that women who delayed marriage to pursue careers would end up alone, infertile, and miserable.

Another grave threat to women came in the area of reproductive rights, as the conservative-dominated Supreme Court supported a spate of restrictive legislation concerning family planning. It is in this area also that the difference in attitudes toward White and Black women become explicit. Conservative commentators expressed no concern about Black women leaving the home. To the contrary, those who received state benefits while staying at home with their children were singled out for criticism.

Rickie Solinger relates how attacks on Black mothers historically have employed tropes that draw on the language and concepts of the marketplace. They are characterized solely in terms of consumers, who produce nothing beneficial for society (300).[103] The cultural imagery surrounding Black motherhood was that of the "welfare queen." Black mothers were stereotyped as lazy, getting rich off the White taxpayer by producing large numbers of illegitimate children, and every effort was made to reduce or remove their social benefits, regardless of the effect this might have upon their families.

The strategy for controlling Black women was diametrically opposed to that for controlling Whites because, firstly, the privilege accorded to Whiteness generally in U.S. society meant that White women could pose a higher threat to traditional White masculine economic privilege. In addition, White masculinity relies upon a certain docile form of White femininity in order to secure its self-image as hetero-patriarch. Finally, Black reproduction is deemed a threat to White interests. This makes White middle-class reproduction essential, and therefore finding ways of compelling White women to again take up traditional spousal and maternal roles becomes crucial to maintaining White male advantages.

David Goldfield refers to the United States in the 1980s as a "colour-obsessed society," but he argues that White America was more selectively racist than in past decades. He cites the increased presence of Blacks in popular culture—the widespread success of figures such as Oprah Winfrey, for example—as proof of the way that class was able to moderate White racial perceptions. Because prosperous Black lifestyles resembled those of the White middle class, Whites could easily bleach these Blacks (282–83). However, White discourse continued to attribute the negative qualities historically associated with Blackness to the growing underclass.

The material impact of the Reagan years on the rank and file of Black communities left them positioned behind Whites on nearly every measure of economic and social wellbeing. Though constituting only 11 percent of the population, Blacks accounted for over 36 percent of the bottom range of income (Shull 193–96).[104] Hacker documents the unacceptable degree of segregation in the education system, with two-thirds of Black children in 1992 attending de facto segregated schools (167). Further, the Reagan administration's reduction in housing aid produced an increase in residential segregation (Shull 197). Drug use in poor Black neighborhoods became a scourge, and Black-on-Black crime soared.

Reagan fundamentally debilitated progressive racial politics in the United States,[105] and African Americans fared no better under Bush Sr.'s government. His 1988 election campaign provided little evidence to support his rhetoric about wanting a "kinder, gentler America." Indeed, it was noteworthy for the way it pandered to racism. The most notorious example was the Willie Horton television commercial, which invoked stereotypes of Black men as sexually rapacious beasts who would prey upon the female progenitors of White society.

Bush's cynical appointment of Clarence Thomas to the Supreme Court in 1991 also illustrates his lack of true commitment to advancing racial equality. Thomas belonged to a new breed of Black accommodationists. Having managed to rise above the general socioeconomic conditions that mitigate against Black progress, Thomas shared the viewpoint of White conservatives when it came to the cause of social inequality: if you were languishing at the bottom of U.S. society, it was due to your lack of individual initiative and not institutionalized prejudice.[106]

Unsurprisingly, relations between Black and White communities worsened in the context of a society being remolded according to a philosophy that tacitly licensed White privilege. This phenomenon included an escalation of hate crimes, with White-on-Black violence rising in the 1980s and '90s. The appearance of organized skinheads in the North and the resurgence of the KKK (newly garbed in corporate attire) in the South formed part of this deteriorating racial landscape. Norman Amaker identifies the 1991 Los Angeles riots that followed the acquittal of the White policemen caught on videotape beating Rodney King as the most chilling example of how racial divides became exacerbated during the Reagan/Bush years ("The Reagan Civil Rights Legacy" 172).

Perhaps the most pernicious effect of continued racial inequality was the "nihilistic threat" to the very existence of Black America identified by Cornel West. Nihilism, in this sense, he writes, "is to be understood . . . not as a philosophical doctrine that there are no rational grounds for legitimate standards or authority; it is, far more, the lived experience of coping with a life of horrifying meaninglessness, hopelessness, and (most important) lovelessness" (14). West attributes the origins of Black nihilism primarily to the saturation of "market moralities" in Black life, with the ascendancy of market values among those living in poverty resulting in a limited capacity to ward off self-hatred as they find themselves unable to realize the American Dream being packaged by the dominant culture (16–17).

The gay community, which had emerged as a force for social change in the early 1970s, was likewise targeted for attack. The gay liberation movement exploded on the cultural scene in 1969 with the Stonewall Riots in Greenwich Village, New York. Stonewall sparked the development of an organized movement that initially, like the women's movement, modeled its action along the lines of Black civil rights groups.

By the 1980s, Alan Sinfield argues, in urbanized areas, at least, the movement had made significant advances in challenging heterosexism. The "years since Stonewall have afforded good opportunity to those who have wanted to be what we have come to recognize as gay or lesbian. We have developed significant institutions and the beginnings of a climate where we may express ourselves without too many restraints" (*Gay and After* 6).

With the rise of the new right, however, and especially the Moral Majority, these advances were at risk.[107] As Leo Bersani identifies, although gay men and women had never been so visible as in the 1980s and '90s, their increased visibility was met with an equivalent increase in homophobic virulence (11, 15). The religious right was repulsed by the very existence of gays and lesbians in U.S. society, and the movement sought to eradicate evidence of their presence in the cultural life of the nation.

The Moral Majority and similar fundamentalist groups campaigned at local and state levels to have books about gays and lesbians banned in schools and removed from public libraries (63). Sarah Schulman notes also how gay and lesbian lives were held to be cheaper than those of "normal" people: many police forces ignored assaults on homosexuals, refusing to recognize violence against them as hate crimes (263). Further, conservatives sought to prevent the production of "perverse" art by pressuring the National Endowment for the Arts (NEA) to withhold funding from gay men and women artists.

The truly vicious nature of the campaign waged against gay men in particular is illustrated most clearly by the way the new right, both secular and sacral, reacted to the AIDS epidemic. Most politicians were content to ignore AIDS as long as it could be viewed as a "gay disease," and money for research into treatment would not be forthcoming until it became clear that heterosexuals were at risk as well.

AIDS was interpreted by the religious right as a modern-day divine thunderbolt, shot into the heart of the gay community by a God who was disgusted by the perversion of gay sexuality. Sinfield interprets the virulence of the hostility toward gay men released by the AIDS pandemic as proportionate to the success of gay subculture in gaining a measure of tolerance, and even envy, for some aspects of the gay lifestyle. Considering that traditional heterosexual marriage and family life had been in crisis since at least the mid-1960s, the idea that gays were doing better on the home front, especially on the sex and love question, began to circulate. Thus AIDS came in handy for "countermanding, precisely, any perceived gay advantage." Neoconservatives could use the epidemic to argue that "It had all been a fantasy—'the family' should set the limits of human experience" (*Cultural Politics* 77).

With the election of Bill Clinton in 1992, the tone of U.S. political rhetoric does alter, but the myths of the American Dream and melting pot in no way disappear. Like Reagan, Clinton promised the U.S. electorate a national regeneration. In his first inaugural address, he proposed a new "American Covenant," described by David Procter and Kurt Ritter as an "obligation to put the community ahead of individual aspirations" (9). In this way, Clinton's vision of U.S. renewal differed from that of his immediate predecessors, encompassing as it did the needs of disenfranchised groups. Frequently, however, Clinton did not possess the necessary political capital to push through social reform. He often wavered in his support of controversial changes, such as ending the ban on gays in the military, for fear of damaging his popularity.

Moreover, the right remained a strong force in national life. White rights continued to be championed. Consider the Republican's 1994 "Contract with America":

[T]his has been the most successful civilization in the history of the human race at liberating people to pursue happiness. There is no other society in history where as many people from as many cultures speaking as many languages could come together and become a nation, and where they could then be liberated to go off and be who they wanted to be. This is a country where Colin Powell and John Shalikashvili can both be chairman of the Joint Chiefs and nobody even thinks about the remarkable difference in ethnicity because they're Americans, and that's the way it should be.

That means we say to the counterculture: Nice try, you failed, you're wrong. And we have to simply, calmly, methodically reassert American civilization. . . . This is also a muscular society, and we've been kidding ourselves about it. . . . And so we have to think through what are the deeper underlying cultural meanings of being American and how do we reassert them. (190–91)

It is clear that the deeper cultural meanings are those of White America, which, because there is no level playing field in U.S. society, profits by a calculated blindness to ethnic difference. The "contract" disregards the fact that men like Powell are exceptions to the general rule. The majority of people belonging to subcultural groups do not enjoy the same level of freedom *to be who they want to be* as compared to the authors of the "Contract." The continued supremacy of White masculinist values ensures that those who, after liberation, might want to go off and be some other kind of American, perhaps queer, can expect to be penalized.

The document's construction of the "real American" places this individual within the context of a battle against a set of savage forces that would counter the right of *civilized* Whites to control the bulk of the nation's resources. When the values of multiculturalism are derided as the philosophy of "Live free or whine," as opposed to the muscular American belief in fighting to "Live free or die," this implies a core populace that is undeserving of the rewards of U.S. citizenship. The "Contract" contains an implied threat to lash out at anyone who would promote an alternative to the American-way-of-life. It warns that the price for those who will not or cannot be absorbed into the category of the *real American* as constructed by straight White men may be effectively muscled out.

Though the election of Clinton seemed to offer minority communities new hope, the views of his administration also signaled a clear change from any previous liberal values.[108] Eric Lott discusses the way in which the Liberal brain trust surrounding Clinton shared similarities to conservative ideologues when it came to race, for example by viewing "special interest" groups as obstacles to the regeneration of U.S. society. New liberal social critics urged the left to retreat from the "politics of difference," or "stigma," as some named it, and focus instead on economics (223).[109] In many ways, how new liberal ideology perceived the relation between mainstream and "other" social groups coincided with neoconservative viewpoints. Lott notes how new liberalism treated race, as well as gender and sexual, discrimination as a "sideshow fight" that distracted people from "real politics," that is, electorally based, elite-ruled politics (233).

Mainstream politics in the 1990s suggested that all the talk about race over the last twenty years had actually gotten in the way of solving many of the most acute problems afflicting Black communities by detracting attention away from the real source of social inequality, which is economic in origin rather than racist. This either/or approach to race and class functions to subsume race within class difference; in turn, this opens a back door for White interests to be re-placed at the center of political discourse.

This approach also ignores the potency White identity politics held in the nation's consciousness. Frankenberg catalogs the new set of false presumptions about Whiteness that came to the fore in the 1990s. While acknowledging White people as past oppressors, White identity politics suggested they no longer held any advantages because of the civil rights movement's successes. Now White people were in danger from the government overcorrecting past inequalities. White rights groups co-opted civil rights discourse, arguing that Black dissatisfaction, which stemmed from habit, hatred, or the fact that some Black people are simply stuck in history, had led to a reverse racism ("Mirage of an Unmarked Whiteness" 85). While these views are not synonymous with new liberal rhetoric, they encode a concept of national identity equivalent to that which forms the basis of Reagan's second American Revolution. Therefore, even though the Clinton administration did not pursue advantages to Whites with the same bald zeal as its predecessors, the social contract proposed by new liberals entailed a strong degree of White protectionism, a desire to resecure the advantages of Whiteness that had been to some degree eroded in the 1960s and '70s.

Postfeminism and White Womanhood: Wendy Wasserstein's *The Heidi Chronicles*

Theater in the 1980s mirrored in a number of ways the larger political and cultural shift to the right in the United States. Alan Woods describes Broadway as reflecting a "conspicuous consumption and ostentatiously public display of wealth" (254) that was in keeping with new right values.

New York theater was dominated by glitzy musicals that appealed to main-stream tastes. However, while many commercial theaters did increase their profits, it was only by inflating ticket prices and reducing the number of new productions.

The rise of the new right had an even more detrimental impact on non-commercial theater. Independent theaters were starved of resources as cuts were made to the National Endowment for the Arts. This made regional theaters more dependent upon private contributions to stay afloat. Despite seasonal subscriptions and corporate grants, ticket prices rose, making it difficult for any but middle-class patrons to attend performances. This financial straitjacket also resulted in a watering down of content. Theater managers proved less open to provocative material, because corporations did not wish their name brands to be associated with controversial subject matter.

Wendy Wasserstein's *The Heidi Chronicles* (1988) exemplifies the type of women's theater that was deemed acceptable for mainstream production in the 1980s. Described by United Press International as "a play of our time, for our time, and one that, in many ways, defines it," its middle-class aesthetics attracted paying audiences as well as critical acclaim: it was awarded a Tony and the Pulitzer Prize in 1989.

Wasserstein is a self-avowed feminist playwright, but the views expressed in *The Heidi Chronicles* fall somewhere between the liberal position that has characterized U.S. White feminism since the 1960s and the position of 1980s postfeminism. Postfeminist opinion resembles in many ways neoconservative views on women's roles, and the play's popularity may be attributed in part to the way its themes harmonize with the prevailing political climate regarding what women are supposed to want.

At first glance, and despite her background as a middle-class Protestant girl from Chicago, Heidi seems to stand outside the traditional symbolics of White femininity. Scene 1 introduces us to Heidi and her friend Susan at a high school dance. Heidi appears unusually independent for a teenage girl in the mid-1960s, uninterested in being the object of a boy's attention if it means leaving her girlfriend alone. When asked to dance, she refuses, admitting without embarrassment that she and Susan came to the dance together. Compared to Heidi, Susan demonstrates a much greater degree of complicity with conventional gender behavior, lecturing Heidi that the point of a dance is "girl meets boy. They hold hands walking in the sand. Then they go to the Chapel of Love" (Wasserstein 164).

Scene 1 sets us up to believe that Heidi's independent mindset will render her immune to any doctrine that preaches the catastrophic effect of women's liberation. However, first appearances prove deceiving. Even though Heidi's outer lifestyle never exactly fits the dominant image of ideal womanhood, by the time she reaches graduate school she and Susan have swapped personae.

Susan joins a radical women's group and takes Heidi to a consciousness raising session. Although Heidi professes a feminist attitude, it comes out that she lives according to the cultural cliché that a woman is nothing without a man. She allows her sometime-boyfriend Scoop to account for her opinion of herself: "I allow him to make me feel valuable" (Wasserstein 182).

Things do not improve in her thirties. Along the way to becoming a successful academic at an elite university, Heidi regresses into an emotionally frustrated woman. She still claims allegiance to feminist ideas, which she expresses in her working life through her commitment to women's art; nevertheless, without husband or children she finds herself discontented, and the plays hints that her feminist identity is the root cause of her dissatisfaction.

Heidi loses Scoop to another woman, who, he tells her, is willing to "make me a home and family life so secure that I could with some confidence go out into the world each day and attempt to get an A" (Wasserstein 201), whereas Heidi would be competing with him. She loses another potential husband when she refuses to give up her job to move to London.

Scoop consigns Heidi to the "generation of disappointed women," and act 2, which stages some of the scenarios that form the center of postfeminist thought, suggests that a majority of women would agree with his assessment. Heidi's friends obsess over the main themes of backlash propaganda. Betsy bemoans the number of her single women friends, for whom "there's absolutely no one" (Wasserstein 211). April recounts the number of single women she knows who are in a panic because of their biological clocks winding down. This prompts Denise, the group's twenty-something, to declare her intention of avoiding the mistakes that led the previous generation astray by having her children before thirty. These characters replicate the 1980s postfeminist voice and mirror the fact that the principle spokespersons for postfeminism were women and not male social critics. The mainstream media highlighted the opinions of a select group of women who, while adopting the label of feminist, actually promoted the same antifeminist ideas as the new right.

There were two main strands of postfeminism in the 1980s. One dismissed the need for a social movement dedicated to forwarding women's interests, because it was alleged that women had already achieved equality in the public sphere. Friedan's follow-up to *The Feminine Mystique, The*

Second Stage, revises her opinion of the women's movement, arguing that it has transgressed its original remit. Women now enjoy professional freedom, but they have become trapped by a prescriptive feminist politics that is as damaging to them as male supremacy. She colludes with new right efforts to reimpose limits on White women's social roles by warning them against falling prey to the "feminist mystique"—a set of orthodoxies about women's behavior and desires that encourages them to confuse equality with separatism and the renunciation of children (33).

Another strand of postfeminism argues that women's liberation has failed women, if not harmed them, by denying their essential needs, which are not related to the world of work. Sylvia Ann Hewlett argues that feminism has eroded the value of marriage and motherhood without providing the conditions for women to improve their economic standing. Moreover, by championing the sexual revolution, it has damaged women's self-esteem, for the concept of legitimate sex enhances women's social value in their own and other's opinion (51–65).

Heidi accurately reflects the ubiquity of postfeminist discourse in the 1980s and its power to influence some women's feelings and choices. The problem is that it fails to intervene in this discourse in any meaningful opposing way. The plot responds to rightwing antifeminist propaganda, and, on the surface, it seems to resist the push to force White women back into a role of enabler for White male ambitions. In fact, though, it supports the view whereby the feminist movement represents a well-meaning but naïve social experiment. For instance, Susan leaves the collective to become a corporate executive. She delivers a typical postfeminist misreading of the women's movement when she tells Heidi: "I'm not political anymore. I mean, equal rights is one thing, equal pay is one thing, but blaming everything on being a woman is just passé" (226).

Susan exchanges her radical feminism for a new 1980s brand of "power feminism," the incongruous notion that equality means women embracing the philosophy of free-market capitalism, so that by working within the system they might grab as much money and power as men.[110] Heidi backs up Susan's view that feminism got it wrong, complaining that it has left her alone when "the whole point was that we wouldn't feel stranded. I though the point was that we were all in this together" (232). Her response is to seek fulfillment in a woman's traditional role, that of mother; at the end of the play, she adopts a Panamanian baby.

Heidi's character offers more evidence that, while it may not replicate straightforwardly the postfeminist party line, the play colludes in yoking White femininity into a role subsidiary to masculinity. Keyssar calls attention to the way in which Heidi is dominated throughout the play by Scoop and her friend Peter. Heidi reacts more than acts in relation to the men in her life ("Drama and the Dialogic Imagination" 98–99). Her independence is limited to financial freedom; psychologically, she remains dependent on men. While Scoop acts as a barometer for Heidi's self-image, Peter acts as a substitute father/brother figure, dispensing advice and support and eventually acting as the intermediary who provides Heidi with a child.

As I suggest elsewhere, despite having a female protagonist the play's overarching voice, like that of postfeminism, is hominocentric.[111] For example, when Peter and Scoop appear with Heidi on a talk show, they constantly interrupt her, effectively silencing a woman's viewpoint on life in the 1980s, and the female host is happy to take the men's word for Heidi's opinion. The one time Heidi speaks in her own voice, her words are framed within the context of a mental collapse (act 2, scene 4); otherwise, her voice is sublimated throughout to a White masculinist one.

Because the play fails to cast convincing doubt on the politics of gender that inform the dominant construction of White femininity in the 1980s, it necessarily fails in the same way to question the politics of race. Whiteness is a constant unspoken component in the play's representation of femininity. *Heidi* is set in the staid world of solid middle-class White America.

In an interview with Esther Cohen, Wasserstein explains why she focuses her writing on women who inhabit this world.

And I think the thing is the women I write about are kind of middle-class, upper middle-class people, who have good jobs, and they're good looking, and there's no problem . . . they're not sort of working-class . . . there's nothing tragic there. And there's nothing romantic there. So I think that's why they're interesting to write about.

Because you can relate to them. It's like someone you knew in college. (261)

Sinfield alerts us to the ideological incentive behind this kind of normative cultural claim. Allegedly normative cultures and identities work to subordinate other cultures and identities: they are defined "as not special to a locality, gender, sexual orientation, race, nationality." They rise "above such matters, and by just so much push them down" (*Faultlines* 291).

Kate Davy identifies the intersection of class privilege as the site where Whiteness is fully mobilized for women: "The symbology of white womanhood is not that of the fallen, disenfranchised white women; it is at the intersection of gender and race with 'middle-classness' that white women embody and perform an institutionalized whiteness" (213). The play's construction of White femininity then allows Whiteness to claim the name of normality by assuming Whiteness to be a nonracial norm and the middle class to be a social group with no specific characteristics. Interestingly, however, in an interview with Jackson Bryer Wasserstein unconsciously admits that Heidi's White middle class femininity constitutes a distinct racial identity. Moreover, she testifies to its cultural capital when she attributes the play's success to the very fact of Heidi's White femininity: "There is a part of me that thinks *The Heidi Chronicles* was taken more seriously because it was about a Gentile girl from Chicago. It wasn't about Wendy with the hips from New York, even if Wendy with the hips from New York had the same emotional life" ("Wendy Wasserstein" 272). Wasserstein assumes that mainstream audiences have no interest in material dealing with women racially or ethnically marked as "other," in this case, Jewish. Therefore, implicit in this statement is the recognition that some women's ethnic and racial differences render them subordinate to White women in U.S. society.

The play itself does not even imply the recognition of racial or ethnic differences among women, and in this way it reinforces the domination of Whiteness as a discursive category. Because it is oblivious to the life conditions of any but White middle class women, White femininity is rendered the same as capital-F femininity. Thus, the questionable ethics concerning the way in which Heidi achieves personal satisfaction—the adoption of a third-world baby of color by a first-world White woman—can pass without remark.

The blindness to racial difference leaves White middle class women positioned above women of other racial and ethnic groups in the socio-racial hierarchy. Combined with its postfeminist subtext, which allows White masculinity to hold a superior position, *The Heidi Chronicles* reproduces dominant power relations of race, class, and gender and thereby works against a progressive feminist dynamic that might successfully meet the demands of the new right's backlash against women and ethnic minorities.

White Identity Politics: Tony Kushner's *Angels in America*

Tony Kushner's Pulitzer Prize–winning *Angels in America* (1990) challenges the demonization of gay men by the new right. *Angels in America* comprises two related but separate plays: *Part I: Millennium Approaches* and *Part II: Perestroika*. The first part, subtitled *A Gay Fantasia on National Themes,* is set in New York in 1985. I will address my remarks to it. The action centers on two couples' relationships: a married Mormon pair and a gay couple. Joe and Harper's marriage is a sham, a cover for his repressed homosexuality and her neurotic fears of modern life, which are exacerbated by her drug dependency. The relationship of Louis and Prior is also in a sick state, because Louis is unable to cope with his lover's advancing illness from AIDS.

Speaking of his vision for *Angels,* Kushner says that "In America, there's a great attempt to divest private life from political meaning," and part of his aim is to demonstrate how "our lives are fraught with politics" (McNulty 88). *Millennium Approaches* shows the boundary between public and private space to be illusory, demonstrating how changes wrought by the Reagan revolution impinge on the most intimate aspects of people's lives. In Kushner's words, it demonstrates how the absence of an ideology *is* an ideology; that is, the claim by Reagan and neoconservatives that they merely wish to return the country to a natural order of things, as opposed to the 1960s project of socially engineering a "Great Society," represents a dishonest attempt to efface a reactionary program (Kinzer et al. 211).

The play offers an apocalyptic vision of U.S. history, in which the history of Prior's family may be taken as synonymous with the history of White society. Prior's ancestry dates back to the early pilgrims who came to the United States on the Mayflower and beyond that to the Norman Conquest; thus he represents the essence of European Whiteness as well.

The familial history articulated by Prior's ancestors—Prior 1 and 2—is the antithesis of the liberal view of history as a sequence of progression toward greater human happiness. In contrast, *Millennium* represents history as a continuum of human suffering, with AIDS simply the latest in a long line of plagues; barring a radical shake-up of the way U.S. life is currently orchestrated ("The Great Work" to which the Angel refers at the end), the play suggests that the human condition can only get worse.

Despite the play's spectral elements, the source of decay is located in human agents. *Millennium Approaches* suggests that individuals both create and come to mirror the corrosive state of the physical and social environments they inhabit. Harper speaks of "beautiful systems dying, old fixed orders spiraling apart" (Kushner 1089). The characters are literally placed beneath a hole in the ozone layer, and they are fully cognizant of the fact that the natural world they occupy is on the brink of exhaustion. The political order too is rotten: "everywhere things are collapsing, lies surfacing." In this kind of acidic atmosphere, individuals' psychological systems of defense are giving way as well.

If, as Louis suggests, in the new century "we will all be insane," then we will be driven toward this state in part by our own choices. However, Kushner foregrounds the way that everyone's choice does not count equally in

U.S. society. A few possess the power to make choices that influence everyone's lives. These people make up the "White monolith." Martin expresses
the values of this monolith:

> It's a revolution in Washington, Joe. We have a new agenda and finally a real
> leader. . . . By the nineties the Supreme Court will be block-solid Republican ap-
> pointees, and the Federal Bench—Republican judges like land mines, everywhere,
> everywhere they turn. Affirmative action? Take it to court. Boom! Land mine. And
> we'll get our way on just about everything: abortion, defense, Central America,
> family values, a live investment climate.
>
> It's really the end of Liberalism. The end of New Deal Socialism. The end of
> ipso facto humanism. The dawning of a genuinely American political personality.
> Modeled on Ronald Wilson Reagan. (Kushner 1101)

By displaying the extensive tentacles of the new right power bloc, the
play tries to show that if the dominant culture is displaying signs of sickness, then it is the source of its own infection. Matthew Wilson Smith
argues that, although AIDS is never allowed to serve as mere metaphor, it
does "take on an apocalyptic tenor in the play, and becomes one of the
larger web of catastrophes that reads like signs of the Endtime" (154). The
connection between the ravages caused by the epidemic on the individual
body and those caused by the ascendancy of the Reagan right on the national body is accomplished through the figure of Roy Cohn, an obsessive
member of the "White monolith" who suffers from the same disease as
Prior.

The differences between those who make up the White elite and those
who are fully or partially excluded from it are explored in relation to the
dominant definition of a U.S. citizen as the end of the twentieth century
approached. Robert Brustein considers *Angels in America*, "first and fore-
most, a work about the gay community in the Age of Aids" (1191), but its
range is actually much wider.[112] It reflects on the power gap between the
"haves" and an increasing community of "have-nots" in the 1980s that included women, African Americans, immigrants, and the homeless as well
as queers.

Arnold Aronson suggests that Kushner locates the play in New York because, as the historical point of entry for immigrants and the place to go
for those who do not fit elsewhere in the country, it is "the place of the
'other,'" and, thus, "it serves as America's other" (1177). The place and
treatment of the "other" in U.S. society, especially immigrants, is central to
the play's critique of the "White monolith."

Scene 1 tells how immigrants have always often known America as myth—they came from the "villages of Russia and Lithuania" in pursuit of a welcoming haven for the poor, a new world where they would be allowed to comfortably melt into the fabric of U.S. society. In his eulogy for Louis's grandmother, Rabbi Chemelwitz debunks this idea: he says to her descendants: "you do not grow up in America. . . . You do not live in America. No such place exists" (Kushner 1088). The rabbi highlights the fact that acceptance for some immigrants and their U.S.-born children, even those able to assimilate as White, will remain only partial. Many from outside seeking refuge in the United States, like those on the inside working for acceptance, represent the living *dis*proof of the myth that is America, in so far as their difference(s) preclude them from approximating U.S. Man closely enough.

The "genuine American personality" will always require an "other," and, even more than Sarah Ironson, Cohn figures as the "other" who proves ironically that the United States still belongs to men who resemble Prior—heirs of the White European Protestant tradition. When Cohn's doctor informs him that he has AIDS, Cohn admits that some identities are a matter of choice, while others are mandated.

Now to someone who does not understand this, homosexual is what I am because I have sex with men. But really this is wrong. Homosexuals are not men who sleep with other men. Homosexuals are men who in fifteen years of trying cannot get a pissant antidiscrimination bill through City Council. (Kushner 1097)

Where one fits in the pecking order, then, depends on the labels that we attach to ourselves or that others can attach to us.

In the "White monolith," one can *discreetly* engage in same-sex relations and hold on to one's superior rank in the social food chain. Cohn's speech suggests that the tacit acceptance of sexual identity as having its basis not in nature but rather in politics does not threaten the positions of those on the inside of the monolith. Therefore, if Prior were willing to live in the closet like Cohn then he too might visit the White House, where President Reagan would smile and shake hands with him and his lover.

Whiteness, in contrast, cannot be acknowledged safely as a socially constructed identity, because the category of pure Whiteness is necessary for covering the inconsistencies and contradictions in the identity of U.S. Man. Accordingly, the attempt to disbar Cohn and thereby topple him from his place within the "White monolith" is not motivated by homophobic feeling but more by racial prejudice. Jonathan Freedman contends that the play maps the place where the figuration of the Jew meets that of the sexual deviant. He notes that Kushner does not posit a simplistic common alterity between them; rather, because the Jew and the queer serve as metonyms for each other, an interplay of similarity and difference is created (91–92).

Cohn and Prior's different relation to the "genuine American personality" is determined first by their racial identities and second by their sexual orientation. Prior's Whiteness means that he would have to actively dissociate himself from social privilege by openly professing a transgressive sexual identity incompatible with that of U.S. Man. Cohn, as a Jew, starts out already and immutably socially disabled. His Jewishness excludes him from the full privileges accorded to U.S. Man because it bars him from a secure place in the clubhouse of White masculinity in the same way that it makes him ineligible to join the "White Brahmins" in their country clubs: "I'm about to be tried, Joe, by a jury that is not a jury of my peers. The disbarment committee: genteel gentleman Brahmin, lawyers, country-club men. I offend them, to these men . . . I'm what, Martin, some sort of filthy little Jewish troll?" (Kushner 1102). Like Rabbi Chemelwitz, Cohn in his analysis challenges a fundamental tenet of dominant U.S. discourse, the idea that the United States represents a unique social covenant incorporating any and all ethnic types, by insisting instead that the United States remains a WASP supremacist society.[113]

However, Kushner points to some cracks in the façade of the "White monolith" as well. In one sense, Prior's racial identity symbolizes the cultural monolith of White America, which may offer a clue to why the Angel chooses to visit him. Yet the play mentions his ancestor's connection with the Bayeaux Tapestry, making Prior Anglo-Norman rather than pure Anglo-Saxon.[114] In other words, the monolith of racial purity that WASP identity represents in U.S. discourse is shown to be hybrid at its origins, and I suggest that this helps discount Whiteness as a unitary construct.

The play disavows American exceptionalism not only in the way it shatters the myth that ethnic difference makes no difference in contemporary U.S. life but also by questioning the idea that the United States enjoys a unique position in the world order. In the play, Harper and Joe are representative of Americans as God's chosen people. As Mormons, the pair signify the quintessence of U.S. religious practice and the link between the spiritual and political dimensions of U.S. life.

One could argue that it would have been difficult for Joseph Smith to unearth the Mormon's Golden Bible anywhere but on U.S. soil.[115] The success of Mormonism is predicated upon a long history of evangelical belief, religious awakenings, and millenarian prophecy in U.S. religious practice. In addition, by the time Mormonism emerged politically, the ground had long been prepared for the successful implantation of a faith that posited the United States as a New Jerusalem, a nation chosen by God and given a special mission in the world.[116]

In the 1980s the United States underwent one of its periodic religious awakenings, similar to that which gave rise to Mormonism in the early nineteenth century—hence, the rise of the religious right. The awakening was led by groups previously on the religious fringe. A. James Reichley records a sharp decline in mainline religious groups and a dramatic rise in evangelical and fundamentalist Protestant numbers. The Mormon Church grew by 36 percent, making it the nation's seventh largest denomination (278–79).

The principles of the Mormon faith—its strong patriarchal basis and its opposition to changes in sex-gender roles, for instance—melded nicely with the new right's political agenda. In the world of the play, however, because Harper and Joe are alienated from their religious heritage, which also forms an integral part of the nation's political inheritance, the special relationship of the United States with God is represented as under stress. The social order, as it is being refashioned by neoconservative ideology, appears divided, characterized by aggression and egotistical self-regard, and a long way from being "one nation under God."

Millennium Approaches places the United States as a New Jerusalem on very shaky ground; indeed, it resembles more the Kingdom of Ice, the "bottomest part of the world" to which Harper descends in one of her drug-induced hallucinations. In the tradition of U.S. expansionism, Harper dreams of colonizing this virgin territory, building a "city made of frontier forts . . . and bonfires burning on every street corner" (Kushner 1111). She seeks to replicate the action of the Founding White Fathers and rebuild the nation, but her guide, Mr. Lies, points out the futility of this hope: in the Kingdom of Ice there are no trees, no timber, only ice and cold. In other words, the seemingly endless frontier, that provided earlier generations with a remedy for ensuring the health of the U.S. White body politic has been transformed into fantasy. There is no twenty-first-century West available to conquer, no place where one might travel in order to escape problems at home.

Sinfield, in a comment meant to apply some skepticism to the play's political efficacy as a whole, questions "whether a State that has depended on extreme violence in its founding, consolidation, continental expansion and global hegemony can realize, from within the ideology that has shaped it, a future that will be harmonious as well as purposeful" (*Out on Stage* 207). His recognition of the nation's violent past is essential to understanding the futility of Harper's proposal for a new world order. Even if her vision were to materialize, given the way that dominant discourse works to mask its history of violence there is doubt as to whether her reconstructed United States would be much different from the one she wants to flee: "Ice has a way of melting."

The Kingdom of Ice as a metaphor for U.S. society suggests that the exceptional thing about the nation is not that it enjoys a direct line to God but that its Founding White Fathers experienced a fortunate historical accident. The colonists found themselves in an exceptional set of historical circumstances that they ruthlessly played to their advantage. Because these material conditions no longer exist, more and more people, including members of the "White monolith," are floundering without a clear sense of purpose or direction.

The Kingdom of Ice as a metaphor for contemporary U.S. society also locates the characters in a post-apocalyptic moment, and it suggests that the vision of society presented in the play is one in which the greatest number of people live in conditions, subjective and social, that resemble a hell realm. So we might say that they inhabit the end time rather than wait for it. In this sense a useful analogy may be drawn between Kushner's Kingdom of Ice and the lowest circle of Hell envisioned by Dante in the *Inferno*.

There Dante places the souls of traitors—those who betrayed family, friends, and their country—and at the bottom of the pit, wholly encased in ice, reside the souls of those who betrayed the divinity. Commenting on Dante's imagery, Dorothy Sayers argues that his choice of ice is meant to reflect the "cold and cruel egotism" that lies behind the act of betrayal. Such egotism "gradually strikes inward till even the lingering passions of hatred and destruction are frozen into immobility—that is the final state of sin" (275).

This comparison implies that, although Kushner may be happy to present the U.S. notion of God as a myth, he does not wholly relinquish faith in spirituality, in his case a humanist sense of spiritual meaning. The play supports the belief that there is a need to cultivate on a personal and cultural level a state of refined ethical inspiration. While in no way promoting the bullish religiosity of new right fundamentalism, the play does mourn the state of the United States as a soulless nation where "tears freeze," a place that fosters the appearance but rejects the substance of compassion for humanity.

The reigning political animal in the "decade of greed" is motivated, like Dante's sinner, by a cold egotism that makes fraught everyone's lives. Regardless of identity or place along the political spectrum, Louis insists that we are all to some degree Reagan's children, living in a "final state of sin": "Selfish and greedy and loveless and blind" (Kushner 1104). If "history is about to crack wide open" (Kushner 1114), as the ghost of Ethel Rosenberg announces to Cohn, it is because as a nation we refuse a social covenant where the needs of others would be recognized as *at least equal to* if not greater than our own, and no one, and no one *community*, is exempt from the spiritual impoverishment that results from the breaking of this covenant. When we collectively renege on our responsibility to other as well as self, we cede even greater authority to those who would write the social contract exclusively in their own image.

Despite his professed abhorrence of the "heartless macho assholes" with whom he equates Reaganism, Louis's own ethics make him complicit in the 1980s zeitgeist. When he abandons Prior, in his words, he falls "through the cracks . . . that separate what we owe to our selves and . . . what we owe to love" (1103). He attempts to forget his disloyalty and guilt through random sexual encounters, but these are meetings that offer him no real connection with the other person. Instead of warmth and communion, sex comes to signify a way of exercising self-hatred, a means of punishing himself, perhaps even by inviting death. Louis asks the character known only as Man to "hurt me, make me bleed" (1099). When the rubber breaks, he tells him to keep going: "Infect me. I don't care" (1100).

Louis's elevation of self over other is shown to contribute also toward the sovereignty of Whiteness. This comes through most clearly in scene 2, where Louis, Jewish and gay, ironically promotes the same "pale, pale white polemics" we detect in the "Contract with America." Louis admits the existence of a White straight male American monolith, and at the same time he tries to convince Belize that "in America race doesn't count" (1108).

As a Black drag queen, Belize can claim first-hand knowledge of oppression, racial as well as sexual. As James Fisher notes, as an out gay man and a nurse Belize sees both sides of the political and sexual spectrum (69–70). Louis, who might also know better, does not recognize the complexity of the lines of oppression in U.S. society, because he remains unaware of the extent to which he has internalized the dominant White voice in a bid to overcome the handicap that Jewish identity carries. Consequently, his meeting with Belize ends in angry denunciation: Belize labels him racist and Louis charges Belize with anti-Semitism.

Some critics have charged that Kushner offloads the burden of racial difference onto Blackness and thereby masks the operations of Whiteness. Jay Plum, discussing Pomo Afros Homos's *Dark Fruit,* in part a response to *Angels in America,* suggests that Whiteness is so pervasive that it is rendered invisible as a particularizing quality, and that the play fails to adequately examine the complexity of difference within its dramatic universe (236–37)[117]

However, one cannot ignore how Jewishness represents racial difference in the play through the concept of variegated Whiteness. Plum's reading, by way of *Dark Fruit,* which also overlooks the racial difference that Louis represents, fails to note the critical point that Kushner is making in scene 2. What the scene reveals is the way in which the myth of U.S. exceptionalism regarding race and ethnicity functions as a device for dividing people who belong to cultures counter to the dominant.

Framji Minwalla offers an alternative reading of Belize that identifies his pivotal role in setting out the play's political and ethical worldview. Minwalla places Belize at the center of the play's fictive universe, with Kushner playing off the other characters against him. Belize acts as an intermediary, linking, self-intentionally or not, the other characters to each other. Thus, Minwalla argues, Kushner makes identity, especially racial and gender identity, one of the central facts of his drama, for Belize "occupies that space against which we gauge the ideology, morality, actions—perhaps even the very humanity" of the other characters (104).

Belize functions as a prime vehicle through which the play demonstrates how Whiteness maintains its hegemony in U.S. society by denying its relational status. White identity is located at the center, with "other" racial identities shifted to the margins. Kushner, however, undermines the status quo by moving first variegated whiteness and then Blackness to center stage. Where Belize appears, the play privileges Blackness, and in so doing it represents the White self as a detour through the "other" and not as an autonomous or self-defined construct.[118] The play highlights the dangers to self and community when members of subcultural groups internalize the false promises of White conformity, and it undermines some of the force of Whiteness by showing the carrot of assimilation to be a rather hollow offer. Perhaps its most powerful strategy, though, is to refuse the White subject the freedom to deny its identification with the "other," for in this way *Millennium Approaches* limits that subject's ability to place itself above the whole of the U.S. community.

(E)Racing American History: Suzan-Lori Parks's *The America Play*

Sinfield makes the case that it is through stories, or representations, that we develop understandings of our world and how to live in it. These stories, which we use to understand ourselves, are not just outside us; rather, we have been and are in them. They comprise the material labeled fiction or drama but also that labeled politics, religion, or education, and these various but interconnected stories function to transmit power. Stories, then, are structured into the social order, and their criteria of plausibility define, or seem to define, the scope of feasible political change (*Literature, Politics and Culture* 23–25).

In an interview with Steven Drukman, Suzan-Lori Parks says that the starting point for *The America Play* (1994) is the false images of African Americans in White narratives of U.S. national life: "It's the story that you're told that goes, 'Once upon a time you weren't here' . . . You weren't here and you didn't do shit! And it's that, that fabricated absence" (296).

The America Play aims to displace the White subject that resides at the heart of dominant U.S. discourse in order to afford African Americans the novel possibility of writing into being their contributions to the making of the nation. Part of the play is set in a great hole in the middle of nowhere. The hole symbolizes the erasure or distortion of Blacks in White historical narratives. It reflects too the practice of denying African Americans a recognizable U.S. parentage, so that, as orphans, Blacks do not inherit the same privileges as the nation's White descendants. What they inherit instead Parks calls "The Great Hole of History."

In the play, the Great Hole is literalized as a theme park where images and scenes from U.S. history are endlessly replayed:

Ever-y-day you could look down into that Hole and see—ooooo you name it. Amerigo Vespucci hisself make regular appearances. Marcus Garvey. Ferdinand and Isabella. Mary Queen of thuh Scots! Tarzan King of thuh Apes! Washington Jefferson Harding and Millard Fillmore. Mistufer Columbus even. . . . Parading daily in thuh Great Hole of History. (Parks 327)

Una Chaudhuri suggests that it is by means of events reproduced in the Great Hole that the "indiscriminate spatializing of history—the leveling of difference by myth—emerges as the special distortion of America, whose endless frontier holds out the promise of countless replications of the original spectacle of greatness" (262). In terms of dominant logic, the greatness of U.S. Man can only be accurately represented by a White agent. Parks, however, casts a Black man in this role, thereby offering a subversive retelling of a pivotal event in U.S. history: Abraham Lincoln's assassination and his subsequent canonization in White stories about abolition.

The "Great Man," Lincoln, is played by a Black performer in the role of the "Foundling Father." Besides being a factual reference to the way in which African Americans were deprived of family life during slavery, the term "foundling" also calls to mind their dissociation from the political parentage of the nation's Founding White Fathers and other Great Men of U.S. history. S. E. Wilmer argues that the representation of the White Lincoln by a Black actor, who is said ironically to be "nearly identical to the Great Man," helps to foreground the physical costume and performative aspects of the historical Lincoln (446). The artifice of Lincoln's identity as reproduced in historical narratives is further emphasized by situating the Foundling Father between a cardboard cutout and a bust of Lincoln when he adorns himself with various props in order to become a "dead ringer" for Lincoln.

This notion of the stylization of identity is elaborated in Judith Butler's description of gender identity as a performative construction. Butler defines gender as a "repeated stylization of the body, a set of repeated acts within a highly rigid regulatory frame that congeal over time to produce the appearance of substance, of a natural sort of being" (33). This means that those sex-gender forms such as gay and lesbian identities that are held to be "other" to normative heterosexual ones are in fact "*not* as copy is to original, but, rather, as copy is to copy" (31). *The America Play* applies this thinking to racialized as well as sex-gendered subjects.

The play challenges the hegemony of U.S. Man primarily by demonstrating raced identity as a performative construct. The Foundling Father, also referred to as the "Lesser Known," follows in the footsteps of U.S. Man by going West. The Lesser Known's difference from the Great Man is represented through his racially marked manual profession, that of digger, and also by his need to dig for evidence of his own people in history.

While working, he memorizes a few of the Great Man's words, and at the end of a day's labor he stands in his hole and recites them. His early performances are viewed merely as a curiosity and attract few spectators. He enjoys more success with his audiences after tacking up posters that invite people to come along and throw food at him while he plays Lincoln.

After much practice, he becomes so good at his impersonation that someone remarks "he played Lincoln so well that he ought to be shot" (Parks 312), suggesting that his imitation is both accurate and, for this reason, very unnerving. Ignoring the spectator's wariness at witnessing a Black person impersonate a White U.S. president, the Lesser Known takes the comment literally and changes his act. He seats himself in a box and invites the public, for a penny, to enter and reenact the fatal shooting of Lincoln, and he becomes "famous overnight."

The repetition of Lincoln's shooting is a strategy for revealing the persistent instability and unreliability of dominant historical narratives and for enabling the expression of alternative Black subjects in the national story. The tale of Lincoln's death is never told in the same way. For example, different actors (male and female) play Booth and shout different expressions of victory, "Thus to the tyrants!" or other times "The South is avenged!" (Parks 320–21), and the Foundling Father's reaction differs slightly each time too.

Writing of repetition as a practice and strategy as opposed to an incognizant act, Trinh T. Minh-Ha states:

> Repetition as . . . a strategy . . . bears within it the seeds of transformation. When repetition calls attention on itself as repetition, it can no longer be reduced to connote sameness and stagnancy as it usually does. . . . When repetition reflects on itself as repetition, it constitutes this doubling back movement through which language . . . looks at itself exerting power and, therefore, creates for itself possibilities to repeatedly thwart its own power, inflating it only to deflate it better. (190)

> Repetition sets up expectations and baffles them at both regular and irregular intervals. It draws attention, not to the object (word, image or sound), but to what lies between them. (191)

In this sense, *The America Play* is not merely restaging history; rather, it is intervening in the process by which history is created. The Foundling Father is engaged in remaking history with a Black presence and, in the process, remaking Whiteness by denying its authenticity and supposed ahistorical character.

That the Foundling Father can make up such a convincing Mr. Lincoln foregrounds the theatricality of identity itself, specifically here White identity. His success points up how U.S. Man has gained the appearance of a naturalized entity because of its repeated invocation over a long period of time. Therefore, the relation posited between the White Lincoln offstage in history and the Whiteface Lincoln onstage is not one of difference between an original and its reproduction; instead, both are shown to be performative instances of the larger cultural discourse of race.

The ideal figure of U.S. citizenship, that is, the White male subject, is shown in the play to have its genesis in the social sphere of language, not nature, and a language that furthermore may be appropriated for subversive use by a host of different race-gendered subjects. This is evidenced by those instances where Lucy, the Foundling Father's wife, repeats her husband's rendition of Lincoln's words: "He'd say: 'Uh house divided cannot stand!' He'd say: '4 score and 7 years uhgoh.' Say: 'Of thuh people by thuh people and for thuh people.' Say: 'Malice toward none and charity toward all'" (Parks 338).

June Jordan sums up the sociopolitical imperative for Black Americans to adopt White English: "literally accept the terms of the oppressor, or perish: that is the irreducible, horrifying truth of the politics of language" (35). Parks, however, refuses this imperative in an attempt to open up the possibility for a Black play on White discourse that does not reinforce White cultural authority but displaces and deconstructs it. She couches this attempt in Black Vernacular English (BVE).

Writing of Black literary discourse, Henry Louis Gates Jr. describes its characteristic practice of signifyin(g). By this he means that although BVE seems to inhabit White discourse it does so only to disrupt its authority by means of inserting into it a double-voice (*The Signifying Monkey* 44). In the same way that signifyin(g) in BVE is audibly different from the received White pronunciation of "signifying," the meaning denoted by signifyin(g) carries a Black, oppositional difference.

Thus, Lucy's repetition of the Foundling Father's repetition of Lincoln's political truisms calls into question the reliability of the White story. Moreover, the repetition of Lincoln's story (in tandem with Parks's treatment of stage space, costume, and props) does not only further underscore the performativity and instability of raced identities. When Lucy "speeches" the Foundling Father's "speeches" of Lincoln's words and the Foundling Father plays and replays Lincoln's dying, what they are signifyin(g) is that the greatness of U.S. Man and the coherence of the White subject both represent fictional narratives.

The play makes the White subject appear as a very mixed bag of goods. In act 2 Lucy and Brazil conduct a group of visitors through the Hall of Wonders, which contains the debris of U.S. history: "Mr Washingtons bones," his wooden teeth, "uh bust of Mr Lincoln carved of marble lookin like he looked in life," "Uh glass tradin bead," "peace pacts," "freein papers," and so forth (Parks 332–33). These are the tools from which Great White men are crafted in myth.

Parks, though, as Minh-Ha suggests, cites these tools only to use them in a different way, that is, to displace their dominant prescribed function. She shows a self-conscious awareness of how the theater she makes forms part of the discursive social apparatus that precedes and enables the subject—White and/or Black. Hence, the Black or White self is never merely reflected back to the spectator. In viewing Parks's racialized subjects it should be understood that the spectator is being spoken *by* that representation in performance as much as spoken *to*.

Michael Eric Dyson argues that White people live in the "United States of Amnesia":

We've got to revoke our citizenship in the State of Denial. That's an extraordinarily disconcerting process, partly because what is demanded is the rejection of a key premise of liberal racial discourse: Whites, Blacks, and others share a common moral conception of racial justice, an ideal that regulates social practice and promotes the resolution of racial disputes. The politics and history of race have not supported this belief. To shift metaphors, what we've got to do is graft the skin of racial memory to the body of American democracy. (Chennault 312)

The America Play represents a postmodern attempt to regraft African Americans onto U.S. political and cultural life, both historically and in contemporary terms. Its strategy of resistance involves demonstrating how White hegemony uses its power to enforce what gets transmitted as history, which then determines what and who gets forgotten in the present as well as the past. As Chaudhuri notes, "every repetition of one of history's privileged textual fragments rewrites the meaning, the substance and affect, of that fragment" for the spectator (265). Parks not only exposes the White subject in its history as an ideological construct but also appropriates the textual fragments of White history in order to create a new Black-informed narrative that might widen the scope of feasible political change.

chapter 8

"Swamped by People with a Different Culture": Race, Sexuality, and the Active British Citizen

The British Conservative Party's victory in 1979, which saw Margaret Thatcher become the first woman prime minister, was fueled in part by its leaders' talent for exploiting the appeal of imperial nostalgia in a way that often cut across class divides. Thatcher's rhetoric leading up to and after the War in the Falklands is exemplary of this. It brings together three themes that resonated in 1980s popular political discourse—imperialism, nationalism, and race. Before the war, Thatcher declared:

> What has happened is that now once again Britain is not prepared to be pushed around. We have ceased to be a nation in retreat. We have instead a new-found confidence—born in economic battles at home and tested and found true 8,000 miles away. That confidence comes from the rediscovery of ourselves and grows with the recovery of our self-respect. (Gilroy, *There Ain't no Black* 51)

Paul Gilroy interprets the background to these comments as the problems associated with Black settlement at home, a prime battleground for disputes over national identity in 1980s Britain. He notes the rich irony in the contrast between the intimacy of the "natural" relationship with people eight thousand miles away and the perception of the alien intruders on British soil who persisted in disrupting life at home (*There Ain't no Black* 51).

D. Keith Peacock remarks on the anachronistic portrayal of the war in the press, which frequently recalled Victorian imperial excursions (18). This provided Thatcher with the opportunity to represent herself as a modern day heroic Britannia—a symbol of the best of Britishness. After taking the salute at the victory parade for the Falklands soldiers (a role usually played by the queen), she remarked: "What a wonderful parade it has been, surpassing all our expectations as the crowd, deeply moved and sensing the spirit of the occasion, accompanied the band by singing 'Rule Britannia'" (Peacock 19).

Despite her infamous denial of the existence of society, a position that suited her agenda for removing social welfare provision from the realm of government, Thatcher's rhetoric consistently revealed a belief in a trans-historical and collective national identity. This identity had been forged in the production of empire, and it had Whiteness and heterosexuality at its center.

Thatcher believed that the decline in British national prestige, as well as many of its social and economic ills, could be traced to the amorality fostered in the 1960s and '70s. In 1982 she lamented that there had been "no riposte, no reply" to the enemies of "traditional values" who had been allowed to gather strength since the 1960s. "The time for counter-attack is long overdue," she declared,[119] and her time in power was spent working to silence the "enemies within," those who did not live up to the ideal of true Britishness.

Alan Sinfield points out that homosexuals represented the "quintessential enemy within" for the Conservative Party. Unlike Black Britons, they could not be told to go back where they came from, for they emanated from within the center itself. He notes that while ethnicity is transmitted usually through family and lineage, most gays and lesbians are born and/or socialized into heterosexual families, a model from which they consciously move away ("Queer Identities and the Ethnicity Model" 201–2). This contributes to the representation in dominant sexual discourse of the homosexual as a dangerous seducer, one who might lure the "normal" into his/her web and spread homosexuality through social movements.

The British gay rights movement emerged in the early 1970s. It was influenced by its trans-Atlantic counterpart as well as other contemporary social movements for women's and Black's rights. As more people became open about their sexuality, it became easier for others to do so, at least in metropolitan areas, where an expanded and visible gay subculture was rapidly developing. While many of the movement's practical demands were being met on only a partial level, and informally rather than through legal reform, when Thatcher came to power gays and lesbians were enjoying new freedoms and a new measure of self-respect. It was the expression of gay pride, and the claim that gay lifestyles were due the same respect and equal treatment as traditional heterosexual arrangements that so disturbed sexual conservatives in the 1980s.[120] As a result, gay subculture came in for sustained attack by the government.

In 1988, Section 28 of the Local Government Act was passed, which made it illegal to use public monies to "intentionally promote homosexuality" or to "promote the teaching in any maintained school of the acceptability of homosexuality as a pretended family relationship." Madeleine Colvin and Jane Hawksley explain the implications of the law as giving important constitutional legitimacy to greater hostility toward and intolerance of gays and lesbians (61). Prejudice against gays became acute with the emergence of AIDS. The disease was represented in the popular press and by some in government as a "gay plague" and the fault of homosexuals themselves. The chief constable of Manchester, a city with a substantial gay population, went on record in *The Daily Express* (December 12, 1986) with his belief that if gays were dying then it resulted from the degenerate behavior of "people swirling around in a human cesspit of their own making" (Durham 123). Such attacks impacted strongly, both negatively and positively, on the gay community.

Despite the gay liberation movement, there remained a substantial number of people who were still at least partially closeted about their sexual identity. Anna Marie Smith identifies an anti-queer backlash within the gay community among those who thought it best to assimilate quietly into the mainstream (235). However, the majority refused to be pushed back into the closet, with Section 28 helping to mobilize their activism.

Ironically, Smith points out, on one level Thatcher's anti-gay campaign produced the very effect it was designed to eliminate, namely the publication of homosexuality. She quotes an open letter to Thatcher from a member of the Gay and Lesbian Youth Federation (GLYF) that congratulates her for "pulling the lesbian and gay community together in a way never before imagined" and "most of all for promoting homosexuality more widely and more efficiently than we could have ever done ourselves" (234).

The representation of homosexuality as repugnant and threatening was in line with a more generalized increased fear of difference in mainstream society. Consider Paul Johnson's advice to homosexual leaders cautioning that instead of seeking equality they should "keep their heads down" (Eric Evans 128), for he considered that tolerance of people who differed from the British norm can only exist when disgust is kept at bay.[121] The presence of Blacks in Britain, whether immigrants or British-born, was viewed in a similar way, if not with outright repugnance then certainly with a great deal of concern.

The message to Black communities was that small numbers of them could expect tolerance, but only if they did not seek to alter British social practices—in effect, resist the historically embedded processes of racism. Thatcher's rise to power was helped by her willingness to exploit racial prejudice, especially hostility toward new immigrants.[122] In a 1978 interview on *World in Action* she explained her views on immigration:

If we went on as we are then by the end of this century there would be four million people of the New Commonwealth or Pakistan here. Now I think that is an awful lot and I think it means that people are really rather afraid that this country might be rather swamped by people with a different culture, and you know, the British character has done so much for democracy, for law and order, and so much throughout the world that if there is any fear that it might be swamped, people are going to react and be hostile to those coming in. (Krieger 76)

There is a clear continuity here with Powell's "Rivers of Blood" speech. Like him, Thatcher identifies Black people as a kind of social infection that must be kept out, or they will bring chaos into the lives of the naturally law-abiding and orderly White populace. Moreover, she absolves the White British of responsibility for racial prejudice, characterizing them as a benign, benevolent lot whose dedication to the virtues of democracy and fairness is demonstrated, paradoxically, in the history of empire.[123] This makes Black people the guilty ones: if they experience racism, they only bring it on themselves by virtue of being where they do not belong or asking for privileges to which they are not entitled.

Stephen Small, commenting on reverse racism, argues that conservative rhetoric positioned Whites as the victims of misguided social engineering; it was inferred that over time multiculturalism in education, and gay and Black liberation campaigns, had eroded the rights of *real* Britons (93). Thatcher couched her opposition to radical social movements in the language of common sense. She excelled at presenting her ideas as unencumbered by ideology, and throughout her tenure she would claim to speak for "Little England," that silent majority of White Britons whose interests Powell had sought to protect.

She could in fact make this claim with some accuracy, as her views resonated with a significant number of White voters. Joel Krieger notes that her popularity increased by 11 % after her *World in Action* remarks. A follow-up Gallup poll found that 70 % of those interviewed approved of her viewpoint (77). Thatcher's three successive election victories, two of them by large majorities, meant that her regressive views on race would form a refrain to the political program in the 1980s and into the '90s.

Whereas past institutional structures of racism relied on biology to argue for social hierarchy, following Powell, racism in the 1980s was organized primarily on culturalist grounds. Cultural racism was based on a belief that certain nations have authentic histories with discrete cultural fillings. Paul Gilroy explains that this homogeneity was held to endow them with great strength and prestige. Therefore, where large "indigestible" chunks of alien settlement had taken place all manner of dangers were feared, and "conflict was visible, above all, along cultural lines" (*Against*

Race 32). This is evident in the "cricket test" Norman Tebbitt advocated for Asians in Britain. This test linked their national loyalty to the team they supported, warning that "where you have a clash of history, a clash of religion, a clash of race, then it is all too easy for there to be an actual clash of violence" (Foley 75).

Even with this revised culturalist bent, as Small recognizes, skin color continued to serve as an organizational mechanism through which social groups were identified as "other" and around which racist practices were constituted (94). All those not possessing White skin continued to be stigmatized, and this reinforced the equation of Whiteness with Englishness or Britishness, as well as the concomitant exclusion of Black people from the dominant definition of citizenship.

The reliance on skin color as a referent of difference complemented that aspect of 1980s racism that, Gilroy notes, conceived of culture along ethnically absolute lines. Culture was discussed in terms of a fixed property of social groups, not as something intrinsically fluid, changing, unstable, or dynamic ("One Nation under a Groove" 266). One example of this is the way that dominant rhetoric fixed the representation of Blacks as a criminal, parasitical element.

In the 1970s the stereotypical image of the black mugger became the centerpiece for the popular politics of law and order, which continued to form an important element in the concept of national identity in the 1980s. However, the emphasis shifted from the lone black mugger to a plural collective image that encompassed Black political protest in terms of criminality. One way that Blacks were considered to express their difference from Whites was through antisocial acts of various kinds, but particularly violent ones; thus Black culture itself could amount to a criminal culture (Gilroy, *There Ain't No Black* 98–99).[124]

In addition to this kind of stigmatization, Black communities faced the dismal situation produced by Thatcherite economic policies. Black Britons represented a high proportion of the country's poorest members, and as a result they were caught up in the government's smear campaign against the "undeserving" poor.[125] Thatcher and her successor, John Major, accused welfare claimants of robbing the taxpayer by either fraudulently claiming payments or simply being perverse enough to persist in depending on the taxpayer rather than becoming "active citizens" in the new "Enterprise Culture," the cult(ure) of individualism. This mediated against the chances of Black people being incorporated into the nationalist framework of citizenship, or in other words of establishing any clear title to Britishness.

Michael Hill argues that the premiership of John Major (1992–97) "witnessed the continued pursuit of a broadly Thatcherite agenda," though one with a less strident tone (178).[126] Despite her unceremonious dethroning in 1990, Thatcher would prove to have a long shadow, influencing not only Major's policies but also those of the future New Labour Government (installed in 1997). An examination of how the British Labour Party changed in relation to Conservative ideology over the course of the 1980s and '90s patently reveals the fundamental way in which Thatcherism altered the political landscape in Britain, particularly concerning the treatment of raced identities.

Traditionally a left-leaning party with strong historic ties to unionism, Labour's gradual shift toward the center-right marks the end of the postwar consensus on the welfare state in Britain.[127] New Labour policies were designed to appeal to middle England—essentially, the White middle-class taxpayer—while its rhetoric denied that class remained a significant factor in modern British life. The party claimed to champion a communal ethic. New Labour's plan for renewing the nation, which Philip Gould describes as a plan to forge links between the individual and his or her community through a new kind of patriotism based on one's relation to community (252), allowed a person to prove his/her British credentials by the place and role s/he chose to play in the community.

On the surface, this collectivist ethos sounds plausible, almost like a return to a welfare state philosophy. However, the equality of choice within society that it presumed did not exist. Further, when considered in the light of New Labour's fiscal policies the vision of a fully united Britain does not appear viable. Such cooperatism would be hard to accomplish without a commitment to the collective public financing of essential services, and, as Peter Dorey makes clear, above all "Blair endorsed the values of the market and the primacy of private enterprise" ("The Blairite Betrayal" 193).

Raymond Plant accounts for the contradiction in New Labour ideology by arguing that when Blair spoke of the equal worth of all Britons, social responsibility, and community, he was not concerned with equality of opportunity as much as "starting gate equality." This amounts to equalizing the opportunity to become unequal (563). New Labour doctrine rejects trying to secure equality of outcome as a direct aim of government policy (566), and in practice this amounts to a continued social exclusion for many people.

New Labour rarely played the race card in the same manner as the Conservatives. They were in principle favorably disposed toward multicultural initiatives for Blacks and other minorities such as gays and lesbians, yet Terence Morris documents that on the issue of immigration, for example, the party did not diverge from its predecessors. It continued to assume that most refugees were bogus, seeking entry to Britain in order to live off the taxpayer (365). Also, little changed in the criminal justice system, where non-Whites continued to have a disadvantage (378).

Blair's concept of modern British citizenship, in fact, encompasses much of the same criteria as Thatcher's idea of "active" citizenship. Both viewpoints involve a person earning his or her place in one-nation Britain by successfully enacting a set of behavior patterns that equate to responsibility in the dominant discourse. Mainly, this entails proving one's individual fiscal prudence by working within an environment of competitive free enterprise and not drawing financial support from the community. Consequently, even though New Labour rhetoric does not demonize Blacks in the same way as Conservative ideology did, the terms it offers for participating in a renewed Britain do not allow for the inclusion of many people who historically have been excluded from material prosperity or treated as scapegoats.

New Labour ideology casts the White middle class as the most authentic exemplars of modern British citizens, and of national ideals and, therefore, racial ones. On one hand, because there is no appeal to the category of the natural or the biological in their racial discourse, Whiteness is available as a space to be occupied by anyone willing to carry its designated social responsibilities. On the other hand, without a commitment to equality of outcome only a few "others" would ever be able to access the same material privileges accorded to middle England and necessary for appearing socially responsible.

Therefore, New Labour thinking on how to unite Britain actually results in the representation of a number of social groups as unworthy of inclusion. This impacts on the contemporary meaning of Whiteness principally in two ways. Firstly, it leaves White power uncontested by allowing Whiteness to claim the virtues of industriousness, common sense, and decency over and against the values, or lack of values, characteristic of the feckless underclass. Secondly, it reinforces the idea of White identity as normative, ordinary, racially unmarked. Thus, Whiteness in 1990s Britain continued to carry many of the connotations it did in the 1950s and earlier.

White/Black Paradigms and British Gay Subculture: Philip Osment's *This Island's Mine*

Historically, theater has contributed to the development of modern British gay identity. Richard Dyer has written of his coming out and the part that theater played in the constitution of his gay identity, especially his need to overcome stereotypical views of homosexuals. The plays he saw as part of the Almost Free Theatre's *Homosexual Acts* season (1974) served a number of functions. Firstly, they were informative, giving insight into how gays really lived and conducted their relationships. They also provided a focus for meeting other gay people, and the season offered a rare cultural space where one could take one's heterosexual friends, and, for a change, be the one on home ground (*The Culture of Queers* 24).

The *Homosexual Acts* season led to the development of Britain's first gay theater group, Gay Sweatshop. Group member Philip Osment writes that Sweatshop was set up in response to the way homosexuality was usually portrayed onstage. Also, it aimed to afford gay people who wanted to work in theater the chance to do so without having to collude in negative and inaccurate representations of their lives ("Finding Room on the Agenda for Love" ix). Though forced to work on a shoestring budget when the Conservatives cut Arts Council funding (and gay theater came low on the council's list of priorities anyway),[128] Sweatshop produced a number of successful plays that addressed the key political issues of the time.

Given the hostile social climate in the 1980s, theater had a particularly important role alongside the work done by campaign groups in helping gays and lesbians to sustain pride in their sexuality and a sense of community. One play by Osment, *This Island's Mine* (1987), confronts the exclusion of gays from the idea of the British national family, and the continuities between the right's discourse on sexuality and racial otherness. Osment began working on the play in 1985, at the height of hysteria over AIDS. This national mood, he states, was responsible for the play's theme of exile:

I very much wanted to look at exiles and make links between them and people who feel like exiles in their own country. I had also been reading Dickens and was fascinated by the way he uses coincidence and chance to make links between different people's stories and lives which resonate thematically with each other and build up a picture of a whole society. My ambition was to write something which went some way to creating a similar impression of eighties Britain. ("Finding Room on the Agenda for Love" lxi)

David Evans, discussing the way that citizenship became a major preoccupation of establishment British politics in the late 1980s, states that the formal meaning of British citizenship has referred principally to the entitlements of citizens to live and work in the country as opposed to those of aliens, who do not share these rights. As noted above, under Thatcher the concept was refined to include the idea of the "active citizen," a person who is believed to make a productive contribution to British culture. Evans describes this "active citizen" as one who is "normal, moral, and nationalist" (3–4). In addition to working and paying taxes, consuming, and exhibiting a patriotism that includes a *correct* view of empire, the clearest way to demonstrate one's membership in the club of active citizenry was to project a conventional family-centered lifestyle. This aspect of the criteria relegated many sexual minorities to the status of less than fully qualified citizens, or, as Osment comments, rendered them exiles in their own country.

This Island's Mine explores the binding of the homosexual and the ethnic as marginal to "active" Britishness. In scene 4 Mrs. Rosenblum, a Jewish refugee from Nazism, warns Martin that "Last time, Mr. Martin / We were the pestilence, / Now you people are spreading a plague" (88). Unlike the "active" British patriot who contributes toward the communal and national good, gays are here aligned with the dangerous foreigner and represented as a pernicious presence draining the strength and vitality of the nation state.

The cultural dislocation of ethnic and sexual minorities is further demonstrated by the staging of segments from Shakespeare's *The Tempest*. Selwyn, a Black actor who is cast as Caliban, is told that "Caliban is a primitive, / He tried to rape Miranda, / So don't try and give us the noble savage / It just won't work" (Osment, *This Island's Mine* 91).

The White director's interaction with Selwyn evokes the historical relations between colonizer and colonized. Susan Bennett claims it is no coincidence that the credibility the director wishes to attach to his reading of the primitive is given force through the citation of rape. Selwyn is positioned within an overdetermined system of imperialism and masculinism, which gives the director's speech the force of iterability—the accumulated force of repetition (38–39). This is illustrated again by Selwyn's one-line response after being berated: "Who is Selwyn to argue with England's greatest playwright?" (Osment, *This Island's Mine* 91).

Homi Bhabha identifies an important feature of colonial discourse to be its dependence on the concept of "fixity" in the construction of otherness:

Fixity, as the sign of cultural/historical/racial difference in the discourse of colonialism, is a paradoxical mode of representation: it connotes rigidity and an unchanging order as well as disorder, degeneracy, and daemonic repetition. Likewise the stereotype, which is its major discursive strategy, is a form of knowledge and identification that vacillates between what is always "in place" already known, and something that must be anxiously repeated. (66)

This type of discursive strategy is enacted in the play through the director's desire to exploit stereotypical ideas of Black masculinity, derived from colonial discourse, to "Give the punters a treat," as he puts it. Dressing Selwyn up in something skimpy in order to foreground his "raw physicality and sex" signifies an attempt to repeat the objectification of the colonial subject beneath the Western Orientalist gaze. Costuming Selwyn in a loincloth represents a political gesture in which the performative aspects of the Black male body would be made to signify within the fixed confines of White racialist discourse.

The problem occurs when Selwyn fails to match this White fantasy of the Black male body. Even so, the director refuses to recognize the discrepancy between his global naming of Black masculinity as the embodiment of primitive heterosexuality and the actual Black gay subject in front of him. Instead, he interprets Selwyn as a failure of Black manhood, complaining that he has "the only black actor/Who doesn't know how to use his body" (Osment, *This Island's Mine* 91).

The director's desire to force into visibility a stereotypical form of Blackness occurs again in scene 26. Selwyn is rehearsing Caliban's best-known speech in which he turns his master's language back on him, using it to curse him. The director criticizes Selwyn for delivering the words in his normal voice, asking: "Where's the West Indian accent?/I thought we agreed you were going to do it with a strong accent!" (Osment, *This Island's Mine* 115).

This moment repeats, but in reverse, a historical colonial moment in which colonial subjects were encouraged to speak properly the colonizer's language in an effort to disconnect them from their cultures of origin or to produce a collaborative buffer class. However, when on the colonizer's home territory, a Black man's use of the same language as a White man is reconfigured as a violent clash between race, and culture, where Black symbolizes race and culture stands in for White British civilization. To speak the master's language as well as the master him/herself makes a claim on the part of the Black subject to British identity. In dominant terms, such a claim is considered an illegitimate desire on the part of the Afro-Caribbean subject to step above his/her designated place in the socio-racial hierarchy.

The director's dissatisfaction with Selwyn's performance, then, partly stems from an inability either to understand or to accept the complexity of modern Britishness, but also, and even more so, it relates to the way that the conjunction of Black and British remains an oxymoron in British nationalist discourse. Further, he is disturbed by the way in which Black and White cultural codes are simultaneously intertwined and contrasted in the figure of Selwyn, for his cultural mixed-ness underlines the mixed-ness of Whiteness as well as Black British identity.

That White heterosexual masculinity functions as the universal standard of Britishness is again illustrated by Selwyn's experience with a group of homophobic and racist policemen in scene 13. Hurrying home from a library where he has checked out some gay titles, Selwyn takes a shortcut:

> Along tree-lined streets,
> So unlike the streets of his childhood
> Lined with council blocks
> With wafer-thin walls
> And lifts that never worked.
> Selwyn feels pleased with himself
> He's made it in a white man's world,
> No need to feel victimized.
> (Osment, *This Island's Mine* 98)

However, his assumption of a successful cultural crossover is denied in the next moment, when three policeman jump from a van and want to know where he is going in such a hurry. They assume his bag contains the booty of his most recent crime. They hustle him into an alley, search him, and, discovering the books, taunt him—"poof," "black pansy"—then assault him.

In scene 26 cultural anxiety regarding Selwyn's hybridity arises because of the way he represents the intersection of two different racialized cultures. In this scene his racial otherness is read in terms of pure Blackness, in itself enough to get him beaten up. However, when conjoined with his homosexuality, which disturbs the dominant sexual regime, it speaks to the way in which a range of differences and discriminations informing the discursive and social practices of racial and sexual hierarchization is bound in the perceptions and drives of the White British collective consciousness.

His beating by the police symbolizes the institutional apparatuses that result in Selwyn, and others, being forced into the position of internal exiles in Britain. The assault is intended to give him "something to remember," and this message is the truth of the phrase *straight White man's world.* Selwyn's beating implies a relationship of cultural specificity to British national identity in which the binaries of home/exile are fixed to those of Whiteness/Blackness and hetero/homosexual.

This duality is reflected physically in the landscape, as illustrated by Selwyn's equation of the privileged environment surrounding the library with White subjectivity. Later, when he moves out of the flat he shares with his White lover, he reaffirms the linkage between the arrangement of material social space and the existential effect of displacement. He tells Martin he is going to live near his mother because "I don't feel at home over this side of/town" (Osment, *This Island's Mine* 116). His mother makes a similar equation with her neighborhood and Black identity, couching her complaint that she does not see enough of her son in this way: "It's like you're living in another country" (Osment, *This Island's Mine* 100).

However, Selwyn's return migration from a White racialized location to a Black one will not enable him to negotiate his multiple subjectivity with any more facility. Originally, he crossed into the "white man's world" because it offered a more developed gay subculture in which he hoped to find a place. The absence of an adequate gay space in Black British communities is indicated by Selwyn's fear that being gay means "letting the side down" (Osment, *This Island's Mine* 105). One reason he has not been home lately is because his brother threatened to beat him up when he learned he was gay.

Selwyn's identity as a Black gay man means that he is claimed and excluded simultaneously by his community of origin. However, in addition to hegemonic sex-gender structures being reproduced in the Black community with deleterious effect, the dominant racial schema is shown similarly provoking division within the gay community. For example, Martin admits that he may find Selwyn sexually attractive because he sees him in terms of White colonial representations of Blackness—as a figure of sexual exoticism.

Just as his sexual "otherness" means that Selwyn cannot fit comfortably in a Black social location, in the same way his racial "otherness" means that he cannot feel at home in White society, either the straight mainstream or a White-dominated gay subculture. Therefore, an important element of the play is how it reveals that structures of domination are multiple and fluid in relation to the particular difference(s) from the norm that one represents. This is illustrated further by the way that Martin's nephew Luke can move easily from his parent's home, where he cannot be open about his homosexuality, into his uncle's world, where he does not have to hide his identity, because his White racial privilege opens more free space in society for him than Selwyn, who is doubly marked as "other."

In the final scene, Luke literally faces his future, symbolized by a set of distant peaks covered in snow that he views from a hilltop position. He has only two terms to complete at school before he can leave the "dump" that he considers his family neighborhood. The distant hills represent the urban gay subculture to which his uncle Martin has introduced him, and though his future is described as unknown, in fact it is fairly clear that he will go on to live openly as a gay man within his newfound community.

Our final glimpse of Selwyn is very different. Firstly, his last words are delivered as Caliban:

> For I am all the subjects that you have,
> Which first was mine own kind; and here
> you sty me
> In this hard rock, while you do keep
> From me
> The rest of the island.
> (Osment, *This Island's Mine* 120)

Where Luke's future is an open vista of potential, Selwyn's appears to be extremely limited.

The contrast between the two characters' prospects reflects the way that dominant race and sex-gender relations may create barriers among members of subcultural communities. The continuity of historical stereotypical Black racial constructs in British society means that in some instances gay subculture offers a less secure haven for those who cannot claim White identity. Consider that when Mark is dismissed from his job because the other restaurant employees fear working with a gay man, he can at least fall back on the security of his position within his gay social circle. However, when Selwyn is assaulted, he finds he must abandon this connection in order to best cope.

What the comparison/contrast between Martin and Selwyn, and Luke and Selwyn, shows us also is how living as an internal exile creates a desire to belong in the subject, a wish to recover or create home space, but that the potential for moving into a place of relative security is modified firstly by skin color, the sign of difference most easily read. What "stys" Selwyn in both mainstream British society and the gay subculture is the authority that Whiteness continues to carry in each; thus Whiteness can afford the White gay subject (that is, Martin and Luke) some measure of safety in society.

The play shows too that the measure of protection Whiteness provides for gays and lesbians is both limited and fragile. R. Radhakrishnan writes that "the concept of identity is a normative measure that a) totalizes heterogeneous 'selves' and 'subjectivity' and b) that the normative citizenship of any identity . . . is an ideological effect that secures the regime of a full and undivided identity. And in our time, whether we like it or not, the dominant paradigm of identity has been the 'imagined community' of nationalism" (752). Britain in the 1980s offered internally exiled minority groups, and individuals fragmented by conflicting desires and cultural allegiances, scant opportunity to envision themselves within the nationalist framework. Thatcher's "imagined community of nationalism" denied Blacks and homosexuals title to the framework of active citizenry and the privileges that accompanied this designation.

At the same time, Kenneth Plummer proposes that the late twentieth century has provided the opportunity to tell new sexual stories "concerned with all those matters linked to our most intimate desires, pleasures and ways of being in the world," and that these harbor the potential for political change (151). Moving out of a silence, he contends, stories of "intimate citizenship" may help shape a new public language, generate communities to receive and disseminate them, and ultimately create more spaces for them to be heard (149). *This Island's Mine*, by showing a rounded picture of "intimate citizenry," the virtues of gay subculture as well as the problems between intimate citizens raced as Black and White, affords the possibility for the spectator to imagine new ways of forming social and sexual intimacies and weaving new empowering stories in contemporary Britain.

Being Black, Seeing White: Michael Ellis's *Chameleon*

Unlike in the United States, no parallel development of Black British theater accompanied the early protest movements. Peacock considers that it was the collapse of White political theater at the beginning of the 1980s that opened a gap for second-generation Black Britons to develop a theatrical discourse that was uniquely Black and British (174–75). Playwright Tunde Ikoli explains the political rationale behind Black artists' endeavor to stake their claim to Britishness through the arts, arguing that all the talk about "inter-racial this and multicultural that" heard by second-generation children in the 1960s and '70s had simply not materialized (Rees 125). Although a few Black playwrights did have work produced and published in the mid-1970s (for example, Trinidadian Mustapha Matura and Nigerian Wole Soyinka), it was not until the 1980s that an indigenous Black British voice found a significant home on stage.[129]

Actor Trevor Laird contrasts the new Black theater in the 1980s with earlier forms, suggesting that each historical phase of Black theater possessed a different social imperative. Plays by Black immigrants dealt with where Black people came from and how and why they were treated as outsiders in Britain. In contrast, second-generation Black Britons came from inside British society. Hence, Laird argues, the imperative of 1980s Black theater was to ask "Why can't we be part of things? We're from here." (Rees 124).

The early 1980s represented an artistic moment that matched the political juncture in the British Black community between those who claimed

Africa or the Caribbean as home and those who knew only Britain as home. Michael Ellis's *Chameleon* is a timely intervention in both these critical moments. A second-generation Black Briton born in London's East End of Jamaican parents, Ellis addresses the different issues faced by first-wave immigrants and the successive generation of Black British as well as the different visions and expectations the two generations held of White British society. *Chameleon* was first presented at the Oval House in London in January 1985.[130] Ellis notes that reviews were lukewarm or "out-and-out hostile" ("Preface" 10); notwithstanding critical opinion, audiences took to the play, and it toured nationally through January 1986.

The play explores the prospects for Blacks in 1980s Britain within the context of the changes wrought by Thatcherism. The narrative is based on the playwright's personal experience. He recalls once working as an accounts clerk with another Black man who refused to speak to him. Meeting one day in the "great leveler" (the "worker's bog"), the man explained that he did not speak to Ellis because he could not risk being seen chatting to other Blacks—it would damage his chances of getting ahead in the company. The man spoke "as if he was clued-in to the thing that would make me a casualty," Ellis writes, but as he was about to explain what this thing was a white face entered; the conversation ended abruptly, and Ellis never spoke with the man again ("Preface" 10).

Ellis uses this encounter as the basis for creating the character of Benjamin Howard, an emigrant from Jamaica who practices a similar self-imposed exile from the Black community. Benjamin works in a large insurance firm, where he is the token Black member of the management team. The corporation stands in as a mirror for White society and how Blacks are positioned within Britain.

Like Ellis's colleague, Benjamin considers his Blackness a disadvantage, an obstacle to his getting on in the company and the larger majority White society. He tries to overcome it by repressing any outward manifestation of his Black identity, hoping that by mimicking the behavior associated with a White corporate executive type his skin color might be overlooked. Thus he avoids cultural events associated with Blackness, such as blues clubs, opting instead for White-identified pursuits and accoutrements. He plays golf and drives a Mercedes, and he has a trophy girlfriend, the White boss's daughter, and therefore someone ideally situated to improve his career and social prospects.

His accommodating behavior is contrasted to that of Marcia Jackson, who joins the firm as his secretary. Born in Britain, her attitude toward the way that the company treats Black workers is strikingly different from Benjamin's. She too recognizes that Blacks face difficulties in a White racist society, yet she takes pride in her identity and gains the strength to resist racism through maintaining solidarity with her community.

For Marcia, the pursuit of Whiteness is a foolish as well as fruitless enterprise. She points out to Benjamin that the managing director will never allow his daughter to marry him: "He knows your place and he'll make damn certain you'll stay there licking his boots and oiling his arse" (Ellis, *Chameleon* 23). She compares Benjamin to a chameleon that changes color to whatever seems most appropriate and likely to appease the White order.

The notion of identity as something that one performs on a subjective and social level is central to the play's construction of race. Benjamin and Marcia, despite their different worldviews, share a similar understanding of self-presentation in terms of a strategic instrument for establishing a sense of individual belongingness in a particular cultural location and for advertising to others where one's political allegiance lies. Of course, the pair employs this strategy for very different ends.

Marcia aims to resist the forces of White dominance. As a member of the Afro-Asian Committee, she works to correct typecast images of Blackness, the articulation of metaphors of Blackness informed by the historical experiences of White societies. She is willing to keep her son away from school until they remove all of the books containing black stereotypes, for reading *Tom Sawyer* and *The Adventures of Huckleberry Finn* with no Black narratives for counterbalance can only increase his sense of cultural dislocation, alienation, and exclusion.

Marcia conceives of the field of culture as a site of struggle between a diasporic Black community and the forces of White hegemony. Black cultural production is seen as essential to constructing a category of British identity able to fully encompass Blackness and lead to a sense of real belonging in Britain. Her anger at the status quo makes her opt for separatism as a political weapon. Whether or not this strategic disengagement from White society offers a viable mode of resistance is open to question; however, in the world of the play it helps Marcia at least avoid the impossible position of cultural in-between-ness that Benjamin wears himself out trying to occupy.

Her Black power stance makes Marcia less susceptible to the effect White scrutiny has on Blacks' lives. One reason Benjamin can no longer connect with other Black people is his internalization of the White gaze. As Marcia puts it: "I've seen this before. . . . Black people who in normal circumstances would get on so well, fighting like cat and dog once they're at work or in a situation where they're under the close scrutiny of White people" (25).

Benjamin "sees White" in several different ways, firstly in the sense that he shares the dominant White vision of Blacks in Britain, conceiving of them as social "rubbish." He sides with the White forces of law and order, admonishing Marcia for keeping her child away from school because "it's illegal in this country" (12). His patronizing attitude and use of the phrase "this country" implies that he, unlike Marcia, has a superior knowledge of British ways and therefore a more rightful place in Britain. He believes that his "good command of the English language" demonstrates his claim, as it displays his likeness to Whites (16).

Secondly, he assumes a position of willful racial blindness: he adopts the dominant White position whereby national identity is un-raced. This accounts for his refusal to acknowledge Britain's imperial past and how older forms of race relations play out in contemporary society. He reiterates the standard denial of White discourse when challenged about racist practices in Britain—that is, "skin colour makes no difference to me" (17). This reinforces the idea that Britain treats all of its citizens with evenhandedness.[131]

Finally, he shows himself capable of seeing Whiteness from an oppositional perspective. He has a partial realization of the motives behind White rhetoric on race and at times shows an awareness of how unlikely it is that a Black man could attain an equal position with White men in British society. Careful as he is to project the image of a loyal company executive, his bitterness sometimes seeps out. He speaks about the envious White eyes that "wouldn't like to see a Black man on anything better than a pogo stick" (12), much less driving a Mercedes.

He gives expression to the exclusionary make-up of White society most clearly when he admits fearing that he will yet again be passed over for promotion and remain in the "arsehole of the building," a dismal basement without windows or any ventilation system: "Seven bloody years in this basement. . . . I ain't asking for anything that's not mine. I won't be passed over again" (Ellis, *Chameleon* 22). Even with his oblique acknowledgment of the power invested in Whiteness, a power that allows the imposition of a White social will and value system on those it considers "other," Benjamin continues to invest his whole sense of identity in it. He desires the material and psychological trappings that accompany success in Thatcher's new "Enterprise Culture" and realizes that identifying with Whiteness is the best available route. Therefore, he carefully conceals his knowledge of the mechanisms of White power, and it is Marcia's determination to make plain and to confront Whiteness in all of its social meanings for White and Black people that provokes him into sabotaging her position in the company.

He believes that Marcia's behavior places his ambitions in jeopardy because Whites taint all Blacks with the same brush; thus he is furious when she complains about the White tea lady refusing to deliver refreshments to the basement. Benjamin cannot afford to acknowledge that her neglect is racist. Similarly, he is horrified when Marcia gets involved in a dispute with the Managing Director's secretary. In an effort to stay one step ahead of his own Blackness, he circulates a petition among the employees, labeling Marcia a troublemaker and seeking her dismissal.

Though Marcia leaves of her own accord before he can fire her, Benjamin's success in covering up the social facts of Whiteness in his workplace does earn him a reward. The play ends with him informing the audience that "I've got what I want" (29). Benjamin succeeds, therefore, in moving one step closer to the "ambitious social project" that is Whiteness (Bonnett 21).

His final address represents an ironic repetition of dominant anti-Black discourse. He characterizes Marcia as an invader who came into an orderly corporate society and turned everything upside down. His rhetorical: "Order! Order! Take away order and what are you left with?" (Ellis, *Chameleon* 29) echoes Thatcher's *World In Action* remarks about the imminent erosion of Britain's unique culture by the disorderly presence of too many Black immigrants.

Chameleon makes clear that a principal political objective for Black Britons in the 1980s was finding ways to prevail over the sense of cultural alienation, isolation, and psychological dissonance that stemmed from living in an exclusivist White society. The play speaks to the need of British-born Blacks to say what they know about Whiteness and to contest the meaning of Blackness being forwarded in contemporary social discourse. It stages the limited choices for Blacks concerning where to place themselves within the culturalist framework of national identity. Like Marcia, one could make moves into White-dominated areas of British life and hope that maintaining strong ties to Black culture would help offset the effects of discrimination that such forays could bring about. Alternatively, one could take Benjamin's path and dissociate from Black identity in the hope of acquiring at least some economic gains. However, the play makes clear that the gesture of allowing himself to be the token figure that his White superiors can call upon to verify their egalitarian racial principles, the ostensible bedrock of White British culture, will only ever afford Benjamin and others like him an uncomfortable and slippery foothold in mainstream society.

The State of Whiteness: David Hare's *The Absence of War*

David Hare's trilogy of plays—*Racing Demon* (1990), *Murmuring Judges* (1991), and *The Absence of War* (1993)—explores the state of Britain's national health after the changes engineered by Thatcher. It takes the pulse of the nation-state by examining the condition of three of its principal institutions—the Church of England, the judiciary, and electoral politics, respectively. *Racing Demon* addresses how Thatcherite principles have infiltrated some quarters of the church, while other clergy have taken up unofficial roles as welfare officers in response to the urgent problems created by cutbacks in social benefits. *Murmuring Judges* shows the legal system under stress, capable of applying the law, but not justice, because it takes no account of the social determinants of crime. *The Absence of War* explores the Labour Party's response to Thatcherism and questions the causes of Labour's fourth consecutive election defeat in 1992.

Unlike Arden and D'Arcy's Arthurian trilogy, Hare's plays, Lane A. Glenn suggests, "were never meant to function like Aeschylus's *Oresteia:* they don't tell a single story. Their importance may lie rather in their very existence" (234). Here Glenn refers to the unique status of plays offering a systematic political analysis of how society functions within the institution of 1990s British theater that was still dominated by glitzy and vacuous West End musicals. In this discussion I will focus on *The Absence of War.* It anticipates the values that would come to characterize Britain as the millennium approached, and it offers, I think, the most intriguing insight into the state of Whiteness, particularly its equation with state power, in the 1990s.

Hare intended for *The Absence of War* to cover broadly the workings of the machinery of state. He describes how he refines his subject in order to "capture that strange moment at which a small part of the state is compelled, for a few weeks at least, to offer itself up to the public's inspection" (*Asking Around* 161). The plot hinges upon the unsuccessful efforts of the Labour Party leader, George Jones, to become prime minister. The main reason for his loss is down to George's decision to make the party "respectable" in the eyes of the electorate. He believes that as a result of the political sea change wrought by Thatcher the Labour Party, as historically constituted, has been rendered unelectable. For this reason George adopts the language of those in power, and it is his willingness to contest the election on the grounds laid out in Conservative discourse that makes him ineffectual and unappealing.

The play's focus on one party leader during one election led a number of reviewers who covered the trilogy's revival in 2003 to conclude that the play was dated and irrelevant to contemporary audiences.[132] Hare responds to such criticism by stating that despite conventional wisdom telling us that nothing dates faster than the up-to-date, in fact frontline reports can acquire a deeper fascination when considered in hindsight and with a change in perspective:

> With the passage of time, plays born in the heat of political passion can turn out much more interesting than those written with an eye to what are embarrassingly called the "eternal truths." . . . In the days when the trilogy was conceived, carers and copers all over the country felt that their role was being deliberately downgraded by a Conservative government which was nakedly unsympathetic to the common good. Now, under a Labour government which seemed at the outset so much more well-meaning and intelligent, they find themselves apparently not greatly advanced . . . It is perhaps not surprising that the only time that I have been in a room with Tony Blair the only thing he wanted to talk about was his own uneasy memories of a performance of *The Absence of War.* ("A Time and a Place")

One thing many, if not all, British institutions share is that they are controlled by a small clique. Most of those who manage the major political parties, and indeed British society, share similar privileged backgrounds. Often they are the children of upper-middle class or middle-class parents and have been educated at elite public or selective grammar schools. Many have an Oxbridge background, and their work experience is in the specialized and lucrative professions (for example, the law).

Throughout the preceding chapters, I have referred to the way in which Whiteness functions as an unnamed standard for access to or acceptance into the social locations occupied by those who dictate the course of British institutions. These institutions are marked as White space, and they function to maintain the status quo of privilege for a particular social group. David Pattie explains the trilogy's simple if bleak conclusion about the state of the nation: the only way to express the common good is through state institutions which, post-Thatcher, are so damaged that they have become ineffective. Accordingly, the plays make a case for British institutions to be overhauled, though not abolished (370, 373).

How then to explain the attitude that the trilogy, frequently read as a critique of conservative Britain, takes toward British institutions? Where does this place *The Absence of War* within the politics of race in 1990s Britain? Finlay Donesky indicates some of the problems with Hare's perspective. One way that the ruling class legitimizes itself is via a claim to help people. The traditional British constitution is really an unwritten agreement that people will trust in the decency and benevolence of this class. It is "therefore absolutely essential for the legitimacy of the rulers that they be allowed to serve, or at least be perceived to serve, otherwise the game is up. For centuries the discourse of service has effectively shifted attention from the elitist ethos and structure of institutions to the personalities and character of those doing the 'serving'" (181).

Certainly by the mid-1980s people were beginning to question their rulers' beneficence, as well as the efficiency of the institutions they ran, yet Hare makes no reference to the movement for constitutional reform that was active at the time. [133] Instead, he gives us, in George Jones, a portrait of a benevolent individual who seeks to govern in the interest of the "common people," something that could work to reawaken people's earlier, more sympathetic perceptions of their leaders and institutions. If one accepts that British national identity is bound up in what Donesky calls a "mystical pact" between people and their centralized, top-heavy institutions, then Hare's attempt to refresh these institutions could contribute toward the reification of Whiteness as the content of British national identity.

In an essay on political theater, Hare writes that if a play is to be a weapon in the class struggle, the weapon is not the thing that is said; rather, "it is the interaction of what you are saying and what the audience is thinking" ("The Play Is in the Air" 30). In order to determine how *The Absence of War* might intervene not only in class contests but also in the ongoing and interrelated struggles among different racial groups in Britain, it is necessary to consider what its silences about the relation between Whiteness and British identity say, as well as what Blackness signified in dominant discourse at the time of its production.

Firstly, I would like to look at the way in which the meaning of Whiteness as synonymous with state power is conveyed without mentioning race. All those in charge of the state, or those who would like to be, are described in the conventional terms of dominant White discourse. By this I mean that those character traits that are mentioned do not include their racial identities; therefore, Whiteness symbolizes the category of the normative in the play, which marks the British subject, the nation-state wherein the subject is contained, and its institutions as White.

There is too a glaring absence of multiethnic Britain in the play's representation of the nation-state, which accurately reflects the fact of the Whiteness of British institutions (other racial groups tending not to be identified with them). At the same time, however, since the 1970s ethnic minorities have contributed to Labour Party politics, yet this is not reflected in the play either. If nations are imagined communities, then political parties play a central place in guiding the imagination of contemporary Britain. Because only White people are represented as contributing actively to the running of a key national institution, the flawed perception of Britain as a racially homogenous culture goes unchallenged.[134]

There is only one Black character in *The Absence of War.* Trevor Avery, a member of Special Branch, is assigned to protect George during the campaign. He appears several times, usually very briefly, as in act 2, scene 2 and scene 9, where he merely stands silently next to George in a studio or hovers in his shadow. In act 1, scene 3, he is simply a device to move the plot forward, imparting the news that the prime minister is on his way to announce a date for the General Election. In act 2, scene 4, he monitors an angry exchange between George and the broadcaster Linus Frank, ensuring that order is maintained.

He holds the stage alone on only one occasion. In act 2, scene 1, Trevor speaks directly to the audience about the nature of his job and his employers.

It's a good posting. According of course to who you get. There are certain Ministers . . . they're the ones who treat you like dirt.

That isn't George. George is popular. When you go to the theatre, he always asks you what you thought of the play. I always say, "Very good play, sir." That means no one tried to kill him while he was there. (Hare, *The Absence of War* 57)

Trevor's role resembles that of a bodyservant: literally, he looks after the physical wellbeing of those he serves, in historical terms not an unusual role for a Black man to play in relation to a White man. Even though Trevor appears alone and his speech constitutes the whole of this scene, still he is not represented as an individual. The words he delivers are intended to give the spectator more information about his boss than to present him as a fully rounded character. It is partly through Trevor that Hare builds his case for George as the good guy, the proof being that he can connect with people regardless of their social status.

In fact, this scene shows how different George is from Trevor, for it demonstrates George's mistaken assumption that he and Trevor think along the same lines. George believes Trevor's response to his question about the play relates to the merits of the production, when Trevor displays no interest in the play and actually means something completely different. While this scene could be read as an indication that George views everyone on equal terms, a more valid interpretation would be to see it as signifying an instance of condescension, the conventional feeling among those of high social status that it is good form to check whether one's servants are happy. Perhaps it is this that sets George apart from the less obliging ministers, rather than any authentic identification with people of Trevor's rank, much less ethnicity.

Trevor's position on the margins is further emphasized by his exclusion from the category of the "common people." Not only are those who represent the leaders of British society White, the "common people"—represented by Vera Klein—also comprise White subjects. In scene 9 Vera, in her seventies, is brought to a manifesto launch as a symbol of the party's roots and continuity. She serves to remind the spectator of the collective postwar commitment to the welfare state: "The most exciting words of my life? 'Common ownership.' To hold things in common, this was our aim. . . . Another phrase: 'moral imperative.' This was the language of after the war" (Hare, *The Absence of War* 50). She also reminds the audience of the shallowness of contemporary Britain's commitment to the common good, when the leaders of the party forget to bring her onto the platform with them.

The moment before Vera is abandoned on an empty stage, Hare's directions state: "*(At once the music surges in a Wagnerian swell of power and emotion. . . . then as they climb the stage we are confronted with a massive video image of them all raising their joined arms above their heads together in a victory salute)*" (*The Absence of War* 55–56). This moment could prove ideal for calling into question the notion of a benevolent leader class in Britain; however, again Hare does not explore the issue of paternalism within the British state. Instead, as Carol Homden recognizes, Vera serves to emphasize nostalgia for a past form of British society that was more equitable and humane for some (225).[135]

While I would not deny the achievements of those who built the postwar welfare state, it is necessary to consider other aspects of the postwar communal British voice, some less savory than those Vera names. Since the late 1940s there has been a throughline of White racial exclusivity in the collective language of British nationalist discourse, and this includes the expression of values underpinning the idea of the common good as enshrined in the welfare state.

Alastair Bonnett identifies how the appeals to a cross-class national community that characterize mid- to late-twentieth-century racist discourse may evoke welfare structures. For example, the repeated variations of the accusation "they've come to sponge off us" first surfaced after the war. Bonnett notes also that surveys of White attitudes, especially among the working class, who rely most heavily upon welfare structures, have found repeatedly that people believe social benefits such as council housing should be limited to "our own people." In other words, benefits should not be shared with anyone outside of the White (often equated with English) community (41–42). Thus, immigration and the growth of already established Black communities is often opposed in terms of the threat they present to the gains that "common people," such as Vera, won after the war.

From the standpoint of a progressive racial politics, one could argue that the thinking behind British institutions has been flawed long before the rise of the new right ideology of the 1980s. Their ability to function for the common good has been impaired because historically the common has equated to the good of White Britons. The extent to which Vera's claim to speak for the commonality might represent a claim to power on behalf of the White racial group in Britain is not considered in the play. However, its possibility supports the position that British society, *as a whole,* would benefit more from what Hare argues against, that is, the abolition of current institutional arrangements.

The imperial ancestry of Britain's institutional forms are prominently displayed on stage in *The Absence of War.* In scene 2, we watch the speaker's procession, an antiquated ceremony comprising the vestiges of imperial pretensions. The bewigged speaker of the House of Commons is preceded by a man in full eighteenth-century fig-stockings and knickerbockers who is carrying a mace. Hare's stage directions state that the ceremony takes places in silent solemnity, "the public watching in awe" (*The Absence of War* 10), thus reflecting the difference in power and status between the governing class and the governed.[136]

In the following scene, where George has the floor, his criticism of the government includes the charge that "It exists purely for one purpose: it exists in order to continue to exist" (Hare, *The Absence of War* 11). Ironically, one could make the same claim about the party led by George, which is fast becoming indistinguishable from the one he criticizes.

Although he claims an interest in making Britain into "a country where everyone is helped" (Hare, *The Absence of War* 95), and he even recognizes that a key problem for social progress is what he terms the nation's obsession with "ancestor-worship,"[137] George fails to perceive how the changes he is engineering in his own party will prohibit its ability to function practically as an instrument for bettering people's lives. In reality, the party is now better able to fit within the institutional status quo that supports the dominant caste system. For one thing, it is no longer the natural party of people who resemble Vera in terms of class identity. Now people such as Lindsay Fontaine, a publicity advisor hired by George's modernizing minder Andrew, control it. Described as a "win-at-all-costs," "sell-your-own-mother" type, she joins the party only ten days before being hired, with the aim of personally profiting by helping them seize power (Hare, *The Absence of War* 16).

The degree to which George resembles those he ostensibly opposes is evident from the start of the play. In act 1, scene 1, he appears at a remembrance ceremony, standing alongside the leader of the Liberal Party and the prime minister. The stage notes state: "With their backs to us, they are indistinguishable" (Hare, *The Absence of War* 1). This reflects the fact that George's views have become homogenized, even interchangeable with conservative ones. The scene demonstrates the way that George has come to resemble the powerful class, the White Male Monolith in Britain, more than Vera and certainly more than Trevor.

Unintentionally, but very effectively, the idea that George remains part of the common collective is further undermined in one of the play's more amusing moments. In act 2, scene 2, Lindsay reports the results of a focus group. She explains to George why the results may be somewhat unreliable. One member mistook him for *Grace* Jones, the Black female performer, to which he sardonically replies: "Yeah, so presumably I'm up with six-foot black Amazons" (Hare, *The Absence of War* 61). This moment of acute irony works to highlight how finding a comparison between George, in his new incarnation as a "modern" party leader, and Trevor or Vera is just as odd a notion as pairing him with Grace Jones.

Like the other main figures of the White British power bloc, he appears as a mouthpiece of conservatism, mocking the "fine old heroes of the Left" (Hare, *The Absence of War* 84). He refers to the historical Labour Party as a "fantasy factory: "I told this Party it had to grow up. I made it contemplate reality" (Hare, *The Absence of War* 82). The only time George becomes distinguishable from the men at the Cenotaph is at the end of the play, after he has lost power.

George's boasts about "modernizing" the Party, considering what the reality of a *conservative reality* means for those outside the power bloc in British society, are fundamentally incompatible with an inclusive, cooperative ethos. Herein lies an irreconcilable paradox for him. George takes a perverse pride in the rank and file of his party hating him because he "got everything right." In other words, he caught the national mood and played to it. However, the national mindset is typified by an ugly self-interest that is the opposite of the socialism George would like to believe he still represents.

His political advisor, Oliver Dix, concludes that what demographics and statistics tell you about British society is that people are innately conservative. Dix poses a rhetorical question about demographics: "What do they tell you? People want hanging back? That half of them would like to send black people home?" (Hare, *The Absence of War* 30). Considering the social history of the times, the answer may well be yes. The choices George and his advisors make in response reveal that the party has come to signify many of the values trumpeted in conservative rhetoric. The spectator watches George make the Labour Party into a preserver of the status quo of the power relations inherited from a White imperial order and not the symbol of the whole British citizenry, for once again the "people" in Dix's formulation represent the White population.

Richard Dyer contends that Whiteness reproduces itself in all texts all of the time, not only those that explicitly set Whiteness against Blackness (*White* 13). *The Absence of War* represents an instance where White hegemony is reproduced by virtue of the play's racial silences. The play reproduces the classic move in White racial discourse whereby Whites are not named as part of a racial group but equate to the human race. Its silence concerning the Whiteness of Britain's imagined national community sets up an invisible yet very active opposition between any color other than White and Britishness, and, as I have shown in previous chapters, the invisibility of Whiteness is what helps maintain inequalities between different racial groups in society. Thus, by replicating the exclusionary racial dynamic that is endemic to British culture, *The Absence of War* succeeds in refreshing at least one institution as a social force—that of Whiteness.

notes

1. For more detail on the historical correspondence between Victorian and early-twentieth-century racial attitudes, see Lorimar.

2. For example, John Hawkins, who in 1562 reached Cape Verde, had this to say of the people he encountered: "These people are all black . . . and are called Negroes, . . . and are of nature very gentle and loving." Hawkins's relatively benign views of the indigenous inhabitants did not, however, prevent him from enslaving many of these "gentle and loving" people. (Quoted in Johnson et al., 10–11.)

3. Some historians trace the first instance of a connection between race and physical difference back to the crusades, in which case the way that race became tied to the body over the course of the sixteenth and seventeenth centuries actually represents the resuscitation of a residual construct.

4. It should be noted that although Ireland was a part of Great Britain at the time, the Irish continued to be excluded from British Whiteness and were often referred to as "white negroes." For a fuller explanation of the link between race and culture in Victorian thought, see Bolt.

5. For instance, in 1864 Alfred Russell Wallace interpreted Darwin's theory of natural selection to mean that the higher European races would displace the lower, degraded races, forecasting a continuous historical process of biological improvement until the world was populated by a single homogenous race.

6. Alter notes that British ethnologists viewed their discipline as a branch of natural history. Conceptually, zoology, race, and language were intertwined in Victorian racial discourse. Linguistic study was paired with ethnology and through the ethnological domain remained linked to the biological domain. In other words, while Victorian ethnology classified people as White or "other" according to blood descent, its racial schema depended concomitantly on linguistic evidence (31–32).

7. For a discussion of white racial primitivism, see Malchow.

8. This describes Shaw's belief in evolutionary eugenics. Ultimately, "the socialization of the selective breeding of man" would lead to the replacement of man, as history has so far recognized him, with a "more highly evolved animal—in short, by the Superman" (Shaw's "The Revolutionist's Handbook" 772, 776).

9. Interestingly, this is the same position Shaw occupied in British society by virtue of his Irishness.

10. As Jacobson rightly points out, there is an element of economic determinism in Allen's argument. His analysis of the relation between racial oppression, capital, and social control overlooks race as a psychocultural formation; that is, race as a subjective or unconscious construct also plays a role in the formation of White identities.

11. For more detail on the way that aspects of the human body are socialized, see Mercer.

12. This is not to say that there were no supplementary or alternative representations of Whiteness and Blackness; for example, subcategories of Whiteness such as "crackers" and "white trash" were well established in nineteenth-century discourse. And, too, there was the minority Quaker view, which espoused the idea of human equality regardless of race or nation. However, the dominant configuration of Black identity as sub-human and degenerate remained largely unaffected by these views.

13. See also Fredrickson, and Stepan and Gilman.

14. Josiah C. Nott, a leading ethnologist, tapped into anxieties concerning a fractured White class. He asserted the equality and racial superiority of Whites regardless of socio-economic origin and occupation: "It is not to the children of the educated class alone that we look for ruling intellects . . . but *nature's noblemen,* on the contrary, more often spring from the families of the backwoodsmen, or the sturdy mechanic." Quoted in Fredrickson, 80.

15. This also reflects British stereotypes of the Irish as Black during this period. For more detail on the similarities between African American and Irish immigrant stereotypes, see Roediger's *The Wages of Whiteness,* 133–44.

16. I would suggest that the connection was less exactly defined in the seventeenth century, when Black and White indentured servants performed similar types of labor, and even in the eighteenth century this link was not yet solidified.

17. Horsman attributes the term "Manifest Destiny" to John L. O'Sullivan, a Democratic politician in the 1840s. The phrase was first used to criticize other nations for interfering with the "natural process" of U.S. expansion: "our manifest destiny to overspread the continent" (219).

18. Note the transformation in Gilpin's portrait of nature and its relation to race compared to Bradford's. Now nature represents the settler's benevolent comrade in the great enterprise of expansion as opposed to a potentially malevolent force likely to be in league with the Indians.

19. For an overview of White writers' use of the "primitive," see Cooley.

20. Though the play was a commercial success, touring for eight months in 1935, it was not published until 1963.

21. The "one-drop theory" refers to the way in which race was believed to be present in the blood. In the South, a person with any degree of Black ancestry was considered Black under the law, regardless of appearance.

22. Robert's own family adopts the same position, believing that accepting his designated place is Robert's only chance of surviving in a White supremacist society.

23. My reading contradicts Wilder's belief about the relation of U.S. identity to place: in "Toward an American Language," he states that "Americans can find in environment no confirmation of their identity." (16).

24. George also must be persuaded to marry, on the basis that marriage forms part of his social duty as a man. His experience shows how in one sense conventional gender identities can also be a prison for younger men, although, of course, marriage also forms part of the route by which George will one day join the ranks of the Selectmen.

25. Quoted in Beebe. His article originally appeared in the *New York Herald Tribune* (20 March 1939: 6, 1, 2).

26. The play has been considered a simple melodramatic fable of good versus evil, an expression of Hellman's private political views and therefore an attack on the capitalist system, and as autobiographical, the characters based on Hellman's own family (as discussed in her memoirs *An Unfinished Woman* and *Pentimento*). See also Lederer (37–49) and William Wright (300–303).

27. This vision is exemplified by Churchill's statement in the House of Commons in March 1946. Speaking of India, he said: "It is with deep grief that I watch the clattering down of the British Empire with all its glories and all the services it has rendered to mankind" (quoted in Philip Murphy 30).

28. In addition to increasing unemployment levels in the 1950s, Britain would experience a number of "sterling crises."

29. In a British context, the term "Black" encompasses emigrants from South Asian as well as Afro-Caribbean origins, as opposed to U.S. racial discourse, which applies Black specifically to persons of African origin.

30. First published in *Hudson Review,* autumn 1950.

31. See, for example, Peter (1950), Hinchliffe, and volume 3 of *T. S. Eliot: Critical Assessments,* particularly E. M. Forster's comments.

32. There were also concerns over the increasing "Americanization" of British culture in the 1950s and how this was impacting youthful attitudes toward Queen and country—for example, new popular dance forms, rock and roll music, and Hollywood cinema.

33. See McQuire.

34. Furthermore, Black men and women in the services faced a catalog of mistreatment: they were often denied the basic privileges attached to military service; they were insulted and brutalized by White officers; and they could be unfairly discharged or court-martialed.

35. The use of racially insulting language was banned by the military in 1942. By 1945, Black schools could participate for the first time in enlistment programs; there were more Blacks in officer training programs; and there came about mixed-race combat units. Racial discrimination was legally banned in the military in 1948.

36. By 1930, 2.3 million African Americans were living north of the Mason-Dixon Line; during the Great Depression and World War II, another two million emigrated from the South. See Olson.

37. The New Deal refers to the progressive politics of the Roosevelt administrations, which saw the beginnings of a social welfare state in the United States.

38. The case for the Black middle class was very different. Black churches opposed communism because they viewed it as a godless doctrine; also many Blacks wished to integrate fully into White society, believing that it was possible to advance socially and economically within the existing order.

39. This data is taken from Oakley.

40. Twenty to twenty-five percent of the population lived in poverty, with another ten percent balanced on the poverty line (Oakley 203–4). The poor consisted mainly of Blacks in urban ghettos, rural White poor in the deep south and Midwest, and recent immigrants of color such as Chicanas/os.

41. For details of the play's genesis and sources, see Black and Frazier.

42. A number of contemporary reviews are reproduced in Cargill, Fagin, and Fisher.

43. Gillett notes that O'Neill follows European American tradition by making his "everyman" characters White (45).

44. Today, of course, *Iceman* occupies an eminent position in the U.S. dramatic canon. Its rise in status may be traced to José Quintero's 1956 landmark revival. Critics variously attribute this change in viewpoint to a different national mood that was more ready to entertain O'Neill's fatalistic vision, and a new dramatic context within which to locate the play, provided by playwrights such as Beckett. Accordingly, the play has garnered a great deal of critical attention as to its internal meanings and the relation of its themes to the playwright's earlier works and to his own psychobiography. My reading focuses on responses to the play's initial run, those elements that may explain why White mainstream audiences found it a disturbing spectacle just after the end of the war.

45. He is distinguished from the other choral characters by virtue of possessing more insight about the conditions in which he finds himself, being, with Larry (the *choregos*), the first to dismiss Hickey's program as "bughouse." He possesses a greater measure of self-control: he is the sole occupant of the saloon who is not subservient to alcohol. Further, Rocky's management ensures that the saloon runs as smoothly as it does.

46. Consider also that her name signifies "white woods."

47. Here Savran draws upon Lacanian theory, within which the phallus is defined as a signifier of masculine privilege.

48. In Lacanian terms, the phallus symbolizes active power, with the lack of power symbolized by castration. These symbols are socially constructed or grafted onto masculine and feminine categories respectively—the male conceptualized as the active subject and the female as the passive object.

49. Lacan writes that there is "a relation of the subject to the phallus that is es-

tablished without regard to the anatomical difference of the sexes, and which, by this very fact, makes any interpretation of this relation especially difficult in the case of women" (*Écrits,* 282).

50. See Kolin.

51. Kevles addresses the roots of eugenics in late-nineteenth-century social Darwinism, noting that findings were widely disseminated in U.S. society through popular books, articles, and lectures, and that by the end of the 1930s the ideas and language of eugenics had made their way into common culture.

52. This is cemented when Stella returns to Stanley as the end of the play with their child, enabling him to assume the role of head of the nuclear family unit.

53. Comparing the two versions, Miller states: "I had originally conceived Eddie as a phenomenon . . . a kind of biological sport, and to a degree a repelling figure not quite admissible into the human family. In revising I found it possible to move beyond the contemplation of the man as a phenomenon into an acceptance for dramatic purposes of his aims themselves" ("Introduction" 51).

54. Braun gives a thoughtful account of the play as a response to Miller's personal experiences.

55. For further analysis on the institution of White womanhood, see Davy.

56. For a more detailed discussion of Eddie and Catherine's relationship from a Freudian perspective, see Centola.

57. The reference to Rodolfo as Blondie refers to more than physical coloring. It associates him with Dagwood's Blondie, the stereotypical dumb but all-American blonde woman from the comic strip who was later a featured character in a series of B movies.

58. Writing of his one-act version, Miller ("On Social Plays" 66) identifies homosexuality as one of the motifs that provides a reason for expanding to two acts.

59. The Black Panthers used armed patrols in Black neighborhoods to combat police brutality and used proceeds from extralegal activities to fund local groups.

60. However, by the late 1960s even the most radical of the Black power groups had seen the advantages, usually financial, of limited partnerships with White liberals. For example, after Eldridge Cleaver became leader of the Black Panther party (previous leaders Huey Newton and Bobby Seale having been jailed), he attempted to form a loose coalition of Black and White radicals.

61. See Sellers.

62. For details of the White reactions, see Cook and Jack E. Davis.

63. There were other equally influential reasons for racial tensions within campaigning groups. For instance, the media tended to focus more attention on White volunteers, which could lead to resentment. Other tensions resulted from interracial sexual relationships, all of which exacerbated racial tensions and placed pressure on Whites to alter their behavior or sometimes leave the movement.

64. Albee explicitly states a fondness for Grandma's character and acknowledges that she is partly based on his own grandmother (Bryer, "Interview: Edward

Albee" 21–22). Albee, an adopted child, felt little sympathy with his parents' values but admits admiring those of his grandmother.

65. For a discussion of race as a set of coded looking relations, see Erickson.

66. See also Werner Sollors, who interprets Clay's speech as positing "a Black mystique, an inner identity of repressed murderous instincts held back forcefully by masks and sublimated by artistic expression" (109). He writes that "Clay's address is often cited as the pumping Black heart of the New Black Aesthetic." Clay functions as a Black nationalist spokesman who rejects his middle class background to affirm a restoration of sanity for the wretched of the earth (110).

67. For a comparison of the two versions, see Cohn.

68. The play moved to Broadway in 1972. It was awarded a Tony for Best Play in 1973, when it was also adapted for screening on public television.

69. By the late 1960s many people were coming to share Ozzie's view of the family as a trap, and the family unit as embodied by the Nelsons was becoming an anachronism. Nevertheless, the myth of the happy nuclear family still held pervasive power in U.S. culture, and its appeal is expressed in the play by the characters' frantic attempts to perform what they perceive to be happy normality.

70. For a more detailed account, see Sara Evans.

71. By mainstream feminism, I mean U.S. liberal feminism, which is dedicated primarily to enabling some women to succeed economically as well as some men do in a consumer capitalist system. In the 1960s and '70s, there were alternative White feminist voices, but these were in the minority. The liberal position was the defining position of the movement.

72. For a more detailed analysis, see my article entitled "Betty Friedan: A Literary Biography."

73. Taken from an article first published in the *New York Times* in June 1970.

74. In Ross's terminology, "examinability" indicates the unfavorable attention paid to some social groups, both overtly hostile forms of attention such as racism and misogyny and more covert ones such as derivedness, deviation, and secondariness, all of which function as indices of disempowerment (189). In contrast, "unexaminability" refers to privileges attached to normalcy that are enjoyed by White persons in U.S. society. Consequently, one occupies a privileged space of the unexamined through the act of examining the "other" (194).

75. I make reference to this elsewhere, in my essay "Violating the Seal of Race."

76. Here I draw upon the idea of binary oppositions being violently hierarchized as posited in poststructuralist thought.

77. As conceived in the 1948 British Nationality Act.

78. The equation of Blacks with apes repeats earlier pseudo-Darwinian conceptions of race. Stepan and Gilman argue that race in British science was sidelined after World War II (141). However, as in the United States this did not mean that the findings of earlier race sciences did not continue to impact on popular thought.

79. Vron Ware marks a tendency in British politics of place to emphasize the

nation's island status, with the use of "Island" representing a metonymic substitution for the nation as a whole. In racist literature this national community refers to one of long-suffering, angry Whites who feel surrounded and besieged on all sides by the forces of multiculturalism ("Island Racism" 284, 303).

80. It was delivered at the West Midlands Conservative Centre in Birmingham in 1968.

81. Powell's speech is reproduced on <www.Sterlingtime.org/powell-speech. doc>. The site, sympathetic to Powell, is a good source for tracing how Powellism impacts on contemporary debates about immigration in Britain.

82. Even before Powell's speech, a number of grassroots movements dedicated to keeping Britain White sprang up in response to increased immigration. Some, including the British National Party and the Greater Britain Movement, had roots in German fascism. Others, such as the Racial Preservation Society, were modern outgrowths of earlier eugenics societies. For more detail, see Patterson.

83. Though it was not produced until 1968, Bond began writing *Early Morning* at the beginning of 1965.

84. See Kowalski 54–55.

85. After the abolition of the Lord Chamberlain's office, *Early Morning* received another run at the Royal Court in March/April 1969, when it also received the George Devine Award.

86. See Martin Esslin, who argues that the play is ineffective as a polemical piece because it places us in the "realm of fantasy," with the references to cannibalism signifying an expression of early infantile sexuality (26).

87. In addition to the Royal Court's difficulties over the play, Methuen expressed serious concerns over publishing the text, fearing libel suits stemming from Bond's prefatory comments (Spencer 153).

88. Writing on Bond's use of the double, Castillo remarks that "these characters represent real antitheses, but the difference is also, at the same time, illusory in the way a Dostoevskian double is both a real physical presence and a psychological projection" (79).

89. The connection between female sexuality and Blackness is repeated in twentieth-century medical discourse as well, most notably in the allusion Freud makes to femininity as the dark continent of the human psyche. Sander Gilman's work has been instrumental in racially contextualizing Freudian theory—see *Freud, Race and Gender.*

90. The trilogy has a prolonged genesis. Arden began working on a play about the Arthurian age in 1953, then revised it in 1956, but neither version attracted a producer. In 1966 he used the material on Arthur as the basis for new plays commissioned by the BBC, but they were never produced. In 1972, collaborating with D'Arcy, he saw this considerably revised Arthur cycle staged by the Royal Shakespeare Company in London.

91. This is particularly evident in the 1960s in both stage and screen versions of Arthurian history—for example, Lerner and Lowe's musical *Camelot* and Dis-

ney's adaptation of White's novel *The Once and Future King,* retitled *The Sword in the Stone.* It is also evident in British television productions, for example, the twenty-four episodes of *Arthur and the Britons* (1972–73).

92. CND: Campaign for Nuclear Disarmament.

93. This is not to say that local groups did not sometimes unite, when pooling resources for a campaign on a single common issue might improve their chances of success, as in, for example, the National Abortion Campaign.

94. This is evidenced also in the passage where Clive refers to Joshua as "my boy": "He has saved my life. He is devoted to me and to mine" (Churchill, *Cloud Nine* 254). Here Clive signals a sense of gratitude, camaraderie, and even emotional attachment between himself and Joshua, certainly more than he feels for his wife.

95. In Act 1, scene 1, Edward performs the role of White patriarch, mimicking Clive in chiding Joshua for showing disrespect to his mother. Edward's rejection of Betty at the end of this scene produces a similar impression on the spectator.

96. Harding refers to the acting workshops as "truth sessions" that reflect the relation between sex, gender, and power as understood through the personal testimony of those involved. According to Innes, the workshop comprised a straight married couple, a straight divorced couple, a gay couple, a lesbian, a woman in the process of coming out, and two bisexual men (*Modern British Drama* 461). The participants' racial identities are not specified. Given the common practice in Anglo-U.S. writing of clarifying race only when the race is question is not White, it is likely that most if not all of the participants were White. Also, given that the first production was done by an all-White cast, one can assume the same racial homogeneity for the workshops. Because the "break-away and leaps" explored in act 2 derive largely from the racially homogenous workshop sessions, perhaps this accounts for why we do not get to see Joshua's character progress in modern Britain. Still, it does not make the failure to develop Joshua's character any less problematic in terms of the play's racial politics.

97. In an introduction to the play, Churchill states that any arrangement of doubling may set up interesting resonances between the two acts. She states a preference for the format chosen in the first production: Clive-Cathy, Betty-Edward, Maud-Victoria, Mrs. Saunders-Ellen-Lin, Joshua-Gerry, Harry-Martin ("Introduction" 247).

98. Gray explains the origin of the title. "Cloud nine" was the term for orgasm used by the caretaker of the rehearsal room, who was drawn into the workshop at one point. For her, orgasm meant a transforming experience. Churchill translated this to mean personal and political freedom for the characters (52).

99. The essential philosophy of supply-side economics attributes growth to the demands stimulated by producers of goods. In this scheme, the best way of running the economy is to give capitalists rather than consumers more money via lower taxes, less regulation, and other incentives, to encourage them to invest more heavily.

100. Reagan used the phrase "evil empire" in a speech to evangelical Christians

in March 1983. The speech is also notable for how it pays lip service to the "legacy of evil" in U.S. history (i.e., racism, anti-Semitism) and then confidently asserts that the glory of the United States has been "its capacity for transcending the moral evils of our past" (Watts and Israel 365–66).

101. Scapegoating, while led by neoconservative spokespeople, was not limited to one side of the political spectrum in the 1980s, for Reagan enjoyed support among conservative Democrats as well.

102. Women were also producing anti-feminist discourse in the 1980s—see Hewlett, Paglia, and Wolf.

103. See also Jewell.

104. See also McClain and Stewart 30.

105. For details of specific legislation vetoed/passed during Reagan's presidency, see Amaker's *Civil Rights and the Reagan Administration.*

106. The 1980s saw a growth in Black conservatism. Shelby Steele epitomizes it when he states: "If conditions have worsened for most of us as racism has receded, then much of the problem must be of our own making" (15).

107. The Moral Majority, led by the Reverend Jerry Falwell, was an affiliation of evangelical, mostly Southern-based churches. As a religious lobby group, it aimed to inject fundamentalist beliefs into political practice, and many of its aims threatened the constitutional separation of church and state.

108. See Caesar and Busch 41.

109. See also Hamilton and Hamilton 138.

110. Power feminism was endorsed most notably by Wolf in *Fire with Fire.*

111. See my reading in *Race, Sex and Gender in Contemporary Women's Theatre.*

112. His review of the 1993 New York production first appeared in *The New Republic.*

113. It is this skepticism toward the narrative of U.S. exceptionalism, Una Chaudhuri argues, that lends the play a 1990s sensibility: Even though it is set in the decade of Reagan/Bush it is reflective also of national sentiment in the 1990s— a decade equally defined by the approach of the millennium (255).

114. The significance of Prior's Anglo-Norman ancestry is discussed further by Allen Frantzen, who takes a less optimistic view of the way Kushner uses the split in Prior's White identity.

115. According to Mormon doctrine, in 1823 Joseph Smith was visited by an angel called Moroni, who told him of a book of gold that was hidden in the side of a hill outside the village of Manchester in New York. The Book of Mormon is meant to represent the "fullness of the gospel," that is, to be the final supplement to the Old and New Testaments (Bartley 14–15).

116. For a more detailed elaboration of the connection between Mormon doctrine and Manifest Destiny, see Wald.

117. David Román similarly notes that Kushner makes Belize carry the "burden of representation." He notes also that Belize functions as the play's ethical center and that this could mean that he does not necessarily support the amorphous

power of Whiteness. Belize could also critically mirror the lived experience of people of color in the gay movement as signifiers of racial difference (213).

118. Diana Fuss contends that the psychical mechanism that produces self-recognition is a question of relations, of self to other, subject to object, and inside to outside. She draws a distinction between identity and identification: identity is defined as "the self that identifies the self" and identification as "the detour through the other" that is necessary to the process of defining the self (1–3).

119. Quoted in Dollimore, 81.

120. Prejudice against gays and lesbians was not limited to those on the right. Some in the Labour movement feared that they would lose votes if they were associated too closely with gay rights. During a London by-election campaign in 1983, a gay candidate was attacked by the shadow education secretary Neil Kinnock, who stated: "I am not in favour of witch hunts, but I do not mistake bloody witches for fairies" (Anna Marie Smith 186).

121. Johnson spoke on BBC's *Weekend World* in January 1988.

122. Joel Krieger records that Thatcher gained the greatest number of swing votes in constituencies that had witnessed the most sustained National Front organizing. One National Front leader concurred that "Mrs. Thatcher's apparent anti-immigration stance was the central cause of NF's electoral decline" (80–81).

123. Thatcher did not share Powell's view of empire as a disruption to the natural order of English society.

124. Gilroy notes that the association of Blackness with violent behavior does reflect earlier biological-based racism that proposed Blacks as being closer to animals than Whites (*There Ain't No Black* 104).

125. For precise statistics, see Andrews and Jacobs, and Riddell.

126. See also Dorey, "Despair and Disillusion Abound."

127. See Heffernan.

128. Thatcher's first arts minister stated the government's attitude as follows: "The arts world must come to terms with the fact that Government policy in general has decisively tilted away from the expansion of the public to the private section" (*The Observer,* October 14, 1979; Peacock 36). While the government would continue to fund the arts, it would be at a standstill rate, and any shortfalls would have to be made up in the private sphere.

129. For a more detailed trajectory of how Black theater developed in Britain, see Khan.

130. Peacock notes that British Black theater was largely confined to areas with large immigrant and/or second-generation populations, chief among which was London (183).

131. This is aptly reflected in one of the most memorable images of the 1983 British General Election campaign. A Conservative Party poster pictured a young Black male with the caption: "Labour Say He's Black. Tories Say He's British." Reproduced in Gilroy, *There Ain't No Black* 58.

132. For example, see the collection of reviews in *Record,* 26 March–8 April 2003.

133. For example, Charter 88's campaign for a new written constitution containing a bill of rights.

134. The multiethnic constitution of British society would encompass Scottish, Welsh, and Northern Irish identities as well. In the 1990s, Vron Ware points out, one of the factors that precipitated public discussions of what constitutes national character, particularly White English identity, was the movements for devolution among Britain's internally colonized peoples ("Perfidious Albion" 189–90). However, space does not permit a detailed exploration of the nuances in constructions of Whiteness in these cultures, nor do I consider it necessary, as Hare does not make it an issue in the play, though he easily could have, given that George Jones is modeled on Neil Kinnock, who was born in a South Wales industrial village. In contrast, Hare chooses Kennington as the birthplace for his character, and his South London working background squarely locates George in a British-as-English paradigm.

135. In addition, as the voice of the "common people" Vera's character has another important function in the play. She provides a contrast to George, who has lost the ability to speak authentically (that is, in terms of historic Labour discourse). Hare emphasizes this in scene 8, when George, departing from his scripted speech, finds himself unable to make the words that would express his concern for the poor.

136. Other signs of the caste system inherited from the days of empire appear in the lobby of the House of Commons, where to one side there is a desk "attended by men in tails and white ties" (Hare, *The Absence of War* 3).

137. In scene 9 George declares: "This country will never, *can* never prosper until it escapes from its past" (Hare, *The Absence of War* 99).

works cited

Achilles, Jochen. "Allegory and Iconography in African American Drama of the Sixties: Imamu Amiri Baraka's *Dutchman* and Alice Childress's *Wine in the Wilderness.*" *American Studies* 45 (2000): 219–38.

Albee, Edward. "Preface." *New American Drama.* 1961. Harmondsworth: Penguin, 1965, 21–22.

———. *The American Dream. New American Drama.* Harmondsworth: Penguin, 1965, 19–60.

Allen, Charles. *Tales from the Dark Continent: Images of British Colonial Africa in the Twentieth Century.* London: Andre Deutsch, 1979.

Allen, Theodore W. *The Invention of the White Race.* Vol. 1: *Racial Oppression and Social Control.* London: Verso, 1994.

———. *The Invention of the White Race.* Vol. 2: *The Origin of Racial Oppression in Anglo-America.* London: Verso, 1997.

Alter, Stephen G. *Darwinism and the Linguistic Image: Language, Race, and Natural Theology in the Nineteenth Century.* Baltimore: Johns Hopkins University Press, 1999.

Amaker, Norman C. *Civil Rights and the Reagan Administration.* Washington, D.C.: Urban Institute Press, 1988.

———. "The Reagan Civil Rights Legacy." *Ronald Reagan's America.* Vol. 1. Ed. Eric J. Schmertz, Natalie Datlof, and Alexej Ugrinsky. Westport, Conn.: Greenwood, 1997, 163–74.

Amoko, Apollo. "Casting Aside Colonial Occupation: Intersections of Race, Sex, and Gender in *Cloud Nine* and *Cloud Nine* Criticism." *Modern Drama* 42 (1999): 45–57.

Anderson, Martin. "Reagan's Long-Term Legacy." *Ronald Reagan's America.* Vol. 1. Ed. Eric J. Schmertz, Natalie Datlof, and Alexej Ugrinsky. Westport, Conn.: Greenwood, 1997, 31–40.

Anderson, Michael. *Anger and Detachment: A Study of Arden, Osborne, and Pinter.* London: Pitman, 1976.

Andrews, Kay, and John Jacobs. *Punishing the Poor: Poverty under Thatcher.* London: Macmillan, 1990.

Arden, John. "Author's Preface (I)." *The Island of the Mighty.* London: Eyre Methuen, 1974, 9–16.

Arden, John, with Margaretta D'Arcy. *The Island of the Mighty.* London: Eyre Methuen, 1974.

Aronson, Aaron. "Design for Angels in America: Envisioning the Millennium." *The Harcourt Brace Anthology of Drama.* 3rd ed. Ed. W. B. Worthen. Fort Worth: Harcourt Brace, 2000, 1175–82.

Arrowsmith, William. "Notes on English Verse Drama II: *The Cocktail Party.*" *T. S. Eliot: Critical Assessments.* Vol. 3. Ed. Graham Clarke. London: Christopher Helm, 1990, 383–98.

Asher, Kenneth. *T. S. Eliot and Ideology.* Cambridge: Cambridge University Press, 1995.

Auden, W. H., and Christopher Isherwood. *The Ascent of F6.* London: Faber and Faber, 1958.

Aziz, Razia. "Feminism and the Challenge of Racism: Deviance or Difference?" *Black British Feminism: A Reader.* Ed. Heidi Safia Mirza. London: Routledge, 1997, 70–7.

Banton, Michael. *The Idea of Race.* London: Tavistock, 1977.

Baraka, Amiri. "The Revolutionary Theatre." *The Harcourt Brace Anthology of Drama.* 2nd ed. Ed. W. B. Worthen. Fort Worth: Harcourt Brace, 1996, 1036–37.

———. *Dutchman. The Harcourt Brace Anthology of Drama.* 2nd ed. Ed. W. B. Worthen. Fort Worth: Harcourt Brace, 1996, 873–80.

Barczewski, Stephanie L. *Myth and National Identity in Nineteenth-Century Britain: The Legends of King Arthur and Robin Hood.* Oxford: Oxford University Press, 2000.

Barksdale, Richard K. "Miscegenation on Broadway: Hughes' *Mulatto* and Edward Sheldon's *The Nigger.*" *Critical Essays on Langston Hughes.* Ed. Edward J. Mullen. Boston: G. K. Hall, 1986, 191–99.

Barthes, Roland. *Mythologies.* 1957. London: Paladin, 1973.

Bartley, Peter. *Mormonism: The Prophet, the Book, and the Cult.* Dublin: Veritas, 1989.

Bassnett, Susan. *Feminist Experiences: The Women's Movement in Four Cultures.* London: Allen and Unwin, 1986.

Beebe, Lucius. "Stage Asides: Miss Hellman Talks of Her Latest Play, *The Little Foxes.*" *Conversations with Lillian Hellman.* Ed. Jackson R. Bryer. Jackson: University Press of Mississippi, 1986, 7–10.

Bennett, Susan. "Rehearsing *The Tempest,* Directing the Post-Colonial Body: Disjunctive Identity in Philip Osment's *This Island's Mine.*" *Essays in Theatre* 15, no. 1 (1996): 35–44.

Benston, Kimberly W. *Performing Blackness: Enactments of African-American Modernism.* London: Routledge, 2000.

Berg, Rick, and John Carlos Rowe. "Introduction: The Vietnam War and American Memory." *The Vietnam War and American Culture*. Ed. Rick Berg and John Carlos Rowe. New York: Columbia University Press, 1991, 1–17.

Berlin, Norman. "The Late Plays." *The Cambridge Companion to Eugene O'Neill*. Ed. Michael Manheim. Cambridge: Cambridge University Press, 1998, 82–95.

Bersani, Leo. *Homos*. Cambridge, Mass.: Harvard University Press, 1995.

Bhabha, Homi. *The Location of Culture*. London: Routledge, 1994.

Bigsby, C. W. E. *Confrontation and Commitment: A Study of Contemporary American Drama, 1959–66*. London: MacGibbon and Kee, 1967.

———. *Albee*. Edinburgh: Oliver and Boyd, 1969.

———. *A Critical Introduction to Twentieth-Century American Drama*. Vol. 2: *Williams/Miller/Albee*. Cambridge: Cambridge University Press, 1984.

———. *Modern American Drama: 1945–1990*. Cambridge: Cambridge University Press, 1992.

———. "Introduction." *David Rabe: Plays I*. London: Methuen, 2002.

Black, Stephen A. *Eugene O'Neill: Beyond Mourning and Tragedy*. New Haven: Yale University Press, 1999.

Bleier, Ruth. *Science and Gender: A Critique of Biology and Its Theories on Women*. New York: Pergamon, 1984.

Blum, John Morton. *Years of Discord: American Politics and Society, 1961–1974*. New York: W. W. Norton, 1991.

Bogard, Travis. *Contour in Time: The Plays of Eugene O'Neill*. Oxford: Oxford University Press, 1972.

Boland, Bridget. *The Cockpit. Plays of the Year: 1948–49*. London: Paul Elek, 1949.

Bolt, Christine. *Victorian Attitudes to Race*. London: Routledge and Kegan Paul, 1971.

Bond, Edward. *Early Morning*. 1968. *Bond: Plays: One*. London: Eyre Methuen, 1977.

———. "Author's Note: On Violence." *Bond: Plays: One*. London: Eyre Methuen, 1977.

Bonnett, Alastair. *White Identities: Historical and International Perspectives*. Harlow, Essex: Prentice Hall/Pearson Education, 2000.

Bradford, William. *Of Plymouth Plantation. The Norton Anthology of American Literature*. Vol. 1. 5th ed. Ed. Nina Baym. New York: W. W. Norton, 1998, 165–204.

Brauer, Carl M. *John F. Kennedy and the Second Reconstruction*. New York: Columbia University Press, 1977.

Braun, Andrea England. "Eddie Wrecks: Probing the Author's Unconscious in *A View from the Bridge*." *CEA Critic* 58, no. 1 (1995): 74–83.

Breines, Wini. *Young, White and Miserable: Growing Up Female in the Fifties*. Boston: Beacon, 1992.

Brewer, Mary. *Race, Sex and Gender in Contemporary Women's Theatre: The Construction of "Woman."* Brighton: Sussex Academic Press, 1999.

———. "Betty Friedan: A Literary Biography." *Twentieth-Century American Cul-*

tural Theorists. Ed. Paul Hansom. New York: Buccoli Clark Layman, 2001, 128–39.

———. "Violating the Seal of Race: The Politics of (Post)Identity and the Theater of Adrienne Kennedy." *Exclusions in Feminist Thought: Challenging the Boundaries of Womanhood.* Ed. Mary Brewer. Brighton: Sussex Academic Press, 2002, 73–91.

Brooke, Stephen. *Reform and Reconstruction.* Manchester: Manchester University Press, 1995.

Brown, John Russell. *Theatre Language: Arden, Osborne, Pinter, Wesker.* London: Penguin, 1972.

Brustein, Robert. "Review of *Angels in America—Part I: Millennium Approaches.*" *The Harcourt Brace Anthology of Drama.* 3rd ed. Ed. W. B. Worthen. Fort Worth: Harcourt Brace, 2000, 1191–93.

Bryan, Beverley, Stella Dadzie, and Suzanne Scafe. *The Heart of the Race: Black Women's Lives in Britain.* London: Virago, 1985.

Bryer, Jackson R. "Interview: Edward Albee." *The Playwrights' Art: Conversations with Contemporary American Dramatists.* Ed. Jackson R. Bryer. New Brunswick: Rutgers University Press, 1995, 1–23.

———. "Interview: Wendy Wasserstein." *The Playwrights' Art: Conversations with Contemporary American Dramatists.* Ed. Jackson R. Bryer. New Brunswick: Rutgers University Press, 1995, 257–71.

Bunge, Nancy. "The Social Realism of *Our Town:* A Study in Misunderstanding." *Thornton Wilder: New Essays.* Ed. Martin Blank, Dalma Hunyadi Brunauer, and David Garret Izzo. West Cornwall, Conn.: Locust Hill, 1999, 349–64.

Butler, Judith. *Gender Trouble: Feminism and the Subversion of Identity.* London: Routledge, 1990.

Caesar, James W., and Andrew E. Busch. *Losing to Win: The 1996 Elections and American Politics.* Lanham: Rowman and Littlefield, 1997.

Carby, Hazel V. "White Woman Listen! Black Feminism and the Boundaries of Sisterhood." *The Empire Strikes Back: Race and Racism in 70s Britain.* London: Routledge/University of Birmingham, 1982, 221–35.

Cargill, O., N. B. Fagin, and W. J. Fisher. *Eugene O'Neill and His Plays: A Survey of His Life and Works.* London: Peter Owen, 1962.

Carmichael, Stokely, and Charles V. Hamilton. *Black Power: The Politics of Liberation in America.* New York: Vintage, 1967.

Cashmore, E. Ellis. *United Kingdom? Class, Race, and Gender since the War.* London: Unwin Hyman, 1989.

Castillo, Debra A. "Dehumanized or Inhuman: Doubles in Edward Bond." *South Central Review: Journal of the South Central Modern Language Association* 3 (1986): 78–89.

Centola, Steven R. "Compromise as Bad Faith: Arthur Miller's *A View from the Bridge* and William Inge's *Come Back, Little Sheba.*" *Midwest Quarterly: A Journal of Contemporary Thought* 28 (1986): 100–113.

Chafe, William H. *The American Woman: Her Changing Social, Economic, and Political Roles, 1920–70.* London: Oxford University Press, 1972.

Chakrabarty, Dipesh. "Postcoloniality and the Artifice of History." *The Post-Colonial Studies Reader.* Ed. Bill Ashcroft, Gareth Griffiths, and Helen Tiffin. London: Routledge, 1997, 383–88.

Chambers, Ross. "The Unexamined." *Whiteness: A Critical Reader.* Ed. Mike Hill. New York: New York University Press, 1997, 187–203.

Chaudhuri, Una. *Staging Place: The Geography of Modern Drama.* Ann Arbor: University of Michigan Press, 1997.

Chennault, Ronald E. "Giving Whiteness a Black Eye: An Interview with Michael Eric Dyson." *White Reign: Deploying Whiteness in America.* Ed. Joe L. Kincheloe, Shirley R. Steinberg, Nelson M. Rodriguez, and Ronald E. Chennault. Houndmills: Macmillan, 1998, 299–328.

Churchill, Caryl. *Cloud Nine.* 1979. *Churchill: Plays: One.* London: Methuen, 1986.

———. "Introduction: Cloud Nine." *Churchill: Plays: One.* London: Methuen, 1986.

Cohen, Esther. "Uncommon Woman: An Interview with Wendy Wasserstein." *Women's Studies* 15 (1988): 257–70.

Cohn, Ruby. *New American Dramatists: 1960–1980.* London: Macmillan, 1992.

Colvin, Madeleine, with Jane Hawksley. *Section 28: A Practical Guide to the Law and Its Implications.* London: National Council for Civil Liberties, 1989.

Combs, James. *The Reagan Range: The Nostalgic Myth in American Politics.* Bowling Green: Bowling Green State University Popular Press, 1993.

Contract with America: The Bold Plan by Rep. Newt Gingrich, Rep. Dick Armey, and the House Republicans to Change the Nation. New York: Times Books, 1994.

Cook, Robert. *Sweet Land of Liberty: The African-American Struggle for Civil Rights in the Twentieth Century.* London: Addison Wesley Longman, 1988.

Cooley, John. "White Writers and the Harlem Renaissance." *Harlem Renaissance: Reevaluations.* Ed. A. Singh. New York: Garland, 1989, 13–22.

Cooper, Pamela. "David Rabe's Sticks and Bones: The Adventures of Ozzie and Harriet." *Modern Drama* 29, no. 4 (1986): 613–25.

Costello, Donald P. "Arthur Miller's Circles of Responsibility: A View from the Bridge and Beyond." *Modern Drama* 36, no. 3 (1993): 443–53.

Coult, Tony. *The Plays of Edward Bond.* 1977. London: Eyre Methuen, 1979.

Cousin, Geraldine. *Churchill: The Playwright.* London: Methuen, 1989.

Darby, Phillip. *Three Faces of Imperialism: British and American Approaches to Asia and Africa, 1870–1970.* New Haven: Yale University Press, 1987.

Darwin, John. *Britain and Decolonisation: The Retreat from Empire in the Post-War World.* Houndmills: Macmillan, 1988.

———. *The End of the British Empire: The Historical Debate.* London: Blackwell, 1991.

Davis, Jack E. *The Civil Rights Movement.* London: Blackwell, 2001.

Davis, Tracy C. *George Bernard Shaw and the Socialist Theatre.* Westport, Conn.: Praeger, 1994.

———. "Shaw's Interstices of Empire: Decolonizing at Home and Abroad." *The Cambridge Companion to George Bernard Shaw.* Ed. Christopher Innes. Cambridge: Cambridge University Press, 1998, 218–39.

Davy, Kate. "Outing Whiteness: A Feminist/Lesbian Project." *Whiteness: A Critical Reader.* Ed. Mike Hill. New York: New York University Press, 1997, 204–225.

de Jongh, Nicholas. *Not in front of the Audience: Homosexuality on Stage.* London: Routledge, 1992.

Diamond, Elin. "(In)Visible Bodies in Churchill's Theatre." *Making a Spectacle: Feminist Essays on Contemporary Women's Theatre.* Ed. Lynda Hart. Ann Arbor: University of Michigan Press, 1992, 259–81.

———. "Adrienne Kennedy." *Speaking on Stage: Interviews with Contemporary American Playwrights.* Ed. Philip C. Kolin and Colby H. Kullman. Tuscaloosa: University of Alabama Press, 1996, 125–37.

———. *Unmaking Mimesis: Essays on Feminism and Theatre.* London: Routledge, 1997.

Dollimore, Jonathan. "The Challenge of Sexuality." *Society and Literature: 1945–1970.* Ed. Alan Sinfield. New York: Holmes and Meier, 1983, 51–86.

Donesky, Finlay. *David Hare: Moral and Historical Perspectives.* Westport, Conn.: Greenwood, 1996.

Dorey, Peter. "Despair and Disillusion Abound: The Major Premiership in Perspective." *The Major Premiership: Politics and Policies under John Major, 1990–97.* Ed. Peter Dorey. Houndmills: Palgrave, 1999, 218–49.

———. "The Blairite Betrayal: New Labour and the Trades Unions." *The Impact of New Labour.* Ed. Gerald R. Taylor. Houndmills: Macmillan, 1999, 190–207.

Drabble, Margaret. *For Queen and Country: Britain in the Victorian Age.* London: Andre Deutsch, 1978.

Drukman, Steven. "Doo-A-Diddly-Dit-Dit: An Interview with Suzan-Lori Parks and Liz Diamond." *A Sourcebook of African-American Performance: Plays, People, Movements.* Ed. Annemarie Bean. London: Routledge, 1999, 284–306.

Du Bois, W. E. B. *Black Reconstruction: An Essay toward a History of the Part Which Black Folk Played in an Attempt to Reconstruct Democracy in America, 1860–1880.* New York: Russell and Russell, 1962.

Durham, Martin. *Sex and Politics: The Family and Morality in the Thatcher Years.* Houndmills: Macmillan, 1991.

Duster, Troy. "The 'Morphing' Properties of Whiteness." *The Making and Unmaking of Whiteness.* Ed. Birgit Brander Rasmussen, Eric Klinenberg, Irene J. Nexica, and Matt Wray. Durham: Duke University Press, 2001, 113–37.

Dyer, Richard. *White.* London: Routledge, 1997.

———. *The Culture of Queers.* London: Routledge, 2002.

Eliot, T. S. *The Idea of a Christian Society.* London: Faber and Faber, 1939.

———. *The Cocktail Party.* London: Faber and Faber, 1950.

Ellis, Michael. "Author's Preface." *Black Plays.* Ed. Yvonne Brewster. London: Methuen, 1987, 10.

———. *Chameleon. Black Plays.* Ed. Yvonne Brewster. London: Methuen, 1987.

Elsom, John. *Post-War British Theatre.* London: Routledge and Kegan Paul, 1976.

Engelhardt, Tom. 1995. *The End of Victory Culture: Cold War America and the Disillusioning of a Generation.* 2nd ed. Amherst: University of Massachusetts Press, 1998.

Erickson, Paul. *Reagan Speaks: The Making of an American Myth.* New York: New York University Press, 1985.

Esslin, Martin. "A Bond Honoured." *Plays and Players* 15, no. 9 (1968): 26–63.

Evans, David. *Sexual Citizenship: The Material Construction of Sexualities.* London: Routledge, 1993.

Evans, Eric J. *Thatcher and Thatcherism.* London: Routledge, 1997.

Evans, Sara. *Personal Politics: The Roots of Women's Liberation in the Civil Rights Movement and the New Left.* New York: Vintage, 1980.

Faludi, Susan. *Backlash: The Undeclared War Against Women.* London: Chatto and Windus, 1991.

Farber, David. *The Age of Great Dreams: America in the 1960s.* New York: Hill and Wang, 1994.

Feldman, Leslie. "Ronald Reagan and Machiavelli: Appearance vs. Reality." *Ronald Reagan's America.* Vol 2. Ed. Eric J. Schmertz, Natalie Datlof, and Alexej Ugrinsky. Westport, Conn.: Greenwood, 1997, 805–811.

Fenton, Steve. *Ethnicity: Racism, Class and Culture.* London: Macmillan, 1999.

Fisher, James. *The Theater of Tony Kushner: Living Past Hope.* London: Routledge, 2001.

Fitzsimmons, Linda. *File on Churchill.* London: Methuen, 1989.

Foley, Conor, with Liberty. *Human Rights, Human Wrongs: The Alternative Report to the United Nations Human Rights Committee.* London: Rivers Oram, 1995.

Foucault, Michel. *Power/Knowledge: Selected Interviews and Other Writings, 1972–1977.* Ed. Colin Gordon, Leo Marshall, John Mepham, Kate Soper. Brighton: Harvester Press, 1980.

———. *The History of Sexuality: Vol. 1.* New York: Vintage, 1980.

Frankenberg, Ruth R. *The Social Construction of Whiteness: White Women, Race Matters.* London: Routledge, 1993.

———. "The Mirage of an Unmarked Whiteness." *The Making and Unmaking of Whiteness.* Ed. Birgit Brander Rasmussen, Eric Klinenberg, Irene J. Nexica, and Matt Wray. Durham: Duke University Press, 2001, 72–96.

Frantzen, Allen J. "Prior to the Normans: The Anglo-Saxons in *Angels in America.*" *Approaching the Millennium: Essays on Angels in America.* Ed. Deborah R. Geis and Steven F. Kruger. Ann Arbor: University of Michigan Press, 1997, 134–50.

Frazier, Winifred L. "'Revolution' in *The Iceman Cometh.*" *Modern Drama* 22 (1979): 1–8.

Fredrickson, George M. *The Black Image in the White Mind: The Debate on Afro-American Character and Destiny, 1817–1914.* Middletown, Conn.: Wesleyan University Press, 1987.

Freedman, Jonathan. "Angels, Monsters, and Jews: Intersections of Queer and Jewish Identity in Kushner's *Angels in America.*" *PMLA* 113, no. 1 (1998): 90–102.

Friedan, Betty. *The Feminine Mystique.* 1963. London: Victor Gollancz, 1971.

———. *The Second Stage.* London: Michael Joseph, 1982.

Fuss, Diana. *Identification Papers.* London: Routledge, 1995.

Gaston, Georg. "An Interview with John Arden." *Contemporary Literature* 32, no. 2 (1991): 147–70.

Gaston, Paul M. *The New South Creed: A Study in Southern Mythmaking.* New York: Alfred A. Knopf, 1970.

Gates Jr., Henry Louis. *The Signifying Monkey: A Theory of African-American Literary Criticism.* Oxford: Oxford University Press, 1988.

Gilleman, Luc. *John Osborne: Vituperative Artist.* New York: Routledge, 2002.

Gillett, Peter J. "O'Neill and the Racial Myths." *Eugene O'Neill: A Collection of Criticism.* Ed. Ernest G. Griffin. New York: McGraw-Hill, 1976, 45–58.

Gilman, Sander. *Inscribing the Other.* Lincoln: University of Nebraska Press, 1991.

———. *Freud, Race and Gender.* Princeton: Princeton University Press, 1993.

Gilpin, William. "Mission of the North American People." *The American Frontier: A Social and Literary Record.* Ed. C. Merton Babcock. New York: Holt, Rinehart, and Winston, 1965, 232–33.

Gilroy, Paul. *There Ain't No Black in the Union Jack: The Cultural Politics of Race and Nation.* 1987. London: Routledge, 1995.

———. "One Nation under a Groove: The Cultural Politics of 'Race' and Racism in Britain." *Anatomy of Racism.* Ed. David Theo Goldberg. Minneapolis: University of Minnesota Press, 1990, 263–82.

———. *Against Race.* Cambridge, Mass.: Harvard University Press, 2001.

Glenn, Lane A. "Playwright of Popular Dissent: David Hare and the Trilogy." *David Hare: A Casebook.* Ed. Hersch Zeifmann. New York: Garland, 1994, 217–35.

Goldfield, David. "America's Changing Perceptions of Race, 1946–1996." *Living with America, 1946–1996.* Ed. Cristina Giorelli and Rob Kroes. Amsterdam: VU University Press, 1997.

Gordon, Vivian. *Black Women: Feminism and Black Liberation: Which Way?* 1987. Chicago: Third World Press, 1991.

Goulbourne, Harry. *Ethnicity and Nationalism in Post-Imperial Britain.* Cambridge: Cambridge University Press, 1991.

———. *Race Relations in Britain since 1945.* Houndmills: Macmillan, 1998.

Gould, Philip. *The Unfinished Revolution: How the Modernisers Saved the Labour Party.* London: Abacus, 1998.

Gray, Frances. "Mirrors of Utopia: Caryl Churchill and Joint Stock." *British and Irish Drama since 1960.* Ed. James Acheson. Houndmills: Macmillan, 1993, 47–59.

Griffin, Alice. *Understanding Arthur Miller.* Columbia: University of South Carolina Press, 1996.

Hacker, Andrew. *Two Nations: Black and White, Separate, Hostile, Unequal.* New York: Ballantine, 1995.

Hall, Catherine. *White, Male and Middle-Class: Explorations in Feminism and History.* Cambridge: Polity, 1992.

Hall, Stuart. "Cultural Identity and Diaspora." *Identity: Community, Culture, Difference.* Ed. Jonathan Rutherford. London: Lawrence and Wishart, 1990, 222–37.

Hamilton, Dona Cooper, and Charles V. Hamilton. "The Dual Agenda of African American Organizations since the New Deal: Social Welfare Policies and Civil Rights." *Critical Issues for Clinton's Domestic Agenda.* Ed. Demetrios Caraley. New York: Academy of Political Science, 1994, 137–54.

Harding, James M. "Cloud Cover: (Re)Dressing Desire and Comfortable Subversions in Caryl Churchill's *Cloud Nine.*" *PMLA* 113, no. 2 (1998): 258–72.

Hare, David. "The Play Is in the Air: On Political Theatre." *David Hare: Writing Left-Handed.* London: Faber and Faber, 1991, 24–36.

———. *The Absence of War.* London: Faber and Faber, 1993.

———. *Asking Around.* London: Faber and Faber, 1993.

———. "A Time and a Place: David Hare and His Inspiration for *The Hare Trilogy.*"
Program Notes: The Hare Trilogy. Birmingham Repertory Theatre, March 7–19, 2003.

Hargreaves, Robert. *Superpower: America in the 1970s.* London: Hodder and Stoughton, 1973.

Harris, Angela P. "Race and Essentialism in Feminist Legal Theory." *Representing Women: Law, Literature, and Feminism.* Ed. Susan Sage Heinzelman and Zipporah Batshaw Wiseman. Durham: Duke University Press, 1994, 106–46.

Hayman, Ronald. *Edward Albee.* London: Heinemann, 1971.

Heale, M. J. *The Sixties in America: History, Politics and Protest.* Edinburgh: Edinburgh University Press, 2001.

Heffernan, Richard. *New Labour and Thatcherism: Political Change in Britain.* Houndmills: Palgrave, 2000.

Hellman, Lillian. *The Little Foxes.* 1939. Harmondsworth, Middlesex: Penguin, 1982.

Hertzbach, Janet S. "The Plays of David Rabe: A World of Streamers." *Essays on Contemporary American Drama.* Ed. Hedwig Bock and Albert Wertheim. München: Max Hueber Verlag, 1981, 173–87.

Hewison, Robert. *Too Much: Art and Society in the Sixties: 1960–75.* London: Methuen, 1986.

Hewlett, Sylvia Ann. *A Lesser Life: The Myth of Women's Liberation.* 1986. Bungay, Suffolk: Sphere, 1988.

Hill, Michael. "Rolling Back the (Welfare) State: The Major Governments and Social Security Reform." *The Major Premiership: Politics and Policies under John Major, 1990–97.* Ed. Peter Dorey. Houndmills: Palgrave, 1999, 165–78.

Hinchliffe, Arnold P. *British Theatre: 1950–70.* Oxford: Blackwell, 1974.

Hiro, Dilip. *Black British/White British: A History of Race Relations in Britain.* 1971. Hammersmith: Paladin, 1992.

Homden, Carol. *The Plays of David Hare.* Cambridge: Cambridge University Press, 1995.

hooks, bell. "Representing Whiteness in the Black Imagination." *Cultural Studies.* Ed. Lawrence Grossberg, Cary Nelson, Paula A. Treichler. New York: Routledge, 1992, 338–46.

Horsman, Reginald. *Race and Manifest Destiny: The Origins of American Racial Anglo-Saxonism.* Cambridge, Mass.: Harvard University Press, 1981.

Houswitschka, Christoph. "The Christian Perspective: War and Ritual Sacrifices in David Rabe's *Sticks and Bones.*" *Modern War on Stage and Screen.* Ed. Wolfgang Görtschacher and Holger Kleim. Lampeter: Edwin Mellon Press, 1995, 117–34.

Howe, Stephen. *Anticolonialism in British Politics: The Left and the End of Empire 1918–1964.* Oxford: Oxford University Press, 1993.

Hughes, Langston. *Mulatto: A Tragedy of the Deep South.* 1935. *Three Negro Plays.* New York: Penguin, 1969.

Hunt, Albert. *Arden: A Study of His Plays.* London: Eyre Methuen, 1974.

Ignatiev, Noel. *How the Irish Became White.* London: Routledge, 1995.

Innes, Christopher. *Modern British Drama, 1890–1990.* Cambridge: Cambridge University Press, 1992.

———. "The Political Spectrum of Edward Bond: From Rationalism to Rhapsody." *Contemporary British Drama: 1970–90.* Ed. Hersch Ziefman and Cynthia Zimmerman. Houndmills: Macmillan, 1993, 81–100.

Jacobson, Matthew Frye. *Whiteness of a Different Color: European Immigrants and the Alchemy of Race.* Cambridge, Mass.: Harvard University Press, 1998.

Jameson, Fredric. *The Political Unconscious: Narrative as a Socially Symbolic Act.* London: Methuen, 1991.

Jann, Rosemary. "Darwin and the Anthropologists: Sexual Selection and Its Discontents." *Sexualities in Victorian Britain.* Ed. Andrew H. Miller and James Eli Adams. Bloomington: Indiana University Press, 1996, 79–95.

Jewell, K. Sue. *From Mammy to Miss America and Beyond: Cultural Images and the Shaping of US Social Policy.* London: Routledge, 1993.

Johnson, Charles, Patricia Smith, and the WGBH Series Research Team. *Africans in America: America's Journey through Slavery.* San Diego: Harcourt Brace, 1998.

Jordan, June. "White English/Black English: The Politics of Translation." *Moving toward Home: Political Essays.* 1972. London: Virago, 1989.

Jordan, Winthrop D. *White over Black: American Attitudes toward the Negro, 1550–1812.* Chapel Hill: University of North Carolina Press, 1968.

Karnow, Stanley. *Vietnam: A History.* New York: Penguin, 1983.

Kennedy, Adrienne. *A Movie Star Has to Star in Black and White. Adrienne Kennedy: In One Act.* 1976. Minneapolis: University of Minnesota Press, 1997.

Kevles, Daniel J. "Eugenics in North America." *Essays in the History of Eugenics.* Ed. Robert A. Peel. London: Galton Institute, 1998, 208–26.

Keyssar, Helene. *Feminist Theatre.* Houndsmill: Macmillan, 1984.

———. "Drama and the Dialogic Imagination: The Heidi Chronicles and Fefu and Her Friends." *Modern Drama* 34 (1991): 88–106.

Khan, Naseem. "The Public-Going Theatre: Community and 'Ethnic' Theatre." *Dreams and Deconstructions: Alternative Theatre in Britain.* Ed. Sandy Craig. Derbyshire: Amber Lane, 1980, 59–75.

King Jr., Martin Luther. "I Have a Dream." *I Have a Dream: Writings and Speeches That Changed the World.* Ed. James M. Washington. San Francisco: Harper, 1992.

Kinzer, Craig, Sandra Richards, Frank Galati, and Lawrence Bommer. "The Theater and the Barricades." *Tony Kushner in Conversation.* Ed. Robert Vorlicky. Ann Arbor: University of Michigan Press, 2001, 188–216.

Kolin, Philip C. "Williams in Ebony: Black and Multi-Racial Productions of *A Streetcar Named Desire.*" *Black American Literature Forum* 25, no. 1 (1981): 147–81.

Kowalski, Jennifer. "Politics and Poetics in the Plays of Edward Bond: The First Two Series." Ph.D. dissertation, The Shakespeare Institute, University of Birmingham, 1990.

Krieger, Joel. *Reagan, Thatcher and the Politics of Decline.* Cambridge: Polity, 1986.

Kritzer, Amelia Howe. *The Plays of Caryl Churchill.* London: Macmillan, 1991.

Kushner, Tony. *Angels in America: A Gay Fantasia on National Themes. Part One: Millennium Approaches. The Harcourt Brace Anthology of Drama.* 3rd ed. Ed. W. B. Worthen. Fort Worth: Harcourt Brace, 2000, 1087–1115.

Lacan, Jacques. *Écrits: A Selection.* Trans. Alan Sheridan. London: Routledge, 1997, 281–91.

Langland, Elizabeth. *Nobody's Angels: Middle-Class Women and Domestic Ideology in Victorian Culture.* Ithaca: Cornell University Press, 1995.

Lederer, Katherine. *Lillian Hellman.* Boston: Twayne, 1979.

Londraville, Richard. "*Our Town:* An American Noh of the Ghosts." *Thornton Wilder: New Essays.* Ed. Martin Blank, Dalma Hunyadi Brunauer, and David Garret Izzo. West Cornwall, Conn.: Locust Hill, 1999, 365–78.

Londré, Felicia Hardison. "A Streetcar Running Fifty Years." *The Cambridge Companion to Tennessee Williams.* Ed. Matthew C. Roudané. Cambridge: Cambridge University Press, 1997, 45–66.

Loomba, Ania. *Colonialism/Postcolonialism.* London: Routledge, 1998.

Lorimar, Douglas A. "Race, Science and Culture: Historical Continuities and Discontinuities, 1850–1914." *The Victorians and Race.* Ed. Shearer West. Aldershot: Scolar, 1996, 12–31.

Lott, Eric. "The New Liberalism in America: Identity Politics in the 'Vital Center.'" *The Making and Unmaking of Whiteness.* Ed. Birgit Brander Rasmussen, Eric Klineberg, Irene J. Nexica, and Matt Wray. Durham: Duke University Press, 2001, 214–33.

MacDonald, Robert H. *The Language of Empire: Myths and Metaphors of Popular Imperialism, 1880–1918.* Manchester: Manchester University Press, 1994.

Malchow, H. L. *Gothic Images of Race in Nineteenth-Century Britain.* Stanford: Stanford University Press, 1996.

Malcom X. *The End of White World Supremacy: Four Speeches.* New York: Merlin House, 1971.

Malick, Javed. *Toward a Theater of the Oppressed: The Dramaturgy of John Arden.* Ann Arbor: University of Michigan Press, 1995.

Malick, Kenan. *The Meaning of Race: Race, History and Culture in Western Society.* London: Macmillan, 1996.

Marable, Manning. *Race, Reform and Rebellion: The Second Reconstruction in Black America, 1945-1982.* Houndmills: Macmillan, 1984.

Marowitz, Charles. "Introduction." *Penguin Plays: New American Drama.* Harmondsworth: Penguin, 1965, 7–17.

Marwick, Arthur. *Culture in Britain since 1945.* London: Blackwell, 1993.

———. *The Sixties: Cultural Revolution in Britain, France, Italy, and the United States: c. 1958–c. 1974.* Oxford: Oxford University Press, 1998.

Massey, Douglas S., and Nancy A. Denton. *American Apartheid: Segregation and the Making of the Underclass.* Cambridge, Mass.: Harvard University Press, 1993.

Maugham, W. Somerset. *The Explorer.* London: William Heinemann, 1912.

———. *East of Suez. The Collected Plays of W. Somerset Maugham.* Vol. 3. Melbourne: William Heinemann, 1931.

McAdam, Doug. *Freedom Summer.* Oxford: Oxford University Press, 1988.

McClain, Paula D., and Joseph Stewart Jr. *"Can We All Get Along?": Racial and Ethnic Minorities in American Politics.* Boulder: Westview, 1995.

McNulty, Charles. "Angels in America: Tony Kushner's Theses on the Philosophy of History." *Modern Drama* 39, no. 1 (1996): 84–96.

McQuire, Phillip. *TAPS for a Jim Crow Army: Letters from Black Soldiers in World War II.* Santa Barbara: ABC-Clio, 1983.

Mercer, Kobena. "Black Hair/Style Politics." *New Formations* 3 (1987): 33–54.

Merrill, Lisa. "Monsters and Heroines: Caryl Churchill's Women." *Caryl Churchill: A Casebook.* Ed. Phyllis R. Randall. New York: Garland, 1988, 71–89.

Meyer, Susan. *Imperialism at Home: Race and Victorian Women's Fiction.* Ithaca: Cornell University Press, 1996.

Miller, Arthur. *A View from the Bridge.* London: Penguin, 1961.

———. "Introduction." *Arthur Miller: Collected Plays.* London: Secker and Warburg, 1974.

———. "On Social Plays." *The Theater Essays of Arthur Miller.* Ed. Robert A. Martin. New York: Viking, 1978.

Miller, Keanne-Marie A. "Black Women Playwrights from Grimke to Shange: Selected Synopses of Their Works." *All the Women Are White, All the Blacks Are Men, but Some of Us Are Brave.* Ed. Gloria T. Hull, Patricia Bell Scott, and Barbara Smith. New York: Feminist Press, 1982, 280–96.

Millett, Kate. *Sexual Politics.* 1971. London: Abacus, 1972.

Minh-Ha, Trinh T. *When the Moon Waxes Red: Representation, Gender and Cultural Politics.* New York: Routledge, 1991.

Mintz, Steven. *A Prison of Expectations: The Family in Victorian Culture.* New York: New York University Press, 1985.

Minwalla, Framji. "When Girls Collide: Considering Race in *Angels in America.*" *Approaching the Millennium: Essays on* Angels in America. Ed. Deborah R. Geis and Steven F. Kruger. Ann Arbor: University of Michigan Press, 1997, 103–17.

Mitchell, Juliet, and Jacqueline Rose. *Feminine Sexuality: Jacques Lacan and the École Freudienne.* Trans. Jacqueline Rose. Houndmills: Macmillan, 1982.

Morgan, Kenneth O. *Britain since 1945: The People's Peace.* 1990. 3rd ed. Oxford: Oxford University Press, 2001.

Morris, John. *The Age of Arthur: A History of the British Isles from 350 to 650.* Trowbridge: Redwood, 1973.

Morris, Terence. "Crime and Penal Policy." *The Blair Effect: The Blair Government, 1997–2001.* Ed. Anthony Seldon. London: Little, Brown, 2001, 355–81.

Morrison, Toni. *Playing in the Dark: Whiteness and the Literary Imagination.* London: Picador, 1993.

Moscucci, Ornella. "Clitoridectomy, Circumcision, and the Politics of Sexual Pleasure in Mid-Victorian Britain." *Sexualities in Mid-Victorian Britain.* Ed. Andrew H. Miller and James Eli Adams. Bloomington: Indiana University Press, 1996, 60–78.

Mullard, Chris. *Black Britain.* London: George Allen and Unwin, 1973.

Murphy, Brenda. *Congressional Theater: McCarthyism on Stage, Film, and Television.* Cambridge: Cambridge University Press, 1999.

Murphy, Philip. *Party Politics and Decolonization: The Conservative Party and British Colonial Policy in Tropical Africa, 1951–1964.* Oxford: Clarendon Press, 1995.

Murray, Keat. "O'Neill's *The Hairy Ape* and Rodin's *The Thinker.*" *Journal of Evolutionary Psychology* 19, nos. 1–2 (1998): 108–15.

Neal, Larry. "The Black Arts Movement." *A Sourcebook of African-American Performance: Plays, People, Movements.* Ed. Annemarie Bean. London: Routledge, 1999, 55–67.

Oakley, J. Ronald. "Good Times: The American Economy in the Fifties." *The Eisenhower Presidency and the 1950s.* Ed. Michael S. Mayer. Boston: Houghton Mifflin, 1998, 189–204.

O'Connor, Sean. *Straight Acting: Popular Gay Drama from Wilde to Rattigan.* London: Cassell, 1998.

Olson, James S. *The Ethnic Dimension in American History.* 2nd ed. 1979. New York: St. Martin's, 1994.

Omolade, Barbara. "Black Women and Feminism." *The Future of Difference.* Ed. Hester Eisenstein and Alice Jardine. New Brunswick, N.J.: Rutgers University Press, 1994, 247–57.

O'Neil, James F. "How You Can Fight Communism." *The Age of McCarthyism: A Brief History with Documents.* Ed. Ellen Schrecker. Boston: Bedford, 1994, 109–12.

O'Neill, Eugene. *The Hairy Ape.* 1922. Harmondsworth: Middlesex, 1960.

———. *The Iceman Cometh.* 1947. London: Jonathan Cape, 1958.

Osborne, John. *The Entertainer.* London: Faber and Faber, 1961.

Osment, Philip. "Finding Room on the Agenda for Love: A History of Gay Sweat-shop." *Gay Sweatshop: Four Plays and a Company.* London: Methuen, 1989, vii–lxviii.

———. *This Island's Mine. Gay Sweatshop: Four Plays and a Company.* London: Methuen, 1989.

OWAAD. "Black Women and Health." *No Turning Back: Writings from the Women's Liberation Movement, 1975–1980.* London: Women's Press, 1981, 145–49.

Paglia, Camille. *Sexual Personae: Art and Decadence from Nefertiti to Emily Dickinson.* 1990. London: Penguin, 1992.

Parks, Suzan-Lori. *The America Play. A Sourcebook of African-American Performance: Plays, People, Movements.* Ed. Annemarie Bean. London: Routledge, 1999, 307–48.

Patsalidis, Savas. "Adrienne Kennedy's Heterotopias and the (Im)Possibilities of the (Black) Female Self." *Staging Difference: Cultural Pluralism in American Theater and Drama.* Ed. Marc Maufort. New York: Peter Lang, 1995, 301–21.

Patterson, Sheila. *Immigration and Race Relations in Britain, 1960–1967.* London: Oxford University Press, 1969.

Pattie, David. "The Common Good: The Hare Trilogy." *Modern Drama* 42 (1999): 363–73.

Peacock, D. Keith. *Thatcher's Theatre: British Theatre and Drama in the Eighties.* Westport, Conn.: Greenwood Press, 1999.

Pearlman, Mickey. "What's New at the Zoo?" *Feminist Rereadings of Modern American Drama.* Ed. June Schlueter. London: Associated University Presses, 1989, 183–91.

Peter, John. "Sin and Soda." *T. S. Eliot: Plays: A Casebook.* Ed. Arnold P. Hinchliffe. Houndmills: Macmillan, 1985, 150–55.

Peters, Sally. *Bernard Shaw: The Ascent of the Superman.* New Haven: Yale University Press, 1996.

Phelan, Peggy. *Unmarked: The Politics of Performance.* London: Routledge, 1993.

Phillips, Mike, and Trevor Phillips. *Windrush: The Irresistible Rise of Multi-Racial Britain.* London: HarperCollins, 1998.

Piggford, George. "Looking into Black Skulls: Amiri Baraka's *Dutchman* and the Psychology of Race." *Modern Drama* 40, no. 1 (1997): 74–85.

Plant, Raymond. "Blair and Ideology." *The Blair Effect: The Blair Government, 1997–2001.* Ed. Anthony Seldon. London: Little, Brown, 2001, 555–68.

Plum, Jay. "Attending Walt Whitman High: The Lessons of Pomo Afro Homos' *Dark Fruit." African-America Performance and Theater History: A Critical Reader.*

Ed. Harry. J. Elam Jr. and David Krasner. Oxford: Oxford University Press, 2001, 235–48.

Plummer, Kenneth. *Telling Sexual Stories: Power, Change and Social Worlds*. London: Routledge, 1995.

Pratt, Minnie Bruce. "Identity: Skin, Blood, Heart." *Yours in Struggle: Three Feminist Perspectives on Anti-Semitism and Racism*. New York: Long Haul, 1984.

Procter, David E., and Kurt Ritter. "Inaugurating the Clinton Presidency: Regenerative Rhetoric and the American Community." *The Clinton Presidency: Images, Issues, and Communication Strategies*. Ed. Robert E. Denton Jr. and Rachel L. Holloway. Westport, Conn.: Praeger, 1996, 1–16.

Pugh, Patricia. "Bernard Shaw, Imperialist." *Shaw and Politics*. Ed. T. F. Evans. University Park: University of Pennsylvania Press, 1991.

Quigley, Austin E. "Character in the Plays of Caryl Churchill." *Feminine Focus: The New Women Playwrights*. Ed. Enoch Brater. Oxford: Oxford University Press, 1989, 26–46.

Rabe, David. *Sticks and Bones. David Rabe: Plays 1*. London: Methuen, 2002.

Radhakrishnan, R. "Postcoloniality and the Boundaries of Identity." *Callaloo* 16 (1993): 750–71.

Rahman, Aishah. "To Be Black, Female and a Playwright." *Freedomways* 19 (1979): 256–60.

Ranald, Margaret Loftus. "From Trial to Triumph (1913–1924): The Early Plays." *The Cambridge Companion to Eugene O'Neill*. Ed. Michael Manheim. Cambridge: Cambridge University Press, 1998, 51–68.

Rawick, George P. *From SunDown to SunUp: The Making of the Black Community*. Westport, Conn.: Greenwood, 1972.

Rebellato, Dan. *1956 and All That: The Making of Modern British Drama*. London: Routledge, 1999.

Rees, Roland. "Black Theatre Two." *Fringe First: Pioneers of Fringe Theatre on Record*. Ed. Roland Rees. London: Oberon, 1992, 117–34.

Reichley, A. James. *Religion in American Public Life*. Washington, D.C.: Brookings Institution, 1985.

Rickenbacker, Captain Eddie. "America Must Return to Fundamentals." *Documents of American Prejudice: An Anthology of Writings on Race from Thomas Jefferson to David Duke*. Ed. S. T. Joshi. New York: Basic Books, 1999, 554–55.

Riddell, Peter. *The Thatcher Era and Its Legacy*. Oxford: Blackwell, 1991.

Roediger, David R. *The Wages of Whiteness: Race and the Making of the American Working-Class*. Rev. ed. 1991. London: Verso, 1999.

———. *Toward the Abolition of Whiteness: Essays on Race, Politics, and Working-Class History*. London: Verso, 1994.

———. "White Looks: Hairy Apes, True Stories, and Limbaugh's Laughs." *Whiteness: A Critical Reader*. Ed. Mike Hill. New York: New York University Press, 1997, 35–46.

Román, David. *Acts of Intervention: Performance, Gay Culture, and AIDS.* Bloomington: Indiana University Press, 1998.

Rutherford, Jonathan. *Forever England: Reflections on Masculinity and Empire.* Ed. Jonathan Rutherford. London: Lawrence and Wishart, 1997.

Said, Edward. *Orientalism.* New York: Random House, 1978.

Sanders, David. *Losing an Empire, Finding a Role: British Foreign Policy since 1945.* Houndmills: Macmillan, 1990.

Savran, David. *Communists, Cowboys, and Queers: The Politics of Masculinity in the Work of Arthur Miller and Tennessee Williams.* Minneapolis: University of Minnesota Press, 1992.

Sayers, Dorothy L. "Commentaries." Dante: *The Divine Comedy: 1: Hell.* Trans. Dorothy L. Sayers. Harmondsworth: Penguin, 1981.

Scharine, Richard. *The Plays of Edward Bond.* Cranbury, N.J.: Associated University Presses, 1976.

Schulman, Sarah. *My American History: Lesbian and Gay Life during the Reagan/Bush Years.* London: Cassell, 1994.

Sedgewick, Eve Kosofsky. *Between Men: English Literature and Male Homosocial Desire.* New York: Columbia University Press, 1985.

Sell, Mike. "The Black Arts Movement: Performance, Neo-Orality, and the Destruction of the 'White Thing.'" *African-American Performance and Theater History: A Critical Reader.* Ed. Harry J. Elam Jr. and David Krasner. Oxford: Oxford University Press, 2001, 56–80.

Sellers, Cleveland. *The River of No Return: The Autobiography of a Black Militant and the Life and Death of SNCC.* New York: William Morrow, 1973.

Shaw, George Bernard. *Captain Brassbound's Conversion. The Bodley Head Bernard Shaw: Collected Plays with Their Prefaces.* Vol. 2. London: Max Reinhardt, 1971, 317–430.

———. "The Revolutionist's Handbook and Pocket Companion." *The Bodley Head Bernard Shaw: Collected Plays with Their Prefaces.* Vol. 2. London: Max Reinhardt, 1971, 736–803.

Shull, Steven A. *A Kinder, Gentler Racism? The Reagan-Bush Civil Rights Legacy.* Armonk, N.Y.: M. E. Sharpe, 1993.

Sinfield, Alan. *Literature, Politics and Culture in Postwar Britain.* Oxford: Basil Blackwell, 1989.

———. *Faultlines: Cultural Materialism and the Politics of Dissident Reading.* Oxford: Clarendon Press, 1992.

———. *Cultural Politics—Queer Reading.* London: Routledge, 1994.

———. "Queer Identities and the Ethnicity Model." *New Sexual Agendas.* Ed. Lynne Segal. Houndmills: Macmillan, 1997, 196–204.

———. *Gay and After.* London: Serpent's Tail, 1998.

———. *Out on Stage: Lesbian and Gay Theatre in the Twentieth Century.* New Haven: Yale University Press, 1999.

Small, Stephen. *Racialised Barriers: The Black Experience in the United States and England in the 1980s*. London: Routledge, 1994.

Smith, Anna Marie. *New Right Discourse on Race and Sexuality: Britain, 1968–1990*. Cambridge: Cambridge University Press, 1994.

Smith, John Kares. "'Why Shouldn't We Believe That? We Are Americans': Rhetorical Myths and Fantasies in the Reagan Inaugurals." *Ronald Reagan's America*. Vol. 2. Ed. Eric J. Schmertz, Natalie Datlof, and Alexej Ugrinsky. Westport, Conn.: Greenwood, 1997, 813–25.

Smith, Matthew Wilson. "Angels in America: A Progressive Apocalypse." *Theater* 29, no. 3 (1999): 152–65.

Solinger, Rickie. "Race and 'Value': Black and White Illegitimate Babies, 1945–65." *Mothering: Ideology, Experience, and Agency*. Ed. Evelyn Nakano Glenn, Grace Chang, 2nd Linda Rennie Forcey. New York: Routledge, 1994, 287–310.

Sollors, Werner. "Amiri Baraka (LeRoi Jones)." *Essays on Contemporary American Drama*. Ed. Hedwig Bock and Albert Wertheim. München: Max Hueber Verlag, 1981, 105–22.

Solomos, John. *Race and Racism in Contemporary Britain*. Houndmills: Macmillan, 1990.

Solomos, John, Bob Findlay, Simon Jones, and Paul Gilroy. "The Organic Crisis of British Capitalism and Race: The Experience of the Seventies." *The Empire Strikes Back: Race and Racism in 70s Britain*. London: Routledge/University of Birmingham, 1982, 9–46.

Spencer, Jenny S. *Dramatic Strategies in the Plays of Edward Bond*. Cambridge: Cambridge University Press, 1992.

Spivak, Gayatri Chakravorty. *The Post-Colonial Critic*. London: Routledge, 1990.

Steele, Shelby. *The Content of Our Character: A New Vision of Race in America*. New York: St. Martin's Press, 1990.

Stepan, Nancy Leys, and Sander Gilman. "Appropriating the Idioms of Science: The Rejection of Scientific Racism." *The Bounds of Race*. Ed. Dominick La Capra. New York: Cornell University Press, 1991.

Sterling, Eric. "Albee's Satirization of Societal Sterility in America." *Studies in Contemporary Satire* 15 (1987): 30–39.

Summerfield, Penny. "Patriotism and Empire: Music Hall Entertainment, 1870–1914." *Imperialism and Popular Culture*. Ed. John M. Mackenzie. Manchester: Manchester University Press, 1986, 17–48.

Swanson, Michael. "Mother/Daughter Relationships in Three Plays by Caryl Churchill." *Theatre Studies* (1985–86): 49–66.

Taylor, John Russell. *Anger and After: A Guide to the New British Drama*. 1962. London: Methuen, 1978.

Timpane, John. "Gaze and Resistance in the Plays of Tennessee Williams." *Mississippi Quarterly* 48, no. 4 (1995): 751–61.

Trewin, J. C. "Introduction." *Plays of the Year: 1948–49.* London: Paul Elek, 1949, 7–24.

Turville-Petre, Thorlac. *England the Nation: Language, Literature and National Identity, 1290–1340.* Oxford: Clarendon Press, 1996.

Wald, Kenneth D. *Religion and Politics in the United States.* 3rd ed. Washington, D.C.: CQ Press, 1997.

Wallace, Alfred Russell. "The Origin of Human Races and the Antiquity of Man Deduced from the Theory of 'Natural Selection.'" *Images of Race.* Ed. Michael D. Biddis. Leicester: Leicester University Press, 1979, 37–54.

Walton, Anthony. "Patriots." *Lure and Loathing: Essays on Race, Identity, and the Ambivalence of Assimilation.* Ed. Gerald Early. New York: Penguin, 1993, 245–63.

Ward, Brian. "Racial Politics, Culture and the Cole Incident of 1956." *Race and Class in the American South since 1890.* Ed. Melvyn Stokes and Rick Halpern. Oxford: Berg, 1994, 181–208.

Ware, Vron. *Beyond the Pale: White Women, Racism and History.* London: Verso, 1992.

———. "Island Racism: Gender, Place, and White Power." *Displacing Whiteness: Essays in Social and Cultural Criticism.* Ed. Ruth R. Frankenberg. Durham: Duke University Press, 1997.

———. "Perfidious Albion." *The Making and Unmaking of Whiteness.* Ed. Birgit Brander Rasmussen, Eric Klinenberg, Irene J. Nexica, and Matt Wray. Durham: Duke University Press, 2001, 184–213.

Wasserstein, Wendy. *The Heidi Chronicles. The Heidi Chronicles and Other Plays.* New York: Vintage, 1990.

Watts, J. F., and Fred L. Israel. *Presidential Documents: The Speeches, Proclamations, and Policies That Have Shaped the Nation from Washington to Clinton.* New York: Routledge, 2000.

Weeks, Jeffrey. *Coming Out: Homosexual Politics in Britain, from the Nineteenth Century to the Present.* London: Quartet, 1977.

Wellman, David. "Minstrel Shows, Affirmative Action Talk, and Angry White Men: Marking Racial Otherness in the 1990s." *Displacing Whiteness: Essays in Social and Cultural Criticism.* Ed. Ruth Frankenberg. Durham: Duke University Press, 1997, 311–31.

Wertheim, Albert. "A View From the Bridge." *The Cambridge Companion to Arthur Miller.* Ed. Christopher Bigsby. Cambridge: Cambridge University Press, 1997, 101–14.

West, Cornel. *Race Matters.* Boston: Beacon, 1993.

Wilder, Thornton. "Preface." *Our Town.* Harmondsworth: Penguin, 1962.

———. *Our Town.* 1938. Harmondsworth: Penguin, 1962.

———. "Toward an American Language." *American Characteristics and Other Essays.* Ed. Donald Gallup. London: Harper and Row, 1979.

———. "Joyce and the Modern Novel." *American Characteristics and Other Essays.* Ed. Donald Gallup. London: Harper and Row, 1979.

Wilkerson, Margaret B. "Critics, Standards and Black Theatre." *The Theater of*

Black Americans. Vol. 2. Ed. Errol Hill. Englewood Cliffs, N.J.: Prentice-Hall, 1980, 120–28.

———. "Diverse Angles of Vision: Two Black Women Playwrights." *Intersecting Boundaries: The Theatre of Adrienne Kennedy*. Ed. Paul K. Bryant-Jackson and Lois More Overbeck. Minneapolis: University of Minnesota Press, 1992, 58–75.

Williams, Raymond. *Drama from Ibsen to Eliot*. 1952: Harmondsworth: Middlesex, Penguin, 1964.

Williams, Tennessee. 1946. *A Streetcar Named Desire*. London: Penguin, 1959.

Wills, Garry. *Reagan's America*. 1987. New York: Penguin, 1988.

Wilmer, S. E. "Restaging the Nation: The Work of Suzan-Lori Parks." *Modern Drama* 43 (2000): 442–52.

Wilson, W. J. *The Declining Significance of Race*. 2nd ed. Chicago: University of Chicago Press, 1980.

Wittner, Lawrence S. *Cold War America: From Hiroshima to Watergate*. New York: Praeger, 1977.

Wolf, Naomi. *Fire with Fire: The New Female Power and How It Will Change the 21st Century*. London: Chatto and Windus, 1993.

Woods, Alan. "Commercial American Theatre in the Reagan Era." *The American Stage: Social and Economic Issues from the Colonial Period to the Present*. Ed. Ron Engle and Tice Miller. Cambridge: Cambridge University Press, 1993, 252–66.

Worth, Katherine J. *Revolutions in Modern English Drama*. London: G. Bell and Sons, 1972.

Wray, Matt, and Annalee Newitz. *White Trash: Race and Class in America*. London: Routledge, 1997.

Wright, Esmond. *The American Dream: From Reconstruction to Reagan*. Oxford: Blackwell, 1996.

Wright, William. *Lillian Hellman: The Image, the Woman*. New York: Simon and Schuster, 1996.

Wynn, Neil A. *The Afro-American and the Second World War*. New York: Holmes and Meier, 1976.

Young, Robert M. *White Mythologies: Writing History and the West*. London: Routledge, 1990.

index

Achilles, Jochen, 99
active citizens, 174–75, 177–78, 183. *See also* Thatcher, Margaret
Adventures of Huckleberry Finn, 185
Adventures of Ozzie and Harriet, 100
Aeschylus, *The Oresteia,* 188
African-Americans: and class, 65; and community identity, 115; and internal colonialism, 86; and nihilism, 148; and non-violent resistance, 85
Afrocentrism, 116
AIDS, 149, 177. *See also* Kushner, Tony; religious right
Albee, Edward: *The American Dream,* 90–94; and anti-consumerism, 100
Albert, Prince, 119, 129
Allen, Charles, 16
Allen, Theodore W., 2, 20
Almost Free Theatre, 177
Amaker, Norman, 148
American apartheid, 24, 84
American Covenant, 149. *See also* Clinton, Bill
American Dream, myth of, 29, 33, 34, 67, 68–69, 84, 85–86, 92, 94, 100, 143, 145, 149
American Revolution, 144. *See also* Reagan, Ronald
American way of life, 33, 34, 36, 63, 64, 65, 67, 69, 71, 81, 87, 88, 89, 91, 100, 143, 145
americong, 90. *See also* counterculture movement
Amoko, Apollo, 140
Anderson, Martin, 145

Anderson, Michael, 38
Anti-Nazi League, 117
antiwar movement, 88, 89; and Black British feminism, 134
Arden, John. See *Island of the Mighty, The* (Arden and D'Arcy)
Aronson, Arnold, 158
Arrowsmith, William, 51
Arthurian legend, 128–29
Arts Council of Great Britain, 50
Ascent of F6, The (Auden and Isherwood), 14–17
Asher, Kenneth, 51
assimilation: and Afro-Caribbeans in Britain, 114–15; and aim of U.S. civil rights movement; and Aryan racialist beliefs, 132, 133–34; and Asians in Britain, 114–15, 116; and immigrants in United States, 63, 65, 158–59, 164; and West Indians in Britain, 116
Auden, W. H. See *Ascent of F6, The* (Auden and Isherwood)
Aziz, Razia, 136

Banton, Michael, 4
Baraka, Amiri, 86; and Dutchman, 95–100. *See also* Black Power movement
Barczewski, Stephanie, 131
Barksdale, Richard, 30
Barthes, Roland, 5, 37
Bassnett, Susan, 134
Bennett, Susan, 178
Benston, Kimberly, 96

Berg, Rick, 101
Berlin, Norman, 67
Bersani, Leo, 148
Bhabha, Homi, 178
Bigsby, C. W. E., 76, 78, 80, 91–92, 93, 97
Black Arts movement, 95–96; and Black women, 106. *See also* Baraka, Amiri
Black consciousness, 95. *See also* Black Power movement
Black diaspora, 185
Black feminism: and U.S. women's movement, 104–6; and UK women's movement, 134–36
Blackness: and Black Arts movement, 95–96; and Black Power movement, 84–86; and category of sub-human, 21; and Christianity, 20–21; and civilized/primitive binary, 67, 113, 123, 178–79, 198n; and colonialism, 138, 140, 179; and commonwealth immigration, 112–17; and criminality, 174; and cultural difference, 184–85; and degeneracy, 25; and diasporic community, 185; and eighteenth-century thought, 3; and Elizabethan England, 2; and gender, 74, 104–10, 134–36; and hetero/homosexual binary, 180; and homosexuality, 180–83; and masculine/feminine binary, 76–77; and nature/culture binary, 179; and otherness, xii, 164; and female promiscuity, 124; and performativity, 65–69, 108–10; and rock and roll, 65; and sexual degeneracy, 123–24; and sexual exoticism, 181; and skin color, 20–21, 32; and socio-political space, 57–58, 72, 142; and underclass, 147; and variegated Whiteness, 22–26; and White/Black binary, 2, 26, 31, 45, 61, 76, 95, 98–99, 123, 180, 195; and White gaze, 31, 99–100, 185–86
Black Power movement, 85–86; and anti-colonialist struggle, 86; and influence in Britain, 116. *See also* Black Arts movement
Black pride, 116
Black vernacular English, 168

Blair, Tony, 175, 176. *See also* active citizens
Bleir, Ruth, 76–77
Bloolips, *Belle Reprieve,* 73
Blum, John Morton, 89
Bogard, Travis, 66
Boland, Bridget, *The Cockpit,* 46–49
Bond, Edward: *Early Morning,* 117–25; *Saved,* 118
Bonnett, Alastair, 192
Bradford, William, *Of Plymouth Plantation,* 19
Brando, Marlon, 107
Brauer, Carl, 86
Breines, Wini, 65
British constitution, 189–90
British Council, 52
British Empire, 42–43, 45; and gender, 6–11, 12–13, 51, 120–25, 137–42; and representation in theatre, 6–17, 50–60, 136–42
British imperial discourse: and colonial subjects, 44, 45, 51–53, 126, 137–42, 179–80; and European identity, 46–49; and Ireland, 126; and middle-class identity, 53; and racialist propaganda, 15; and Roman Empire, 129; and Thatcherism, 171–72; and Victorian domestic ideology, 121, 137; and working-class identity, 6, 9, 42
British welfare state, 42, 192–93
Broadway, 90
Brooke, Stephen, 112
Brown, John Russell, 55
Brustein, Robert, 158
Bryan, Beverley, 135
Bryer, Jackson, 156
Bunge, Nancy, 33
Burns, Sir Alan, 15–16
Bush, George H. W., 147
Butler, Judith, 166

Campaign for Nuclear Disarmament, 134
Carby, Hazel, 138
Carmichael, Stokeley, 84, 85
Cashmore, E. Ellis, 42
Chafe, William H., 104
Chakrabarty, Dipesh, 133–34

Chambers, Ross, 108, 109
Charter, 88
Chaudhuri, Una, 165, 169
Chennault, Ronald E., 169
Churchill, Caryl, *Cloud Nine,* 136–42
Civil Rights Act, 84
Civil Rights movement, 61, 64, 87–88; and U.S. gay liberation movement, 148, 171; and U.S. women's movement, 104
Clift, Montgomery, 107
Clinton, Bill, 149; and racial ideology, 150–51
Cohen, Esther, 155
Cold War, xv, 44, 63, 64, 82
Colorism, 80–81, 131–32
Colvin, Madeleine, 171–72
Combs, James, 143–44
Commonwealth immigration, 45, 111–17
Commonwealth Immigration Act, 112
Confederacy, 39. *See also* Old South
Conservative Party (UK), 112, 170, 171
Cooper, Pamela, 101
corporate capitalism, 88
Costello, Donald P., 79
Coult, Tony, 119
counterculture movement: and Europe, 125; and anti-Vietnam movement, 89–90. *See also* White backlash
Cousin, Geraldine, 137
"Cricket test," 174. *See also* Tebbitt, Norman
Crow, Jim, 86

Dadzie, Stella, 135
Daily Express, 172
Dalton, Hugh, 45
Dante, *The Divine Comedy: Hell,* 162
Darby, Phillip, 5
D'Arcy, Margaretta. See *Island of the Mighty, The* (Arden and D'Arcy)
Darwin, John, 43, 52
Davis, Bette, 107
Davis, Jack E., 201
Davis, Tracy C., 7, 8
Davy, Kate, 155
Declaration of Independence, 68, 143. *See also* Reagan, Ronald

De Jongh, Nicholas, 84
Denton, Nancy, 62
de Troy, Chrètien, 129
Diamond, Elin, 106, 108, 138
Donesky, Finlay, 189, 190
Dorey, Peter, 175
Drabble, Margaret, 119
Drukman, Steven, 165
Du Bois, W. E. B., 23, 42
Durham, Martin, 172
Duster, Troy, xiii
Dyer, Richard, xi, 176–77, 195
Dyson, Michael Eric, 168–69

Edinburgh Festival, 50
Eliot, T. S., *The Cocktail Party,* 50–53; "The Idea of a Christian Society," 50; *Murder in the Cathedral,* 50
Ellis, Michael, *Chameleon,* 183–87
Elsom, John, 50
Empire Windrush, 44, 112
Engelhardt, Tom, 65, 89, 90
Enterprise Culture, 174, 186. *See also* Thatcher, Margaret
Equal Rights Amendment, 105
Erickson, Paul, 144
Evans, David, 177
Evans, Eric J., 172
evil empire, 145
exchange value, 91–92

Faludi, Susan, 146
Farber, David, 84
FBI. *See* Federal Bureau of Investigation (FBI)
Federal Bureau of Investigation (FBI), 87
Feldman, Leslie, 144
feminine mystique, 104. *See also* Friedan, Betty
feminist mystique, 154. *See also* Friedan, Betty
Fenton, Steven, 3
Findlay, Bob, 114
Fisher, James, 163
Fitzsimmons, Linda, 137
Foley, Conor, 174
Foucault, Michel, 48, 96
Frankenberg, Ruth, xii, 133, 151

Freedman, Jonathan, 159
Friedan, Betty, 104, 153–54

Gaston, Georg, 127–28
Gaston, Paul M., 37
Gates, Henry Louis, Jr., 168. *See also* Signifyin(g)
Gay and Lesbian Youth Federation, 172
gay liberation movement, 148, 171
Gay Sweatshop, 177
generation gap, 100
Genet, Jean, 137
Geoffrey of Monmouth, 131
ghettoization: process of, 62; and violent protest, 86
Gilleman, Luc, 56
Gilman, Sander, 54
Gilpin, William, 24
Gilroy, Paul, 112, 114, 170, 174
Gingrich, Newt, "Contract with America," 150
Glenn, Lane A., 188
Goldfield, David, 147
Gordon, Vivian, 105
Goulbourne, Harry, 111, 112
Gould, Philip, 175
Gray, Frances, 142
Griffin, Alice, 79

Hacker, Andrew, 26, 147
Hall, Catherine, 121
Hall, Stuart, 68
Hamilton, Charles V., 85
Happy Days, 65
Hare, David: *The Absence of War*, 188–95; *Murmuring Judges*, 188; *Racing Demon*, 188
Hargreaves, Robert, 217
Harris, Angela, 144
hate crimes, 148
Hawksley, Jane, 171–72
Hayman, Ronald, 93
Heale, M. J., 83
Heffernan, Richard, 206n
Hellman, Lillian, *The Little Foxes*, 37–41
Henreid, Paul, 107
Hertzbach, Janet, 100–101
Hewison, Robert, 118
Hewlett, Syliva Ann, 154

Hill, Michael, 174
Hinchliffe, Arnold P., 50
Hiro, Dilip, 117
Homden, Carol, 192
homosocial, concept of, 14, 82
hooks, bell, 97–98
Horton, Willie, 147
House of Commons, 193
House Un-American Activities Committee, 64. *See also* McCarthyism
housewife syndrome, 104. *See also* Friedan, Betty
Houswitchka, Christoph, 103
Howe, Stephen, 43
Hughes, Langston, *Mulatto*, 30–32
Humanism, 94
Hunt, Albert, 128
Hunt, James, 3
Hybridity, 180. *See also* Bhabha, Homi

Idylls of the King, 129
Ignatiev, Noel, 23
Ikoli, Tunde, 183
Individualism, 91, 145; and anti-individualism, 91–94
Innes, Christopher, 118
intimate citizenry, 183
Iran hostage crisis, 145
Isherwood, Christopher. See *Ascent of F6, The* (Auden and Isherwood)
Island of the Mighty, The (Arden and D'Arcy), 125–34, 188

Jacobson, Matthew Frye, 19
Jameson, Fredric, 93
Jann, Rosemary, 124
Jefferson, Thomas, 68. *See also* Declaration of Independence
Johnson, Paul, 172
Joint Stock Theatre, 136
Jones, Grace, 194
Jones, Simon, 114
Jordan, June, 168
Jordan, Winthrop D., 2

Karnow, Stanley, 89
Kazan, Elia, 76
Kennedy, Adrienne, *A Movie Star Has to Star in Black and White*, 106–10

Keyssar, Helene, 136, 154–55
King, Martin Luther, Jr., 84, 85
King, Rodney, 148
Kingsley, Mary, 7
Kinzer, Craig, 157
Krieger, Joel, 173
Ku Klux Klan, 76, 148
Kushner, Tony, *Angels in America,* 156–64

Labour Party (UK), 112, 188–95
Lacan, Jacques, and phallicism, 73
Laird, Trevor, 183
Langland, Elizabeth, 121
Lerner and Lowe, *Camelot,* 203
Lincoln, Abraham, 165–66
Londraville, Richard, 33
Londré, Felicia Hardison, 71
Loomba, Ania, 8
Lott, Eric, 150–51

MacDonald, Robert H., 7
Major, John, 174
Malcolm X, 84–85
Malick, Javed, 128
Malick, Kenan, 5
Malory, Sir Thomas, 129. See also *Morte d'Arthur, Le*
Manifest Destiny, 19, 24, 40, 89; and U.S. imperialism, 71
Manson murders, 100
Maoist Revolution, 65
Marable, Manning, 62
Marowitz, Charles, 94
Marwick, Arthur, 50, 130
Massey, Douglas, 62
Matura, Mustapha, 183
Maugham, W. Somerset: *East of Suez,* 1; *The Explorer,* 11–14; and Oscar Wilde, 11
McAdam, Douglas, 87
McCarthyism, 64, 87; and queer identity, 81
McNulty, Charles, 157
Merrill, Lisa, 142
Meyer, Susan, 8
Miller, Arthur, *A View From the Bridge,* 77–82
Miller, Keane-Marie, 106
Millet, Kate, 104–5

Minh-Ha, Trinh T., 167, 168
Mintz, Steven, 93
Minwalla, Framji, 164
Moral Majority, 148
Morgan, Kenneth O., 42, 54
Mormon religion, 160–61
Morris, John, 129
Morris, Terence, 175–76
Morrison, Toni, 77–78, 93
Morte d'Arthur, Le, 129. See also Malory, Sir Thomas
Moscussi, Ornella, 123–24
Mulatto, category of, 30–33
Mullard, Chris, 112–13
Murphy, Brenda, 78
Murphy, Philip, 42
Murray, Keat, 27
My Lai massacre, 89

National Endowment for the Arts, 149, 152
Nation of Islam, 85. See also Malcolm X
Neal, Larry, 95
neoconservatism, 143–51; and homosexuality, 157. See also Reagan, Ronald
Newitz, Annalee, 72. See also White trash
New Labour, and race relations, 175–76
New Liberalism, and Clinton administration, 151
new right, 152. See also neoconservatism; religious right
New South, 38–41
New York Public Shakespeare Festival, 100, 107
Nightingale, Florence, 120
Nixon, Richard, 89
Now Voyager, 107. See also Kennedy, Adrienne

Oakley, Ronald, 66, 200n
O'Connor, Sean, 11
Oedipal complex, 118
Off-Broadway, 90
Old South, 38–41
Omalade, Barbara, 105
O'Neill, Eugene: *The Hairy Ape,* 27–30; *The Iceman Cometh,* 66–71
O'Neill, James F., 64

Osborne, John: *The Entertainer,* 53–60; *Look Back in Anger,* 53
Osment, Philip: and "Finding Room on the Agenda for Love," 177; *This Island's Mine,* 176–83
"Other," concept of, xii–xiii, xiv, 14; and African Americans, 21, 25–26, 30–32, 34, 51, 69, 76, 94, 164, 165; and Blacks in Britain, 176–83, 186; and British imperial discourse, 1, 6–10, 49, 50–51; and British internal colonization, 127; and British nationalism, 123; and civilized/primitive binary, 123; and colonial subjects, 133; and commonwealth immigrants, 56–57, 112, 115, 131; and cultural difference, 34, 155, 173–74; and Darwin's theory, 4; and dominant White identity, 99–100, 104, 107–8, 109; and dress, 10; and examinability, 108; and femininity, 8–9, 28, 35–37, 136; and "fixity," 178; and homosexuality, 14, 166, 176–83; and immigrants in United States, 158–59; and Irish identity, 22–23; and Italian identity, 79; and Jewish identity, 156, 159; and New Liberalism, 151; and psychosocial integrity, 55–56; and skin color, 74; and Southern Whites, 39–40; and theatrical representation, 6, 32–33; and Victorian racial discourse, 5; and Vietnamese, 102–4; and White English, 115; and U.S. Man, 145, 159; and U.S. socio-political space, 158; and Western expansion, 23–25
Oval House, 184
OWAAD, 134
Oxbridge, 189

Parker, Pam, 87. *See also* McAdam, Douglas
Parks, Suzan-Lori, *The America Play,* 164
Patsalidis, Savas, 108
Patterson, Sheila, 116
Pattie, David, 189
Peacock, D. Keith, 170, 183
Pearlman, Mickey, 92
people's capitalism, 91

Peters, Jean, 107
Peters, Sally, 7
Phelan, Peggy, 109
Phillips, Mike, 45
Phillips, Trevor, 45
Piggford, George, 98
Place in the Sun, A, 107. *See also* Kennedy, Adrienne
Plant, Raymond, 175
Plum, Jay, 163–64
Plummer, Kenneth, 183
Pomo Afro Homos, *Dark Fruit,* 163–64
postfeminism, 151–56
Powell, Colin, 150
Powell, Enoch, 113–17, 122, 131, 173
power feminism, 154
power/knowledge, 96. *See also* Foucault, Michel
Pratt, Minnie Bruce, 103
Presley, Elvis, 65
Procter, David, 149
Protestant work ethic, 84
Pugh, Patricia, 6
Puritans, 143; and ideology, 145

Quigley, Austin, 138

Rabe, David, *Sticks and Bones,* 100–104
Radhakrishnan, R., 182
Rahman, Aisha, 106
Ranald, Margaret Loftus, 27
Rawick, George, 18, 33
Reagan, Ronald: and new right, 143, 157, 158; and equal opportunities, 146; and second American Revolution, 145, 149, 151
Rebellato, Dan, 49
Rees, Roland, 183
Reichley, A. James, 161
religious right, 144–49
repetition, and representation, 167, 168. *See also* Minh-Ha, Trinh T
Republican party, 150
Rickenbacker, Captain Eddie, 63
Ridenhour, Ronald, 89. *See also* Vietnam war
Ritter, Kurt, 149
"Rivers of Blood" speech, 173. *See also* Powell, Enoch

Roediger, David, 23, 28
Rose, Jacqueline, 73
Rowe, John Carlos, 101
Royal Court theatre, 53, 118, 136
Royal Shakespeare Company
Ruskin, John, 121
Rutherford, Jonathan, 113, 114

Said, Edward, 88. *See also* orientalism
Sanders, David, 44
Savran, David, 74, 82
Sayers, Dorothy, 162
Scafe, Suzanne, 135
Scharine, Richard, 119
Schulman, Sarah, 149
Scientific Racism, 3–5, 8, 21–22
Section 28, 171
Sedgewick, Eve Kosofsky, 14
segregation: and housing, 62; and
    schools, 147
Selassie, Haile, 116
Sell, Mike, 95
Sellers, Cleveland, 201
sexual revolution, 100
Shakespeare, William, *The Tempest,* 178
Shaw, G. B.: and *Captain Brassbound's
    Conversion,* 6–11; and "life-force," 8
Shull, Steven A., 147
Signifyin(g), 168. *See also* Gates, Henry
    Louis, Jr.
Sinfield, Alan, 75, 148, 149, 155, 161–62,
    164–65, 171
skinheads, 148
Small, Stephen, 173, 174
Smith, Anna Marie, 172
Smith, John Kares, 144
Smith, Joseph, 160
Smith, Matthew Wilson, 158
Social Darwinism, 144
Solinger, Rickie, 146
Solomos, John, 111–12, 114
Soviet Union, 44, 64, 66, 145. *See also*
    evil empire
Soyinka, Wole, 183
Spencer, Jenny S., 153
Spivak, Gayatri Chakravorty, 9
Split Britches, *Belle Reprieve,* 73
Sterling, Eric, 92
Stonewall Riots, 148

suburbanization, 62, 84. *See also* White
    flight
Suez Crisis, 53–54
Summerfield, Penny, 54
supply-side economics, 145
Swanson, Michael, 140

Taylor, John Russell, 58
Tebbitt, Norman, 174
Tennyson, Alfred (Lord), 129
Terry, Ellen, 7
Thatcher, Margaret: and British class-
    system, 170–74; and economic policy,
    188; and immigration, 172–73, 187;
    and nationalism, 182–83
Thomas, Clarence, 147
Thompson, Dudley, 44–45
Timpane, John, 72
Tom Sawyer, 185
trades union movement, and British
    feminism, 134
Trewin, J. C., 46–47
Turville-Petre, Thorlac, 131

U.S. exceptionalism, 64, 160
U.S. Justice Department, 87
U.S. Man, category of, 40, 68–69, 70,
    76, 78, 89, 145, 159–60, 165
U.S. military: and expansionism, 145;
    and homosexuality, 149; and racial
    discrimination, 62–63
U.S. Supreme Court, 147

verse drama, 50
Victoria, Queen, 119, 121
Vietnam war, 88, 100–104
Viva Zapata, 107. *See also* Kennedy,
    Adrienne
Voting Rights Act, 84

Walton, Anthony, 143
Ward, Brian, 65
Ware, Vron, 139
Wasserstein, Wendy, *The Heidi Chroni-
    cles,* 151–56
Watergate scandal, 89
welfare queens, 146
Wellman, David, 143
West, Cornell, 148

West End, 53
White backlash, 86, 143
Whiteface, 167
White flight, 83
White gaze, 98, 185–86
White monolith, 158, 159, 194
White negroes, 112
Whiteness: and Anglo-Norman identity, 160; and Anglo-Saxon identity, 113, 131–32, 65; and African identity, 18, 51–52; and Black/White binary, 8, 18, 72, 96, 123; and British imperial discourse, 48–49; and cannibalism, 122–23; and capitalism, 3, 66, 91, 119, 122, 130, 134, 144, 154; and Celtic ethnicity, 131–33; and Christianity, 3, 22, 26, 50–51, 103, 121, 132–33, 143–44, 152, 155; and civilized/primitive binary, 67, 69, 72, 121, 123, 150; and class, 9, 20, 23, 27–30, 34, 54–55, 64, 72, 145, 151, 155; and consumerism, 91–94, 102; and Darwinism, 4–5, 25, 36, 51, 74; and death, 103–4; and Edwardian masculinity, 11–12; and Elizabethan England, 2; and English identity, 48, 127–34; and European identity, 157; and feminism, 104–6, 134–36; and gender, 7–11, 28–30, 35–37, 69–70, 72–77, 92–93, 96–98, 107–10, 113–14, 120–25, 134, 137–42, 143, 146–47, 150–56, 166; and genocide, 98; and hetero/homosexual binary, 72, 74; and heterosexuality, 36, 123, 179; and homosexuality, 80–82, 123–25, 137, 139, 143, 145, 148–49, 156–64, 171–76; and homosocial desire, 14, 82; and intermediate Whites, 26; and Irish identity, 2, 22–23; and Jewish identity, 155, 159–63, 178; and labor, 22–23, 62–63, 83–84; and masculine/feminine binary, 72, 74; and motherhood, 146; and mulatto identity, 30; and Native Americans, 19, 24–26, 34, 37, 90; and nature/culture binary, 67, 72, 74, 123, 179; and nuclear family, 36, 100–104, 114–15, 119–20, 149, 202n; and Orien-

talism, 88; and performativity, 166, 185; and Reconstruction, 21–22, 39; and race/gender binary, 110; and rock and roll, 65; and Scottish identity, 207n; and skin color, 21, 30–31, 174, 186; and slavery, 2–3, 20–21, 165; and UK citizenship, 174–75, 177–78, 183; and U.S. citizenship, 22, 26, 33, 40, 150; and U.S. Civil War, 21; and U.S. religious right, 145, 148–49, 157–64; and variegated Whites, 75; and Victorian domestic ideology, 137; and Victorian racial thought, 4–5; and Vietnam war, 87–90, 100–104, 145; and WASP identity, 34, 36, 160; and Western Expansion, 24–25; and White/white binary, 72; and World War II, 2, 42, 46–49, 50, 53, 61–63, 67, 71
White trash, 72, 74
White, T. H., 129
Wilder, Thornton: "Joyce and the Modern Novel," 36; Our Town, 32–37, "Toward an American Language," 36
Wilkerson, Margaret, 106, 107
Williams, Raymond, 53
Williams, Tennessee, A Streetcar Named Desire, 71–77
Wills, Gary, 145
Wilmer, S. E., 166
Wilson, Lanford, 33
Wilson, W. J., 27
Winfrey, Oprah, 147
Winters, Shelley, 107
Wittner, Lawrence S., 81
women's movement: and Black British feminism, 134–36; and raising of consciousness, 153; and U.S. feminism and race, 104–6
Woods, Alan, 151–52
Worth, Katherine J., 57
Wray, Matt, 72
Wright, Esmond, 83
Wynn, Neil, 62

Young, Robert M., 94
Yuppies, 145